Scholarship Schemes for Muslim in India

Scholarship Schemes for Muslim in India

Dr. Fahimuddin
Senior Fellow
Giri Institute of Development Studies
Lucknow-226 024

ADHYAYAN PUBLISHERS & DISTRIBUTORS
New Delhi-110 002

ADHYAYAN PUBLISHERS & DISTRIBUTORS
4378/4B, 105, J.M.D. House, Murari Lal Street
Ansari Road, Daryaganj, New Delhi-110 002
Phones : 011-23263018, 011-23277156, Fax : 23280028
E-mail: adhyayanpublishers@yahoo.com.

Scholarship Schemes for Muslim in India

First Edition 2013

ISBN : 978-81-8435-389-1

PRINTED IN INDIA

Published by Harish Chandra Yadav for Adhyayan Publishers & Distributors, New Delhi-110 002, Laser Typesetting at Net Graphics, and Printed at Tarun Offset Printers, Delhi.

Preface

The Ministry of Minority Affairs, Government of India has been implementing four types of Scholarship schemes for the minority students. These schemes are the Pre-matric Scholarship, Post-Matric Scholarship, Merit-cum Means Scholarship and Free Coaching. All these four types of schemes are being implemented in all states and union territories of the country. These schemes are under implemntaion since quite some time and their impact assessment was eaasential in order to find out their strength and weakness and to suggest suitable remedial measures for effetive implementation of these shemes. The Ministry of Minorty Affairs, Government of India has sponsered this study which was conducted in Rampur district of Uttar Pradesh and Indore district of Madhya Pradesh, both these districts being minority concentrated. The study has tried to make as assessment of all the four scholarship schemes to look at to what extent scholarships schemes have been able to promote the academic environment among the minorities. The purpose of evaluation is also to assess the impact and scope of such scholarships on the overall educational development of the minorities.

The author is grateful to Dr. Sanchita Dutta of the India Council of Social Science Research, New Delhi for entrusting the task of study to our institute. She has supported all through the study and I belive that without her support, it was difficulty for me to complet the task. I am very thankful to the officials of the Ministry of Minority Affairs, Governement of India for sparing their valauable time for holding numureous rounds of discuusions at New Delhi to decide the methodology of the study. I feel grateful to other particiapting institutes for helping me in conduct of the study as the scope of the study was pan India and ICSSR institutes from other states were involved in the conduct of same study in their respecticve states.

I feel highly obliged to our director Prof. A.K. Singh for guiding me in conducting the study. He has been guide of this study and later on sanctioned subsidy grant for publication.

I am thankful to the research staff of GIDS namely Dr. R.K. jaiswal, Dr. Atika Khatoon, Mohd. Kaleem, Surya Prakash and Mohd. Zeeshan for data collection, tabualtiona and analysis.

Last but not the leat I am thankful to Deepak Gupta for helping me in word processing of the manuscript and to R.S. Bist for maintaing the official records of the study.

January 23, 2013

Dr. Fahimuddin
Professor
Giri Institute of Development Studies
Lucknow

CONTENTS

	Preface	*v*
Chapter I	**Introduction**	1-2
1.1	Objectives of Evaluation	1
1.2	Sample of the Study	1
Chapter II	**Characteristics of Sample Students-Pre-matric Scholarship: Rampur District**	**3-51**
2.1	Age of Students	3
2.2	Level of Schools	4
2.3	Type of Schools	4
2.4	Sources of Income and Schooling	5
2.5	Income of Families	5
2.6	Expenditure on Pre-metric Education	6
2.7	Children Attending Schools, Getting Scholarship and Family Features	7
2.8	Housing	8
2.9	Main Findings	9
2.10	Complete Awareness about Pre-metric Scholarship	10
2.11	Sources of Awareness of Pre-metric Scholarship to Rural Students	11
2.12	Sources of Awareness of Pre-metric Scholarship to Urban Students	12
2.13	Sources of Awareness of Pre-metric Scholarship to All Students	12
2.14	Knowledge about Eligibility Conditions	13
2.15	Knowledge of both Eligibility Conditions	14
2.16	Students Receiving Different Amount of Scholarship	14
2.17	Mode of Payment of Scholarship Amount	15
2.18	Scholarship Given by Different Persons	15
2.19	Expenses of Getting Pre-metric Scholarship	16
2.20	Utilization of Pre-metric Scholarship Amount: Students of Class 1-5	16
2.21	Utilization of Pre-metric Scholarship Amount: Students of Class 6-10	17
2.22	Effectiveness of Pre-matric Scholarship: Rural Students	18
2.23	Effectiveness of Pre-matric Scholarship: Urban Students	18
2.24	Effectiveness of Pre-matric Scholarship: All Students	19
2.25	Perception ofRural Students about Pre-matric Scholarship	19
2.26	Perception of Urban Students about Pre-matric Scholarship	20

2.27	Perception of All Students about Pre-matric Scholarship	20
2.28	Main Findings	21
2.29	Students Facing Difficulties while Applying	22
2.30	Level of Difficulty in Obtaining Application Form for Rural Students	22
2.31	Level of Difficulty in Obtaining Application Form for Urban Students	23
2.32	Level of Difficulty in Obtaining Application Form for All Students	24
2.33	Level of Difficulty in Filling Application Form for Rural Students	24
2.34	Level of Difficulty in Filling Application Form for Urban Students	25
2.35	Level of Difficulty in Filling Application Form for All Students	26
2.36	Cooperation of Institution in getting Pre-matric Scholarship: Rural Students	26
2.37	Cooperation of Institution in getting Pre-matric Scholarship: Urban Students	27
2.38	Cooperation of Institution in getting Pre-matric Scholarship to All Students	28
2.39	Role of State Government Officials: Perception of Rural Students	28
2.40	Role of State Government Officials: Perception of Urban Students	29
2.41	Role of State Government Officials: Perception of All Students	30
2.42	Suggestions of Students to Improve the Pre-matric Scholarship Scheme	30
2.43	Main Findings	33
2.44	Sample Parents	34
2.45	Housing and Family Features	34
2.46	Land Size and Income of Beneficiary Parents	35
2.47	Land Size and Income of Non-beneficiary Parents	35
2.48	Awareness about Pre-matric Scholarship	36
2.49	Sources of Awareness of Pre-matric Scholarship	36
2.50	Reasons of untimely payment of Pre-matric Scholarship	37
2.51	Problems Faced by Beneficiary Students: Perception of their Parents	37
2.52	Level of Difficulty Faced in Filling the Application Form: Perception of their Parents	38
2.53	Rating of Various Processes of Pre-matric Scholarship: Beneficiary Parents	38
2.54	Parents Perceptions on Scholarship	40
2.55	Sample Institutions	40
2.56	Type of Sample Institutions	40
2.57	Enrolment, Applied and Award of Pre-matric Scholarship: Rural Areas	41
2.58	Enrolment, Applied and Award of Pre-matric Scholarship: Urban Areas	41
2.59	Enrolment, Applied and Award of Pre-matric Scholarship: All District	42
2.60	Reasons of not getting Scholarship: Perspective of Institutions	42
2.61	Mode of Payment of Scholarship Amount	43
2.62	Time taken in Processing	43
2.63	Level of Difficulty in Processing	44
2.64	Time taken from Proposal to Disbursement of Pre-matric Scholarship	44
2.65	Improvement in Enrolment and Drop out	44

2.66	Level of Satisfaction of Institutions with State and Central Government Agencies	45
2.67	Data Management	45
2.68	Impact of Pre-matric Scholarship Scheme	45
2.69	Most Important Problems and Overall Assessment of Pre-matric Scholarship Scheme	46
2.70	Main Suggestions of Institutions for Improvement of Scheme	46
2.71	District Official	46
2.72	On the Guidelines	46
2.73	Selection Criteria	46
2.74	Awardees of Pre-matric Scholarship	46
2.75	Grants of Pre-matric Scholarship	47
2.76	Strategy of Community Awareness Adopted	47
2.77	Time Spent in Disbursement of Pre-matric Scholarship	48
2.78	Impact of Pre-matric Scholarship Scheme: Officer's Views	48
2.79	Problems in Implementation of Scheme: Officer's Views	48
2.80	Suggestions for Improvement	48
2.81	Main Findings	48
2.82	Field Observations	49
2.83	Key Issues of Pre-matric Scholarship	50
2.84	Suggestions	51
Chapter III	**Introduction: Post-matic Scholarship-Rampur District**	**52-85**
3.1	Sample of the Study	52
3.2	Age of Students	52
3.3	Level of Schools	53
3.4	Type of Institutions	54
3.5	Sources of Income	54
3.6	Income of Students	55
3.7	Expenditure on Education	55
3.8	Attending Schools, Getting Scholarship and Family Features	56
3.9	Housing	57
3.10	Main Findings	58
3.11	Complete Awareness about Post-matric Scholarship	59
3.12	Sources of Awareness of Post-matric Scholarship to Rural Students	59
3.13	Sources of Awareness of Post-matric Scholarship to Urban Students	60
3.14	Sources of Awareness of Post-matric Scholarship to All Students	60
3.15	Detailed Knowledge of Post-matric Scholarship	61
3.16	Knowledge of Eligibility Conditions	61
3.17	Students Receiving Different Amount of Post-matric Scholarship	62
3.18	Mode of Payment	62
3.19	Scholarship Given by Different Persons	62
3.20	Expenses for Applying the Post-matric Scholarship	62

3.21	Utilization of Pre-matric Scholarship Money: Students of Class 11-12	63
3.22	Utilization of Pre-matric Scholarship Money:Graduation and above:	63
3.23	Effectiveness of Post-matric Scholarship	64
3.24	Perception of Rural Students about Pre-matric Scholarship	64
3.25	Main Findings	65
3.26	Students Facing Difficulties while Applying	66
3.27	Level of Difficulty in Obtaining Application Form	66
3.28	Level of Difficulty in Filling Application Form	66
3.29	Level of Cooperation of Institutions	67
3.30	Role of State Government Officials	67
3.31	Suggestions of Students for Improving the Post-matric Scholarship Scheme	68
3.32	Main Findings	68
3.33	Sample Size	69
3.34	Housing and Family Features	69
3.35	Land Size of Parents	70
3.36	Annual Income of parents	70
3.37	Parents Knowledge of Post-matric Scholarship	70
3.38	Sources of Awareness of Post-matric Scholarship	71
3.39	Reasons of Untimely Payment of Post-matric Scholarship	71
3.40	Problems faced by Beneficiary Students: Parents Response	72
3.41	Level of Difficulties	72
3.42	Perception of Beneficiary Parents about various Aspects of Post-matric Scholarship	73
3.43	Perception of Non-beneficiary Parents about various Aspects of Post-matric Scholarship:	73
3.44	Perception of All Parents about various Aspects of Post-matric Scholarship:	74
3.45	Observations of Parents	75
3.46	Main Findings	75
3.47	Enrolment, Applicants and Scholarship Award	76
3.48	Reasons for Non- Award of Scholarship	78
3.49	Method of Scholarship Payment and Processing of Application	79
3.50	Institutions' Satisfaction Level with Govt. agencies Involved	79
3.51	Bottlenecks Faced in the Teaching process and Education System:	80
3.52	Selection of Beneficiary Students	80
3.53	Main Findings	81
3.54	On the Guidelines	81
3.55	Selection Criteria	81
3.56	Problems Regarding Implementations the Scheme	81
3.57	Awardees of Post-matric Scholarship	82
3.58	Criteria for Selecting Institutions	82
3.59	Grants of Post-matric Scholarship	82
3.60	Mechanisms for Community Awareness	82
3.61	Availability and Accessibility of the Scheme	83

3.62	Time Spent in Disbursement of Post- matric Scholarship	83
3.63	Impact of Post- Matric Scholarship	83
3.64	Suggestions for Improvement of Post-matric Scholarship	83
3.65	Main Findings	83
3.66	Field Observations	84
3.67	Key Issues of Post-matric Scholarship	84
3.68	Suggestions	84
Chapter IV	**Characteristics of Sample Students- Merit cum Means based Scholarship: Rampur District**	**86-100**
4.1	Age of Students	86
4.2	Occupations	86
4.3	Location of Previous Institutions	87
4.4	Family Income of Students	87
4.5	Courses of Study of Students	87
4.6	Main Findings	88
4.7	Scholarship Amount Received	88
4.8	Expenditure of Scholarship Amount	89
4.9	Sources of Information of the Scheme	89
4.10	Level of Difficulty in Receiving the Scholarship: Students Perception	89
4.11	Students Satisfied the Amount of Scholarship	90
4.12	Level of Satisfaction with Reimbursement of Course Fee	90
4.13	Perception of Students about Various Aspects of Scholarship	90
4.14	Future Plan of Students	91
4.15	Satisfaction of Students with their Institutions	91
4.16	Satisfaction with the State Government	92
4.17	Satisfaction with the Central Government	92
4.18	Impact of Merit cum Means Scholarship: Perception of Students	92
4.19	Suggestions of Students to Improve the Scheme	93
4.20	Main Findings	93
4.21	About the Educational Institutions	94
4.22	Trend in Enrolment and Processing of Applications for Scholarship	94
4.23	Impact of MCM Scheme	95
4.24	Assessment of Merit cum Means Scheme	96
4.25	Suggestions for Improvement in MCM Scheme	96
4.26	Response of District official (Implementing Agency)	96
4.27	Scholarship Application and Grant	97
4.28	Selection Process of Candidates	97
4.29	Distribution Method of Scholarship Amount	97
4.30	Number of Male and Female Candidates received Scholarship	98
4.31	Suggestions for Better Implementation of the Scheme	98
4.32	Field Observations	99
4.33	Key Issues of Merit cum Means Bases Scholarship	99
4.34	Suggestions	99

Chapter V **Characteristics of Sample Students of Pre-matric Scholarship: Indore District** **101-132**
5.1 Age of Student 101
5.2 Level of Schools 102
5.3 Type of Schools 102
5.4 Sources of Income and Schooling 103
5.5 Income of Families 103
5.6 Expenditure on Pre-matric Education 104
5.7 Children Attending Schools, Getting Scholarship and Family Features: 104
5.8 Housing 105
5.9 Main Findings 106
5.10 Awareness, Utilization and Impact of Pre-matric Scholarship 107
5.11 Complete Awareness about Scholarship 107
5.12 Knowledge about Eligibility Conditions 108
5.13 Knowledge of both Eligibility Conditions 108
5.14 Students Receiving Different Amount of Scholarship 109
5.15 Mode of Payment of Scholarship Amount 109
5.16 Scholarship Given by Different Persons 110
5.17 Expenses of Getting Pre-matric Scholarship 110
5.18 Utilization of Pre-matric Scholarship Amount: Students of Class 1-5 111
5.19 Utilization of Pre-matric Scholarship Amount: Students of Class 6-10 111
5.20 Effectiveness of Pre-matric Scholarship 112
5.21 Perception of Students about Pre-matric Scholarship 113
5.22 Main Findings 113
5.23 Problems in Getting Pre-matric Scholarship and Suggestions of Students 114
5.24 Students Facing Difficulties while Applying 114
5.25 Level of Difficulty in Filling Application Form 115
5.26 Cooperation of Institution in getting Pre-matric Scholarship 116
5.27 Role of State Government Officials: Perception 116
5.28 Suggestions of Students to Improve the Pre-matric Scholarship Scheme 117
5.29 Main Findings 118
5.30 Parents of Beneficiary and Non-Beneficiary Students, Institution and Officials 118
5.31 Sample Parents 118
5.32 Land Size and Income of Beneficiary Parents 119
5.33 Income of Parents 120
5.34 Awareness about Pre-matric Scholarship 120
5.35 Sources of Awareness of Pre-matric Scholarship 120
5.36 Reasons of untimely payment of Pre-matric Scholarship 121
5.37 Problems Faced by Beneficiary Students: Perception of their Parents 121
5.38 Level of Problem Faced by Beneficiary Students: Perception of their Parents 122
5.39 Rating of Various Processes of Pre-matric Scholarship: Beneficiary Parents 122

5.40	Parents Perceptions on Scholarship	123
5.41	Sample Institutions	123
5.42	Type of Sample Institutions	124
5.43	Enrolment, Applied for and award of Pre-matric Scholarship	124
5.44	Reasons of not getting Scholarship: Perspective of Institutions	125
5.45	Mode of Payment of Scholarship Amount	125
5.46	Time taken in Processing	125
5.47	Level of Difficulty in Processing	126
5.48	Time taken from Proposal to Disbursement of Pre-matric Scholarship	126
5.49	Improvement in Enrolment and Drop out	126
5.50	Level of Satisfaction of Institutions with State and Central Government Agencies	127
5.51	Data Management	127
5.52	Impact of Pre-matric Scholarship Scheme	127
5.53	Assessment of Pre-matric Scholarship: Views of Institutions	127
5.54	Main Suggestions of Institutions for Improvement of Scheme	128
5.55	On the Guidelines	128
5.56	Selection Criteria	128
5.57	Awardees of Pre-matric Scholarship	128
5.58	Grants of Pre-matric Scholarship	129
5.59	Time Spent in Disbursement of Pre-matric Scholarship	129
5.60	Impact of Pre-matric Scholarship Scheme: Officer's Views	129
5.61	Problems in Implementation of Scheme: Officer's Views	129
5.62	Suggestions for Improvement	130
5.63	Main Findings : Parents	130
5.64	Main Findings : Institutions	130
5.65	Main Findings : District Official	131
5.66	Field Observations	131
5.67	Key Issues of Pre-matric Scholarship	132
5.68	Suggestions	132
Chapter VI	**Introduction: Post-matric Scholarship-Indore District**	**133-165**
6.1	Sample of the Study	133
6.2	Age of Students	133
6.3	Level of Schools	134
6.4	Type of Institutions	135
6.5	Sources of Income	135
6.6	Income of Students	136
6.7	Expenditure on Education	136
6.8	Attending Schools, Getting Scholarship and Family Features	137
6.9	Housing	138
6.10	Main Findings	139
6.11	Complete Awareness about Post-matric Scholarship	139

6.12	Sources of Awareness of Post-matric Scholarship	140
6.13	Student's Knowledge of Eligibility Conditions	140
6.14	Knowledge about Each Eligibility Conditions	141
6.15	Students Receiving Different Amount of Post-matric Scholarship	141
6.16	Mode of Payment	142
6.17	Scholarship Given by Different Persons	142
6.18	Expenses for Applying the Post-matric Scholarship	142
6.19	Utilization of Post-matric Scholarship Money: Students of Class 11-12	143
6.20	Utilization of Post-matric Scholarship Money: Graduation and above	144
6.21	Effectiveness of Post-matric Scholarship	144
6.22	Perception of Students about Post-matric Scholarship	145
6.23.	Main Findings	146
6.24	Students Facing Difficulties while Applying	147
6.25	Level of Difficulty in Obtaining Application Form	147
6.26	Level of Difficulty in Filling Application Form	148
6.27	Level of Cooperation of Institutions	148
6.28	Role of State Government Officials	149
6.29	Suggestions of Students for Improving the Post-matric Scholarship Scheme	149
6.30	Main Findings	150
6.31	Sample Size	150
6.32	Housing and Family Features	150
6.33	Land Size of Parents	150
6.34	Annual Income of parents	151
6.35	Awareness about Post-matric Scholarship	152
6.36	Sources of Awareness of Post-matric Scholarship	152
6.37	Reasons of Untimely Payment of Post-matric Scholarship	153
6.38	Problems faced by Beneficiary Students: Parents Response	153
6.39	Level of Difficulty Faced in Filling the Application Form: Perception of Parents	154
6.40	Rating of Various Aspects of Post-matric Scholarship by Beneficiary Parents	154
6.41	Rating of Various Aspects of Post-matric Scholarship by Non-beneficiary Parents	155
6.42	Parents Perceptions on Scholarship	156
6.43	Main Findings	156
6.44	Sample Institutions	157
6.45	Award of Post-matric Scholarship to Muslim Students, Government Holkar Science College, Indore	157
6.46	Award of Post-matric Scholarship to Muslim Students, Government Kasturba Girls Higher Secondary School, Indore	158
6.47	Award of Post-matric Scholarship to Muslim Students, Mata Jija Bai Girls P.G. College, Indore	158
6.48	Award of Post-matric Scholarship to Muslim Students, Naurilal Senior Secondary School, Indore	159

6.49	Reasons for Non- Award of Scholarship	159
6.50	Level of satisfaction of Institutions with State Government	159
6.51	Level of satisfaction of Institutions with Central Government	160
6.52	Bottlenecks in the Education System	161
6.53	Data Management	161
6.54	Availability of Guidelines of Post-matric Scholarship	161
6.55	Problems of Post-matric Scholarship: Institutions Views	162
6.56	Main Findings	162
6.57	On the Guidelines	162
6.58	Selection Criteria	163
6.59	Problems Regarding Implementations the Scheme	163
6.60	Awardees of Post-matric Scholarship	163
6.61	Utilization of Grant of Post-matric Scholarship	163
6.62	Satisfaction with MOMA	163
6.63	Time Spent in Disbursement of Post- matric Scholarship	164
6.64	Impact of Post- Matric Scholarship	164
6.65	Main Findings	164
Chapter VII	**Introduction: Merit cum Means based Scholarship–Indore District**	**166-178**
7.1	Sample of the Study	166
7.2	Age of Students	166
7.3	Occupations	167
7.4	Location of Institutions of Students	167
7.5	Family Income of Students	168
7.6	Courses of Study of Students	168
7.7	Students Views about Merit cum Means based Scholarship	168
7.8	Amount of Scholarship	169
7.9	Items of expenditure	169
7.10	Sources of Information of Merit cum Means scholarship	169
7.11	Level of Difficulty Faced by the Students in getting the Scholarship	170
7.12	Satisfaction with Scholarship Amount	170
7.13	Level of satisfaction	171
7.14	Perception about Merit cum Means Scholarship	171
7.15	Future Plan of Students	171
7.16	Level of satisfaction with Institutions	172
7.17	Level of Satisfaction with the State Government	172
7.18	Impact of the Scheme	173
7.19	Suggestions	173
7.20	Main Findings	173
7.21	Award of MCM	174
7.22	Processing of Applications	174
7.23	Impact of Merit cum Means scholarship	175
7.24	Assessment of Scholarship	175

7.25	Selection of Candidates	176
7.26	Process of Selection	176
7.27	Distribution of Scholarship	177
7.28	Main Findings	177
7.29	Field Observations	178
7.30	Key Issues of MCM Scholarship	178
7.31	Suggestions	178
Chapter VIII	**Free Coaching and Allied Scheme**	**179-188**
8.1	Religion-wise Students	179
8.2	Type of Coaching Attended	179
8.3	Annual Income	179
8.4	Type of Institutions	180
8.5	Source of Awareness	180
8.6	Purpose of Joining Free Coaching	181
8.7	Increase in confidence in Competitive Exams	181
8.8	Utility Level of Free Coaching Scheme	182
8.9	Level of Satisfaction of Students with Facilities/Infrastructure of Coaching Centre	182
8.10	Average Expenditure of Scholarship Amount	183
8.11	Mode of Payment of Scholarship	184
8.12	Processing of Application	184
8.13	Coaching Institute	184
8.14	Enrolment of Minority Students in Coaching Centre	185
8.15	Infrastructure of Coaching Centre	185
8.16	Qualification of Faculty	186
8.17	Experience of Faculty	186
8.18	Selection Criteria of Students	186
8.19	Suggestions of Students for better implementation of Free Coaching Scheme	187
8.20	Main Findings	187
8.21	Field Observations	187
8.22	Key Issues of Free Coaching and Allied Scheme	188
8.23	Suggestions	188
	Index	189

List of Tables

Sl. No	Title	Page No.
1.1	Sample Size of the Pre-matric Scholarship: Students	2
2.1	Age-wise Number of Sample Students	3
2.2	Schools Where Sample Students are Studying	4
2.3	Type of Institutions of Sample Students	4
2.4	Sources of Income of Sample Students	5
2.5	Classification of Students According to their Income	6
2.6	Average Expenditure of Education per Student on Different Items	7
2.7	Children Going to Schools, Getting Scholarships and Family Structure	8
2.8	Housing and other Conditions of Sample Students	9
2.9	Students who are Completely Aware of the Pre-matric Scholarship Scheme	11
2.10	Sources of Awareness of Pre-matric Scholarship among Rural Students	11
2.11	Sources of Awareness of Pre-matric Scholarship among Urban Students	12
2.12	Sources of Awareness of Pre-matric Scholarship among All Students	13
2.13	Students Knowing Eligibility Conditions of Pre-matric Scholarship Scheme	13
2.14	Knowledge of Each of the two Eligibility Conditions of Pre-matric Scholarship	14
2.15	Classification of Beneficiary Students According to amount of Scholarship	15
2.16	Mode of Payment of Scholarship Amount	15
2.17	Scholarship Given by Different Persons	16
2.18	Item wise Expenditure for getting Pre-matric Scholarship	16
2.19	Items wise Average Expenditure of Scholarship Amount: Students of Class-1-5	17
2.20	Items wise Average Expenditure of Scholarship Amount: Students of Class-6-10	17
2.21	Effectiveness of Pre-matric Scholarship: Rural Students	18
2.22	Effectiveness of Pre-matric Scholarship: Urban Students	18
2.23	Effectiveness of Pre-matric Scholarship: All Students	19
2.24	Views of Rural Students about Pre-matric Scholarship Scheme	19
2.25	Views of Urban Students about Pre-matric Scholarship Scheme	20
2.26	Views of All Students about Pre-matric Scholarship Scheme	21
2.27	Number of Students Facing while applying for Pre-matric Scholarship	22
2.28	Level of Difficulty in Obtaining Application Form: Response of Rural Students	23
2.29	Level of Difficulty in Obtaining Application Form: Response of Urban Students	23

2.30	Level of Difficulty in Obtaining Application Form: Response of Total Students	24
2.31	Level of Difficulty in filling the Application Form: Response of Rural Students	25
2.32	Level of Difficulty in filling the Application Form: Response of Urban Students	25
2.33	Level of Difficulty in filling the Application Form: Response of Total Students	26
2.34	Level of Cooperation of Institutions in helping Students to get Scholarship: Perception of Rural Students	27
2.35	Level of Cooperation of Institutions in helping Students to get Scholarship: Perception of Urban Students	27
2.36	Level of Cooperation of Institutions in helping Students to get Scholarship: Perception of All Students	28
2.37	Role of State Government Officials: Response of Rural Students	29
2.38	Role of State Government Officials: Response of Urban Students	29
2.39	Role of State Government Officials: Response of All Students	30
2.40	Suggestions of Students in Improving the Scheme: Rural Students	31
2.41	Suggestions of Students in Improving the Scheme: Urban Students	32
2.42	Suggestions of Students in Improving the Scheme: All Students	33
2.43	Sample of the Parents	34
2.44	Housing and Family Conditions of Sample Parents	35
2.45	Land Size and Income of Beneficiary Parents	35
2.46	Land Size and Income of Non-beneficiary Parents	36
2.47	Parents Knowing the Pre- Scholarship Scheme	36
2.48	Sources of Awareness of Pre-matric Scholarship Scheme	37
2.49	Reasons of Pre-matric Scholarship not getting Timely	37
2.50	Problems Faced by Students in getting the Pre-matric Scholarship : Parents Responses	38
2.51	Level of Difficulty in Filling the Application Form	38
2.52	Perception of Beneficiary Parents about various Aspects of Pre-matric Scholarship Scheme: Rural Parents	39
2.53	Perception of Beneficiary Parents about various Aspects of Pre-matric Scholarship Scheme: Urban Parents	39
2.54	Perception of Beneficiary Parents about various Aspects of Pre-matric Scholarship Scheme: All Parents	39
2.55	Location of Sample Institution	40
2.56	Type of Institutions	40
2.57	Type of Institutions	41
2.58	Year-wise Enrolment, Applied and Pre-matric Scholarship Awarded to Students in Sample Institutions of Rampur District (Rural)	41
2.59	Year-wise Enrolment, Applied and Pre-matric Scholarship Awarded to Students in Sample Institutions of Rampur District (Urban)	42
2.60	Year-wise Enrolment, Applied and Pre-matric Scholarship Awarded to Students in Sample Institutions of Rampur District (Rural and Urban)	42
2.61	Reasons of not getting Scholarship	43
2.62	Mode of Payment Scholarship Amount	43
2.63	Average Time Taken in Processing of Application	44

2.64	Level of Difficulty in Processing the Application	44
2.65	Duration of Pre-matric Scholarship Distribution	44
2.66	Level of Satisfaction with State and Central Government Agencies	45
2.67	System of Data Management of Pre-matric Scholarship	45
2.68	Overall Assessment of Pre-matric Scholarship Scheme	46
2.69	Year and Religion wise Number of Awardees Students of Pre-matric Scholarship in Rampur District	47
2.70	Grant Allocation, Approval and Utilization (Rs. Lakhs)	47
2.71	Time Spent in Disbursement of Pre-matric Scholarship	48
3.1	Sample Size of the Post-Matric Scholarship: Students	52
3.2	Age-wise Number of Sample Students	53
3.3	Institutions Where Sample Students are Studying	54
3.4	Type of Institutions of Sample Students	54
3.5	Sources of Income of Sample households: Students Response	55
3.6	Classification of Students According to their Income	55
3.7	Average Annual Expenditure of Education per Student on Different Items	56
3.8	Going to Schools, Getting Scholarships and Family Structure	57
3.9	Housing and other Conditions of Sample Students	58
3.10	Students who are Completely Aware of the Post -matric Scholarship Scheme	59
3.11	Source of Awareness of Post- matric Scholarship among Rural	59
3.12	Source of Awareness of Post -matric Scholarship among Urban Students	60
3.13	Source of Awareness of Post -matric Scholarship among Students	60
3.14	Detail Knowledge of Post-matric Scholarship Scheme: Students Response	61
3.15	Knowledge of Sample Students about Each of the Eligibility Conditions of Post-matric Scholarship	61
3.16	Classification of Beneficiary students According to amount of Scholarship	62
3.17	Scholarship Given by Different Persons	62
3.18	Item wise Expenses for Applying the Post-matric Scholarship	63
3.19	Items wise Average Expenditure of Scholarship Amount: Students of Class-11-12	63
3.20	Items wise Average Expenditure of Scholarship Amount: Graduation and above	64
3.21	Response of Students on the Effectiveness of Post-matric Scholarship	64
3.22	Views of Students about Post-matric Scholarship Scheme	65
3.23	Number of Students Facing problems while applying for Post-matric Scholarship	66
3.24	Level of Difficulty in Obtaining Application Form: Response of Students	66
3.25	Level of Difficulty in Filling the Application Form: Response of Students	67
3.26	Level of Cooperation of Institutions in helping Students to get Scholarship: Perception of Students	67
3.27	Role of State Government Officials: Perception of Students	67
3.28	Suggestions of Students in Improving the Scheme	68
3.29	Sample Parents of Students of Post-matric Scholarship	69
3.30	Housing and Family Features of Sample Parents	69
3.31	Land Size of Parents	70
3.32	Classification of Parents According to their Annual Income	70

3.33	Parents Knowledge of the Post-Matric Scholarship Scheme	71
3.34	Sources of Awareness of Post-Matric Scholarship Scheme	71
3.35	Reasons of Post Matric Scholarship not getting Timely: Beneficiary Responses	72
3.36	Problem Faced by Students in Getting the Post Metric Scholarship: Parents Response	72
3.37	Level of Difficulty in Filling the Application Form: Parent Response	73
3.38	Perception of Beneficiary Parents about various Aspects of Post-Matric Scholarship Scheme	73
3.39	Perception of Non Beneficiary Parents about various Aspects of Post-matric Scholarship Scheme: Non Beneficiary	74
3.40	Perception of All Parents (Beneficiary and Non Beneficiary) about various Aspects of Post-Matric Scholarship Scheme	74
3.41	Observations of Sample Parents about Post-matric Scholarship Scheme	75
3.42	Basic Information on Surveyed Institutions	76
3.43	(A) Information on Students Enrolled Applied and Awarded Scholarship in the Surveyed Institutions	77
	(B) Government Raza Post Graduate College	77
	(C) Government Inter College Shahabad	77
	(D) Shamsi Girls Inter College	77
	(E) Ramrata Degree College, Zahidpur : Shahabad	78
3.44	Important Reasons for Students Not Being Awarded Scholarship	78
3.45	Institutions' Level of Satisfaction with State Government Agencies	79
3.46	Institutions' Level of Satisfaction with Central Government Agencies	80
3.47	Bottlenecks Faced in the Education System	80
3.48	Procedure of Data Management	80
3.49	Availability of Guidelines of Post-matric Scholarship	81
3.50	Year and Religion wise Number of Awardees Students	82
3.51	Grant Approval and utilization	82
3.52	Time Spent in Disbursement of Post- matric Scholarship	83
4.1	Classification of Sample Students according to their Age	86
4.2	Classification of Sample Students according to their Family Occupations	86
4.3	Type and Location of Institutions of Students	87
4.4	Annual Income of Students Households	87
4.5	Students Studying in Different Courses	88
4.6	Amount of Scholarship Received	88
4.7	Item wise Average Expenditure of Scholarship Amount: Beneficiary Students	89
4.8	Sources of Information about the Scheme to Students	89
4.9	Level of Difficulty Faced by Students in receiving the Scholarship	90
4.10	Response of Beneficiary Students on the Satisfaction with Scholarship	90
4.11	Level of Satisfaction with Method the Reimbursement of Course Fee: Beneficiary Students	90
4.12	Perception about various Aspects of Merit Cum Means Scholarship	91
4.13	Future Plans of Students	91
4.14	Level of Satisfaction with Institutions	92
4.15	Level of Satisfaction with State Government	92

4.16	Level of Satisfaction with Central Government	92
4.17	Impact of Scholarship: Students Views	93
4.18	Suggestions for Improvement of Merit cum Means Based Scholarship-Students Views	93
4.19	Enrolment of Minority Students and their Application for MCM	94
4.20	Processing of Applications	95
4.21	Impact of Merit cum Means Scholarship	95
4.22	Assessment of MCM Scheme	96
4.23	Selection of Candidates	96
4.24	Scholarship Application and Grant	97
4.25	Process of Selection	97
4.26	Distribution Method of Scholarship Amount	98
4.27	Year-wise Number of Male and Female candidates	98
5.1	Age wise Number of Sample Students	101
5.2	Schools Where Sample Students are Studying	102
5.3	Type of Institutions of Sample Students	102
5.4	Sources of Income of Sample Students	103
5.5	Classification of Students According to their Income	103
5.6	Average Expenditure of Education per Student on Different Items	104
5.7	Children Going to Schools, Getting Scholarships and Family Structure	105
5.8	Housing and other Conditions of Sample Students	106
5.9	Students who are Completely Aware of the Pre-matric Scholarship Scheme	107
5.10	Sources of Awareness of Pre-matric Scholarship among Students	108
5.11	Students knowing Eligibility Conditions of Pre-matric Scholarship Scheme	108
5.12	Knowledge of Each of the Eligibility Conditions of Pre-matric Scholarship	109
5.13	Classification of Beneficiary Students According to amount of Scholarship	109
5.14	Mode of Payment of Scholarship Amount	110
5.15	Scholarship Given by Different Persons	110
5.16	Item wise Expenditure for getting Pre-matric Scholarship	111
5.17	Items wise Average Expenditure of Scholarship Amount: Students of Class 1-5	111
5.18	Items wise Average Expenditure of Scholarship Amount: Students of Class-6-10	112
5.19	Effectiveness of Pre-matric Scholarship-Beneficiary Students	112
5.20	Views of Students about Pre-matric Scholarship Scheme	113
5.21	Number of Students Facing Problems while applying for Pre-matric Scholarship	114
5.22	Level of Difficulty in Obtaining Application Form: Response of Students	115
5.23	Level of Difficulty in filling the Application Form: Response of Students	115
5.24	Level of Cooperation of Institutions in Helping Students for Scholarship: Perception of Students	116
5.25	Role of State Government Officials: Response of Students	116
5.26	Suggestions of Students for Improving the Scheme	117
5.27	Sample of the Parents	118
5.28	Housing and Family Conditions of Sample Parents	119
5.29	Land Size of Parents	119
5.30	Source of Income of Sample Parents	120

5.31	Parents Knowledge of the Pre- Scholarship Scheme	120
5.32	Sources of Awareness of Pre-matric Scholarship Scheme	121
5.33	Reasons of Untimely Payment of Pre-matric Scholarship: Reasons given by Beneficiaries	121
5.34	Problem Faced by Students in Getting the Pre- Matric Scholarship: Parents Response	122
5.35	Level of Difficulty in Filling the Application Form	122
5.36	Rating of various Aspects of Pre-matric Scholarship Scheme: Parents	123
5.37	Location of Sample Institution	124
5.38	Type of Institutions	124
5.39	Type of Institutions	124
5.40	Year-wise Enrolment, Applied and Pre-matric Scholarship Awarded to Students in Sample Institutions	124
5.41	Reasons of not getting Scholarship	125
5.42	Mode of Payment Scholarship Amount	125
5.43	Average Time Taken in Processing of Application	126
5.44	Level of Difficulty in Processing the Application	126
5.45	Duration of Pre-matric Scholarship Distribution	126
5.46	Level of Satisfaction with State and Central Government Agencies	127
5.47	System of Data Management of Pre-matric Scholarship	127
5.48	Overall Assessment of Pre-matric Scholarship Scheme	128
5.49	Number of Awardees Students of Pre Matric Scholarship in Indore District	128
5.50	Grant Allocation, Approval and Utilization (Rs. In Lakhs)	129
5.51	Time Spent in Disbursement of Pre-matric Scholarship	129
6.1	Sample Size of the Post-Matric Scholarship: Students	133
6.2	Age wise Number of Sample Students	134
6.3	Institution Where Sample Students are Studying	135
6.4	Institution Where Sample Students are Studying	135
6.5	Sources of Income of Sample Students	136
6.6	Classification of Students According to their Income	136
6.7	Average Expenditure of Education per Student on Different Items	137
'6.8	Children Going to Schools, Getting Scholarships and Family Structure	138
6.9	Housing and other Conditions of Sample Students	139
6.10	Students who are Completely Aware of the Post -matric Scholarship Scheme	140
6.11	Source of Awareness of Post- matric Scholarship	140
6.12	Students Knowing Eligibility Conditions of Post -matric Scholarship Scheme	141
6.13	Knowledge of Sample Students about Each of the Eligibility Conditions of Post-matric Scholarship	141
6.14	Classification of Beneficiary students According to amount of Scholarship	141
6.15	Mode of Payment of Scholarship Amount	142
6.16	Scholarship Given by Different Persons	142
6.17	Item wise Expenditure for getting Post-matric Scholarship	143
6.18	Items wise Average Expenditure of Scholarship Amount: Students of Class-11-12	143
6.19	Items wise Average Expenditure of Scholarship Amount: Students of Graduation and above	144

6.20 Responses of Students on Effectiveness of Post-matric Scholarship 145
6.21 Views of Students about Post-matric Scholarship Scheme 146
6.22 Number of Students Facing problems while applying for Post-matric Scholarship 147
6.23 Level of Difficulty in Obtaining Application Form: Response of Students 147
6.24 Level of Difficulty in Filling the Application Form: Response of Students 148
6.25 Level of Cooperation of Institutions in helping Students to get Post-matric Scholarship: Perception of Students 148
6.26 Role of State Government Officials 149
6.27 Suggestions of Students in Improving the Scheme 149
6.28 Sample of the Parents 150
6.29 Housing and Family Conditions of Sample Parents 151
6.30 Land Size of Parents 151
6.31 Annual Income of Parents 152
6.32 Parents Knowing the Post-Matric Scholarship Scheme 152
6.33 Source of Awareness of Post-Matric Scholarship Scheme 153
6.34 Reasons of Post-matric Scholarship not getting Timely 153
6.35 Problems Faced by Students in getting the post-matric Scholarship: Parents Responses 154
6.36 Level of Difficulty in Filling the Application Form 154
6.37 Rating of various Aspects of Post-matric Scholarship Scheme by Beneficiary Parents 155
6.38 Rating of various Aspects of Post-matric Scholarship Scheme by Non-beneficiary Parents 155
6.39 Observations of Sample Parents about Post-matric Scholarship Scheme 156
6.40 Basic Information on Surveyed Institutions 157
6.41 Students Enrolled, Applied and Awarded Scholarship: Government Holkar Science College, Indore 158
6.42 Students Enrolled, Applied and Awarded Scholarship: Government Kasturba Girls Higher Secondary School, Indore 158
6.43 Students Enrolled, Applied and Awarded Scholarship: Mata JijaBai Girls P.G. College Indore 158
6.44 Students Enrolled, Applied and Awarded Scholarship: Naurilal Senior Secondary School, Indore 159
6.45 Important Reasons for Students Not being Awarded Scholarship 159
6.46 Satisfaction Level of Institutions with State Government 160
6.47 Institutions' Level of Satisfaction with Central Government Agencies 160
6.48 Bottlenecks Faced in the Education System 161
6.49 Methods of Data Management 161
6.50 Availability of Guidelines of Post-matric Scholarship 161
6.51 Problems Regarding Implementation of the Scheme 162
6.52 Availability of Guidelines of Post-matric Scholarship 162
6.53 Year and Religion wise Number of Awardees Students of Post-matric Scholarship 163
6.54 Grant Approval and utilization (In Rs. Lakh) 163
6.55 Satisfaction Level with MOMA 164

6.56	Time Spent in Disbursement of Post- matric Scholarship	164
7.1	Sample Size of the Study of Merit cum Means based Scholarship: Students	166
7.2	Classification of Sample Students according to their Age	167
7.3	Classification of Sample Students according to their Family Occupations	167
7.4	Type of Institutions of Students	167
7.5	Annual Income of Students Households	168
7.6	Students Studying in Different Courses	168
7.7	Amount of Scholarship Received	169
7.8	Item wise Average Expenditure of Scholarship Amount: Beneficiary Students	169
7.9	Sources of Information about the Scheme to Students	170
7.10	Level of Difficulty Faced by Students in receiving the Scholarship	170
7.11	Response of Beneficiary Students on the Satisfaction with Scholarship Amount	170
7.12	Level of Satisfaction with Method the Reimbursement of Course Fee: Beneficiary Students	171
7.13	Perception about various Aspects of Merit Cum Means Scholarship	171
7.14	Future Plans of Students	172
7.15	Level of Satisfaction with Institutions	172
7.16	Level of Satisfaction with State Government	172
7.17	Impact of Merit cum Means based Scholarship: Students Views	173
7.18	Enrolment of Minority Students and their Application for MCM	174
7.19	Processing of Applications	175
7.20	Impact of Merit cum Means based Scholarship	175
7.21	Assessment of MCM Scheme	176
7.22	Selection of Candidates	176
7.23	Process of Selection Process of Selection Process of Selection	176
7.24	Distribution Method of Scholarship Amount	177
8.1	Sample Students of Free Coaching and Allied Scheme	179
8.2	Type of Coaching attended by Sample Students	179
8.3	Annual Income of Households of Sample Students	180
8.4	Type of Coaching Institution	180
8.5	Sources of Awareness about Free Coaching Scheme among Students	181
8.6	Purpose of Joining the Free Coaching	181
8.7	Increase in Confidence of Students in Competitive Examinations	182
8.8	Utility of Free Coaching Scheme	182
8.9	Level of Satisfaction with Facilities/Infrastructure in Coaching Centre: Students Responses	183
8.10	Items wise Average Expenditure of Stipend: Students Responses	183
8.11	Mode of Payment of Scholarship	184
8.12	Responses of Students about Processing of Application and Documentation	184
8.13	About the Coaching Institution	185
8.14	Total Enrolment and Enrolment of Minority Students	185
8.15	Availability of infrastructures in the institute	185
8.16	Qualification of the Faculty of Coaching Centre	186
8.17	Teaching Experience of Faculty	186

Chapter I

Introduction

The Ministry of Minority Affairs, Government of India has been implementing four types of scholarship schemes for the minority students. These schemes are the Pre-matricScholarship, Post-MatricScholarship, Merit-cum Means Scholarship and Free Coaching. All these four types of schemes are being implemented in all states and union territories of the country.

1.1 Objectives of Evaluation:

The study tries to make as assessment of the scholarship schemes to look at to what extent scholarships schemes have been able to promote the academic environment among the minorities The purpose of evaluation is also to assess the impact and scope of such scholarships on the overall educational development of the minorities.

1.2 Sample of the Study:

Rampur district of Utter Pradesh and Indore district of Madhya Pradesh were selected for the study. There are six development blocks in the Rampur district.Out of six development blocks, two development blocks namely Swar and Shahabad have relatively larger concentration of minorities in the district. In these two blocks, distribution of each of the three types of scholarships was also higher among all the six blocks. Therefore, these two blocks were selected as sample blocks. In each of two blocks, four institutions were identified where higher numbers of scholarships were awarded. In the catchment area of these institutions (identified on the basis of number of students coming to these institutions) five villages were selected from one block (selection of villages was based on the population of minorities and distribution of number of Scholarships. In each sample village, household listing was prepared to identify the students who obtained different types of scholarships of the Ministry of Minority Affairs, Government of India. Among the identified students who obtained Pre-matric Scholarship, twenty (20) beneficiary students and ten (10) non-beneficiary students were selected from each village for detailed interview.The institutions based selection of beneficiary (20) and non-beneficiary students (10) were also done from each of two urban wards of the district. Adequate representation to girls' students was given in the sample. A total 180 parents were also taken as sample. 13 institutions (8 from rural area and 5 from urban area) and one main official were also taken as sample. Thus, institution based sampling was followed to select beneficiaries and non-beneficiaries of the scholarship schemes. It is to be mentioned here that Free Coaching Scheme was not implemented in Rampur district; therefore the present evaluation has not covered it. All the

scholarships in the district have been given to Muslims only and very few to Sikhs and Christians. Therefore, sample of the study could capture Muslim beneficiaries only.

Indore district which is one of the largest minority concentrated districts of Madhya Pradesh State was selected for the evaluation of Educational Scholarship Schemes of the Ministry of Minority Affairs, Government of India. There are five development blocks in Indore district. Out of five development blocks, two development blocks namely Indore Sadar and Mhow have largest concentration of minorities among all the five development blocks of the district. But the Scholarships of the Ministry of Minority Affair, Government of India were given only in Indore Sadar block. Therefore, Indore Sadar block was selected as sample block. In this block, eight institutions were identified where higher number of scholarships was awarded. It was found that scholarships to minorities have been given to urban based institutions only. In the catchment area of these institutions (identified on the basis of number of students coming to these institutions) ten wards were selected on the basis of population of minorities and distribution of number of Scholarships. In each sample ward, household listing was prepared to identify the students who obtained different types of scholarships of the Ministry of Minority Affairs, Government of India. Among the identified students who obtained Pre-matric Scholarship, twenty (20) beneficiary students and ten (10) non-beneficiary students were selected for detailed interview. 39 per cent representation to girls' students was given in the sample. Thus, a total 300 students were selected as sample which included 200 beneficiaries and 100 non-beneficiary students. Thus, institution based sampling was followed to select beneficiaries and non-beneficiaries of the scholarship schemes. It was found that each type of scholarships in the district have been given mostly to Muslims and very few to Sikhs and Christians. Therefore, sample of the study could capture Muslim beneficiaries only. The detail sample of the study covering both the districts of Rampur and Indore has been shown in following table-1.1.

Table-1.1: Sample Size of the Pre-matric Scholarship: Students

Sex	Number of Students					
	Beneficiary		Non Beneficiary		Total	
	Rampur	Indore	Rampur	Indore	Rampur	Indore
Boys	108	116	67	67	175	183
Girls	132	84	53	33	185	117
Total	240	200	120	100	360	300

Chapter II

Characteristics of Sample Students-Pre-matric Scholarship : Rampur District

2.1 Age of Students:

The data as shown in table-2.1 shows that majority of the beneficiary (53.34 per cent) and non-beneficiary (63.33 per cent) students are in the age of 11-14 years. The similar pattern is evident in case of beneficiary (64.89 per cent) and non-beneficiary (75.38 per cent) boys while around 50 percent +beneficiary and non-beneficiary girls are the age group of 11-14 years. The percentage of girls in the age group of 6-11 years is more than double to that of boys in the same age group. In the total sample, 19.72 per cent students are in the age of 14-17 years and there are negligible difference in percentage terms among the boys and girls falling in this age group.

Table-2.1: Age-wise Number of Sample Students

Sex/ Students		6-11 Years	11-14 Years	14-17 Years	Total
Boys	Beneficiaries	16 (14.89)	63 (64.89)	29 (20.21)	108 (100.00)
	Non-Beneficiaries	9 (10.77)	49 (75.38)	9 (13.85)	67 (100.00)
	Total	25 (13.21)	112 (69.18)	38 (17.61)	175 (100.00)
Girls	Beneficiaries	40 (30.30)	65 (49.24)	27 (20.56)	132 (100.00)
	Non-Beneficiaries	20 (37.74)	27 (50.94)	6 (11.32)	53 (100.00)
	Total	60 (32.43)	92 (49.73)	33 (17.84)	185 (100.00)
Total	Beneficiaries	56 (23.33)	128 (53.34)	56 (23.33)	240 (100.00)
	Non-Beneficiaries	29 (24.79)	76 (63.33)	15 (12.50)	120 (100.00)
	All	85 (23.61)	204 (56.63)	71 (19.72)	360 (100.00)

Note: Figures in brackets indicate percentages.

Source: Primary data based.

2.2 Level of Schools:

Table-2.2 shows that majority of students (86.39 per cent) are studying in primary schools. The proportion of boys (80.57 per cent) studying in primary schools is lower than that of girls (91.89 per cent). When correlated with the age, it indicates two patterns. One is that the Muslim children in general start getting education late and second is that the number of late starter boys is higher than the late starter girls. It also appears that non-beneficiary students are more late starters than beneficiary students.

Table-2.2: Schools Where Sample Students are Studying

Sex/ Students		Primary School	Upper Primary School	High School	Total
Boys	Beneficiaries	86 (79.83)	5 (4.63)	17 (15.74)	108 (100.00)
	Non-Beneficiaries	55 (82.09)	7 (10.45)	5 (77.46)	67 (100.00)
	Total	141 (80.57)	12 (6.86)	22 (12.57)	175 (100.00)
Girls	Beneficiaries	119 (90.15)	8 (6.06)	5 (3.79)	132 (100.00)
	Non-Beneficiaries	51 (96.23)	2 (3.77)	0 (0.00)	53 (100.00)
	Total	170 (91.89)	10 (5.41)	5 (2.70)	185 (100.00)
Total	Beneficiaries	205 (85.42)	13 (5.41)	22 (9.17)	240 (100.00)
	Non-Beneficiaries	106 (88.33)	9 (7.50)	5 (1.57)	120 (100.00)
	All	311 (86.39)	22 (6.11)	27 (7.50)	360 (100.00)

Note: Figures in brackets indicate percentages.
Source: Primary data based.

2.3 Type of Schools:

It is evident that lowest proportion of sample students is found to be going to government schools except at the secondary levels where 15.79 per cent of all sample students reported to be going to government schools as against 10.53 per cent of them going to Madrasas. It is the private

Table-2.3: Type of Institutions of Sample Students

Type of Institution	Type Of Institution				
	Government	Private	Aided	Madrasa	Total
Primary	29 (9.06)	204 (63.75)	45 (14.06)	42 (13.13)	320 (100.00)
Upper Primary	1 (4.76)	12 (57.14)	8 (38.10)	0 (0.00)	21 (100.00)
High School	3 (15.79)	10 (52.63)	4 (21.05)	2 (10.53)	19 (100.00)
Total	33 (9.17)	226 (62.78)	57 (15.83)	44 (12.22)	360 (100.00)

Note: Figures in brackets indicate percentages.
Source: Primary data based.

institutions at primary (63.75 per cent), upper primary (57.14 per cent) and high school (52.63 per cent) levels, where majority of students are found to be studying (Table-2.3). This trend may be emerging due to the fact that people have become quality conscious of the education so preference for private education has also emerged among Muslims as well.

2.4 Sources of Income and Schooling:

There are three major sources of income of households. These are the farming with small land holding, small trade/business and agriculture (Table-2.4). It further reflects that private institutions are the most preferred for schooling irrespective of occupation of families. The household engaged as casual labour mostly prefer private schools but at the same time around 10 per cent of them send their children to Madrasas also. Small farmers mostly like private schools but 4.40 per cent and 2.52 per cent of them send their wards to government aided and private schools respectively. The cultivators mostly like private schools (65.79 per cent) but 34.21 percent of them send their wards to government schools. Most of the artisan (63.33 per cent) sends their children to private schools but 30 per cent of their wards are going to government schools. The schooling institutions of children of salaried households is more or less same as that cultivating households but in case of students belonging to small business/trading households, 18.18 per cent children have reported to be going to Madrasas which is the highest among all categories of households. On the whole, 5.28 per cent of all sample students have reported to be going to Madrasas. The inference is that private institutions are preferred irrespective of source of income of the family.

Table-2.4: Sources of Income of Sample Students

	Source	Type of Institution				
		Government	Private	Aided	Madrasa	Total
1	Casual Labour	3 (5.88)	34 (66.67)	9 (17.65)	5 (9.80)	51 (100.00)
2	Small Farmer	4 (2.52)	148 (93.08)	7 (4.40)	0 (0.00)	159 (100.00)
3	Cultivator	13 (34.21)	25 (65.79)	0 (0.00)	0 (0.00)	38 (100.00)
4	Artisan	9 (30.00)	19 (63.33)	1 (3.33)	1 (3.33)	30 (100.00)
5	Salaried (Government /Private)	6 (37.50)	9 (56.25)	0 (0.00)	1 (6.25)	16 (100.00)
6	Small Business/Trade	19 (28.79)	31 (46.97)	4 (6.06)	12 (18.18)	66 (100.00)
	Total	54 (15.00)	266 (73.89)	21 (5.83)	19 (5.28)	360 (100.00)

Note: Figures in brackets indicate percentages.
Source: Primary data based.

2.5 Income of Families:

The students were asked to report the estimated average annual income of their families and accordingly all of them have been classified according to different income slabs in table-2.5. It is evident from the table that more than 60 per cent of them have average annual income in the range of Rs. 50,000 to Rs. 1, 00,000. The proportion of such families is higher (73.33 per cent) in urban areas versus rural areas (58.67 per cent). In view of the fact that people generally tend to disclose their income lower than the actual one, it can be safely be assumed here that the majority of Muslim families have annual income higher than 50,000 to Rs. 1, 00,000 per annum. In this situation, the income limit of granting Pre-matric scholarship to those students whose parents have annual income not exceeding Rs. 100,000 merits revision.

Table-2.5: Classification of Students According to their Income

Income (Rs.)	Number of Students		
	Rural	Urban	Total
Less than 20,000	2 (0.67)	1 (1.67)	3 (0.83)
20,001 to 50,000	121 (40.33)	15 (25.00)	136 (37.78)
50,001 to 1,00,000	176 (58.67)	44 (73.33)	220 (61.11)
1,00,001 to 1,50,000	1 (0.33)	- (0.00)	1 (0.28)
Total	300 (100.00)	60 (100.00)	360 (100.00)

Note: Figures in brackets indicate percentages.
Source: Primary data based.

2.6 Expenditure on Pre-matric Education:

The Pre-matric education may be classified in two.The first part is from class 1-5 and the other is from class 6-10.The average expenditure incurred by a family on first and second part has been calculated. The average expenditure during class 1- 5 has been estimated to be Rs. 2600 which is Rs. 1998 in rural areas as against Rs. 3201 in urban areas. In the entire expenses on education, course fee and other expenses like clothing and teaching learning materials are the major items of expenditure. The average expenditure for study during classes 6-10 comes around Rs. 4000 which is higher in urban areas as compared to rural areas. In these classes, private coaching, travel and course fee are the major components of expenses (Table-2.6).The schooling in government schools at primary level (Class 1-5) is free and onward education in government institutions is also relatively cheaper but as has been observed above, the families in rural as well as in urban areas irrespective of their source of income largely prefer private schools over government schools, hence expenditures are quite high in view of the average annual income of families in rural and urban areas. Therefore, the amount of Pre-matric scholarship being given at present needs upward revision in view of the current level of expenses incurred by the families on the education at Pre-matric level.

Table-2.6: Average Expenditure of Education per Student on Different Items

Item	Amounts (in Rs.)		
	Rural	Urban	Total
For Class 1-5			
Course Fee	482	725	605
Teaching Learning Materials	365	482	425
Travel	362	664	510
Tuition	246	605	428
Others	543	725	632
Total	1998	3201	2600
For Class 6-10			
Course Fee	725	962	845
Teaching Learning Materials	482	604	541
Travel	718	902	812
Tuition	845	1082	965
Others	722	962	840
Total	3492	4512	4003

Source: Primary data based.

2.7 Children Attending Schools, Getting Scholarship and Family Features:

It was to be assessed that how many children out of total children are going to schools that are in the age group of 6 to 14 years. It was found that at the aggregate level; around 65 per cent of them are attending the schools regularly. The percentage of school attending children is higher in urban areas (72.07) in comparison with the children in rural areas (63.81). The percentage of school attending girls is higher in comparison with schools attending boys. These results appear to be realistic as it was found in the study of Monitoring and Evaluation of SSA Programme in different districts of Uttar Pradesh that roughly 55 to 60 per cent of enrolled children attend their schools regularly.

It was also assessed that out of total children who apply for Pre-matric scholarship, how many of them succeeded in getting the scholarship. As evident in table-2.7 that out of those children who applied for the Pre-matric scholarship, around 40 per cent of them got it. The percentage of Pre-matric scholarship getting children is higher in rural areas of the district as against in urban areas.

The families have largely the younger population and one-fourth family members are working though they are engaged in gainful occupation or not is a different question. The highest education of a family member is high schools in majority of households (Table-2.7).

Table-2.7: Children Going to Schools, Getting Scholarships and Family Structure

Item	Number of Students		
	Rural	Urban	Total
Children Going to School			
Boys	250(63.61)	57(71.25)	307(64.90)
Girls	242(64.02)	54(72.97)	296(65.48)
Total	492(63.81)	111(72.07)	603(65.19)
Students Getting Scholarships			
Boys	92(36.80)	16(28.07)	108(35.18)
Girls	108(44.62)	24(44.44)	132(44.59)
Total	200(40.65)	40(36.36)	240(39.80)
Age Structure of Family Members			
Less than 5 Years	1772(51.95)	355(52.44)	2127(52.03)
5-14 Years	417(12.22)	84(12.41)	501(12.26)
15-23 Years	356(10.44)	72(10.64)	428(10.47)
24-35 Years	177(5.19)	36(5.32)	213(5.21)
36-59 years	118(3.46)	15(2.21)	133(3.25)
60 + years	571(16.74)	115(16.98)	686(16.78)
All Members	3411(100.00)	677(100.00)	4088(100.00)
No. of Earning Members in the Family	850 (24.91)	193 (28.51)	1043 (25.51)
Highest Educational Status of a Member in Family			
High School	54(45.00)	23(46.00)	77(45.30)
Intermediate	43(35.84)	18(36.00)	61(35.88)
Graduate	8(6.67)	3(6.00)	11(6.47)
Post Graduate	3(2.50)	0(0.00)	3(1.76)
Technical/Professional	12(10.00)	6(12.00)	18(10.59)
Total	120(100.00)	50(100.00)	170(100.00)

Note: Figures in brackets indicate percentages.
Source: Primary data based

2.8 Housing:

Sharp difference in housing condition is visible between rural and urban areas. While 87 per cent houses are kachcha in rural area, 91.67 per cent houses are pucca in urban area as evident from table-2.8. While most of the houses are owned in rural areas the same is only 50 per cent in urban areas. In urban areas of the district, around 17 per cent houses have been given by the employers. The average value of a housing unit is Rs. 1.81 lakh in rural areas while it is Rs. 2.50 lakh in urban areas, higher by around 38 per cent. The housing unit has 4 rooms on an average in rural area while the same has 2 rooms in urban area. All the housing units have electricity in urban area. Only 41.67 per cent houses in rural area have electricity. The households holding ration card are 72.22 per cent in rural areas as against 88.33 per cent in urban areas.

Table-2.8: Housing and other Conditions of Sample Students

Housing Type	Rural	Urban	Total
1. Kachcha	261 (87.00)	5 (8.33)	266 (73.89)
2. Pucca	24 (8.00)	55 (91.67)	79 (21,94)
3. Mix	15 (5.00)	0 (0.00)	15 (4.17)
Total	300 (100.00)	60 (100.00)	360 (100.00)
Ownership of the House			
Owned	290 (96.67)	30 (50.00)	320 (88.89)
2. Rented	10 (3.33)	20 (33.34)	30 (8.33)
3. Given by Employer	0 (0.00)	10 (16.66)	10 (2.78)
Value of the House, if owned (Average)	181698	250180	243946
Average Number of Rooms	4	2	3
Houses with Electricity (Yes)	125 (41.67)	60 (100.00)	185 (51.39)
No. of Households with Ration Cards	260 (72.22)	53 (88.33)	313 (86.84)
Percentage of Marginal and Small Land owning Households	241 (80.33)	46 (76.67)	287 (79.72)

Source: Primary Data Based.

2.9 Main Findings:

It is evident that Muslim children in general start getting education late and second is that the number of late starter boys is higher than the late starter girls. It also appears that non-beneficiary (Pre-matric scholarship) students are more late starters than beneficiary students.

It is evident that at all level of schooling, lowest proportion of total sample students are found to be going to government schools except at the secondary levels where 15.79 per cent of all sample students reported to be going to government schools as against 10.53 per cent of them going to Madrasas. The inference is that Muslims also have greater preference for private schooling of their children conforming to the general trend of the Indian society.

It is evident that more than 60 per cent families have average annual income in the range of Rs. 50,000 to Rs. 1,00,000. The proportion of such families is higher (73.33 per cent) in urban areas versus rural areas (58.67 per cent). In view of the fact that people generally tend to disclose their income lower than the actual one, it can be safely assumed here that the majority of Muslim families have annual income higher than 50,000 to Rs. 1, 00,000 per annum. In this situation, the income limit of granting Pre-matric scholarship to those students whose parents have annual income not exceeding Rs. 100,000 merits revision.

It has been observed above, that families in rural as well as in urban areas irrespective of their source of income largely prefers private schools over government schools; hence expenditures are high in view of the average annual income of families in rural and urban areas. Therefore, the amount of Pre-matric scholarship being given at present needs upward revision in view of the current level of expenses incurred by the families on the education at Pre-matric level.

It is found that at the aggregate level; around 65 per cent of schools age children are attending the schools regularly. The percentage of school attending children is higher in urban areas (72.07) in comparison with the children in rural areas (63.81). The percentage of school attending girls is higher in comparison with schools attending boys.

As evident that out of those children who applied for the Pre-matric scholarship, around 40 per cent of them got it. The percentage of Pre-matric scholarship getting children is higher in rural areas of the district as against in urban areas.

Sharp differences in housing conditions are is visible between rural and urban areas. Around one-fourth of total family members are found to be working but whether they are working in gainful occupations or not is a question not enquired here.

Awareness, Utilization and Impact of Pre-matric Scholarship

2.10 Complete Awareness about Pre-matric Scholarship:

The awareness among the sample students about the Pre-matric scholarship was examined and the result has been shown in table-2.9. It is to be mentioned here that the awareness here means complete knowledge of details of Pre-matric scholarship scheme like the name of the scheme, source of availability of its application form, eligibility criteria, knowledge of filling of application form, submission of the form and the date on which the award of the scholarship is known. On the basis of wholesome knowledge of the Pre-matric scholarship scheme, number of beneficiary and non-beneficiary students was found to be not much. However, the fact is that the proportion of beneficiary students who are aware of the details of Pre-matric scheme is higher than the non-beneficiary students as evident from table-2.9. At the aggregate level of rural and urban areas and boys and girls, no major difference in the proportion of scheme knowing students among the beneficiary group and all students is evident.However, the percentage of urban beneficiary boys having awareness of the scheme is higher than the girls in the same group. Similarly, the percentages of non-beneficiary boys and total boys knowing the scheme are higher than of the girls in the respective groups. On the whole, detail awareness about the Pre-matric scholarship among the students is found to be poor in general in Rampur district of Uttar Pradesh and among the girls of the district it is in particular worse than that of the boys. It is to be mentioned here that out of total students (240 students) who were getting Pre-matric scholarship, large number of them were unknown (138 students) that they are getting the Pre-matric scholarshin.

Table-2.9: Students who are Completely Aware of the Pre-matric Scholarship Scheme

Students	No. of Student		
	Rural	Urban	Total
		Beneficiary	
Boys	40 (43.48)	7 (43.75)	47 (43.52)
Girls	46 (42.59)	9 (37.50)	55 (41.67)
Total	86 (43.00)	16 (40.00)	102 (42.50)
		Non-Beneficiary	
Boys	17 (32.69)	8 (53.34)	25 (37.31)
Girls	19 (39.58)	1 (20.00)	20 (37.33)
Total	36 (36.00)	9 (45.00)	45 (37.50)
		All	
Boys	57 (39.58)	15 (48.38)	72 (41.14)
Girls	65 (41.68)	10 (34.48)	75 (40.54)
Total	122 (40.00)	25 (41.67)	147 (40.84)

Note: Figures in brackets indicate percentages.

Source: Primary data based.

2.11 Sources of Awareness of Pre-matric Scholarship to Rural Students:

The sources of awareness of the beneficiary as well as non-beneficiary students of rural areas were obtained from sample students. It is found in table-2.10 that the school teachers are the most important source of awareness to students followed by the fellow students who got scholarship, representative of gram panchayats/urban bodies and radio. It is to be noted here that Newspapers are the least important source of awareness of Pre-matric scholarship to rural students, despite the fact

Table-2.10: Sources of Awareness of Pre-matric Scholarship among Rural Students

Source	Rural (Students)								
	Beneficiary			Non-Beneficiary			Total		
	Boys	Girls	Total	Boys	Girls	Total	Boys	Girls	Total
Teachers	14 (35.00)	17 (36.96)	31 (36.05)	6 (35.29)	7 (36.84)	13 (36.11)	20 (35.09)	24 (36.92)	44 (36.07)
Students who got Scholarship	9 (22.50)	10 (21.74)	19 (22.09)	4 (23.53)	5 (26.32)	9 (25.00)	13 (22.81)	15 (23.08)	28 (22.95)
Gram Panchayat Representatives	7 (17.50)	8 (17.39)	15 (17.44)	3 (17.65)	4 (21.05)	7 (19.45)	10 (17.54)	12 (18.46)	22 (18.03)
Radio/TV	6 (15.00)	7 (15.22)	13 (15.12)	2 (11.77)	2 (10.53)	4 (11.11)	8 (14.03)	9 (13.85)	17 (13.93)
News Papers	4 (10.00)	4 (8.68)	8 (9.30)	2 (11.76)	1 (5.26)	3 (8.33)	6 (10.53)	5 (7.69)	11 (9.02)
Total	40 (100.00)	46 (100.00)	86 (100.00)	17 (100.00)	19 (100.00)	36 (100.00)	57 (100.00)	65 (100.00)	122 (100.00)

Note: Figures in brackets indicate percentages.

Source: Primary data based.

that government officials consider the newspaper as the most important source of spreading awareness about the scholarships. The pattern of awareness is found to be the same across beneficiary and non-beneficiary students of rural areas in the district. The level of awareness from different sources also does not vary much across different groups.

2.12 Sources of Awareness of Pre-matric Scholarship to Urban Students:

The sources of awareness of the beneficiary as well as non-beneficiary students of urban area were obtained from sample students. It is found in the table- 2.11 again that the school teachers are the most important source of awareness to students followed by the fellow students who got scholarship, representative of urban bodies and radio/TV. It is to be noted here that Newspapers are the least important source of awareness of Pre-matric scholarship to urban students about which only 12 per cent students reported that they got information about Pre-matric scholarship.The teachers and fellow students accounted for more than 50 per cent for the sample students as the major source of their awareness for Pre-matric scholarship.

Table-2.11: Sources of Awareness of Pre-matric Scholarship among Urban Students

Source	Urban (Students)								
	Beneficiary			Non-Beneficiary			Total		
	Boys	Girls	Total	Boys	Girls	Total	Boys	Girls	Total
Teachers	2 (28.57)	3 (33.33)	5 (31.25)	2 (25.00)	1 (100.00)	3 (33.33)	4 (26.67)	4 (40.00)	8 (32.00)
Students who got Scholarship	1 (14.29)	2 (22.22)	3 (18.75)	2 (25.00)	- (0.00)	2 (22.22)	3 (20.00)	2 (20.00)	5 (20.00)
Sabhasad	1 (14.29)	- (0.00)	1 (6.25)	- (0.00)	- (0.00)	- (0.00)	1 (6.67)	- (0.00)	1 (4.00)
Radio/TV	2 (28.57)	3 (33.33)	5 (31.25)	3 (37.50)	- (0.00)	3 (33.33)	5 (33.33)	3 (30.00)	8 (32.00)
News Papers	1 (14.28)	1 (11.12)	2 (12.50)	1 (12.50)	- (0.00)	1 (11.12)	2 (13.33)	1 (10.00)	3 (12.00)
Total	7 (100.00)	9 (100.00)	16 (100.00)	8 (100.00)	1 (100.00)	9 (100.00)	15 (100.00)	10 (100.00)	25 (100.00)

Note: Figures in brackets indicate percentages.
Source: Primary data based.

2.13 Sources of Awareness of Pre-matric Scholarship to All Students:

The sources of awareness of the beneficiary as well as non-beneficiary of all sample students were enquired from them. It is found in the table-2.12 that the school teachers are the most important source of awareness to students (35.30 per cent) followed by the fellow students (22.45 per cent) who got scholarship, representative of gram panchayats/urban bodies (15.65) and radio/TV (17.01) and newspapers (9.52 per cent students). The teachers and fellow students accounted for 57.82 per cent of sample students as the major source of their awareness for Pre-matric scholarship. The radio/TV appears to be an important source of spreading awareness about the Pre-matric scholarship.

Table-2.12: Sources of Awareness of Pre-matric Scholarship among All Students

Sources	All Students (Rural and Urban)								
	Beneficiary			Non-Beneficiary			Total		
	Boys	Girls	Total	Boys	Girls	Total	Boys	Girls	Total
Teachers	16 (34.04)	20 (36.36)	36 (35.29)	8 (32.00)	8 (40.00)	16 (35.55)	24 (33.33)	28 (37.33)	52 (35.37)
Students who got Scholarship	10 (21.28)	12 (21.82)	22 (21.57)	6 (24.00)	5 (25.00)	11 (24.44)	16 (22.22)	17 (22.67)	33 (22.45)
Gram Panchayats Representative/Sabhasad	8 (17.02)	8 (14.55)	16 (15.69)	3 (12.00)	4 (20.00)	7 (15.56)	11 (15.28)	12 (16.00)	23 (15.65)
Radio/TV	8 (17.02)	10 (18.18)	18 (17.65)	5 (20.00)	2 (10.00)	7 (15.56)	13 (18.06)	12 (16.00)	25 (17.01)
News Papers	5 (10.64)	5 (9.09)	10 (9.80)	3 (12.00)	1 (5.00)	4 (8.89)	8 (11.11)	6 (8.00)	14 (9.52)
Total	47 (100.00)	55 (100.00)	102 (100.00)	25 (100.00)	20 (100.00)	45 (100.00)	72 (100.00)	75 (100.00)	147 (100.00)

Note: Figures in brackets indicate percentages.

Source: Primary data based.

2.14 Knowledge about Eligibility Conditions:

It has been found above that the teachers are the main source of information of Pre-matric scholarship to students. The teachers generally inform to students that to get the scholarship, a student is to fulfill two conditions. One is that the total annual income of the parents should not

Table- 2.13: Students Knowing Eligibility Conditions of Pre-matric Scholarship Scheme

Students	Rural	Urban	Total
Beneficiary			
Boys	67 (72.82)	13 (81.25)	80 (74.07)
Girls	62 (57.40)	14 (58.34)	76 (57.57)
Total	129 (64.50)	27(67.50)	156 (65.00)
Non-Beneficiary			
Boys	34 (65.38)	13 (86.67)	47 (70.15)
Girls	43 (89.58)	3 (60.00)	46 (86.79)
Total	77 (77.00)	16 (80.00)	93 (77.50)
All			
Boys	101 (70.14)	26 (83.87)	127(72.57)
Girls	105 (67.30)	17 (58.62)	122 (75.95)
Total	206 (68.67)	43 (71.67)	249 (79.17)

Note: Figures in brackets indicate percentages.

Source: Primary data based.

exceed more than 1 lakh in the year and other is that the student should have obtained not less than 50 per cent marks in final examination of last class. When sample students were asked to report their knowledge about these two basis conditions, 69.17 per cent of them reported to be aware of these conditions of Pre-matric scholarship (Table-2.13).

2.15 Knowledge of both Eligibility Conditions:

There are three conditions of getting the Pre-matric scholarship. One is the income limit of Rs. 1 lakh, other is the condition of getting 50 per cent marks in last examination and finally only 2 children are eligible to get the Pre-matric scholarship from a household. When the knowledge of each of three conditions was enquired from the students, they reported what has been placed in table-2.14. The table shows that the substantial percentages of sample students are aware of the first criteria. The same is about second and third conditions. Further, it is evident that the level of awareness about each of the three conditions of getting scholarship was higher in urban areas as against in rural areas of the district.

Table-2.14: Knowledge of Each of the two Eligibility Conditions of Pre-matric Scholarship

Conditions	No. of Students								
	Rural			Urban			Total		
	B.	NB.	Total	B.	NB.	Total	B.	NB.	Total
Household Income not more than Rs. 1 lakh	90 (69.77)	70 (90.91)	160 (77.67)	31 (96.88)	14 (93.33)	45 (95.74)	121 (75.16)	84 (91.30)	205 (81.02)
Marks not less than 50 per cent in last exam	120 (93.02)	75 (97.40)	195 (94.66)	32 (100.00)	15 (100.00)	47 (100.00)	152 (94.41)	90 (97.83)	242 (95.65)
Only 2 students from one household	95 (73.64)	69 (89.61)	164 (79.61)	30 (93.75)	15 (100.00)	45 (95.74)	125 (77.64)	125 (135.87)	250 (98.81)
Total	129 (100.00)	77 (100.00)	206 (100.00)	32 (100.00)	15 (100.00)	47 (100.00)	161 (100.00)	92 (100.00)	253 (100.00)

Note: B- Beneficiary
NB-Non Beneficiary
Note: Figures in brackets indicate percentages.
Source: Primary data based.

2.16 Students Receiving Different Amount of Scholarship:

The sample beneficiary students have reported that 96.25 per cent of them received Pre-matric scholarship between Rs. 1000 to 1500 (Table-2.15).

Table-2.15: Classification of Beneficiary Students According to amount of Scholarship

Amount (Rs.)	Number of Beneficiary Students								
	Rural			Urban			Total		
	Boys	Girls	Total	Boys	Girls	Total	Boys	Girls	Total
1000-1500	89 (96.74)	102 (94.44)	191 (95.50)	16 (100.00)	24 (100.00)	40 (100.00)	105 (97.22)	126 (95.46)	231 (96.25)
1500-2000	3 (3.26)	4 (3.71)	7 (3.50)	-	-	-	3 (2.78)	4 (3.03)	7 (2.92)
More than 2000	-	2 (1.85)	2 (1.00)	-	-	-	-	2 (1.51)	2 (0.83)
Total	92 (100.00)	108 (100.00)	200 (100.00)	16 (100.00)	24 (100.00)	40 (100.00)	108 (100.00)	132 (100.00)	240 (100.00)

Note: Figures in brackets indicate percentages.
Source: Primary data based.

2.17 Mode of Payment of Scholarship Amount:

The beneficiary students have reported that around 55 per cent of them get the scholarship money through the cheque while 45 per cent get in cash. The percentage of rural boys and girls getting in cash is higher than their urban counterparts. Even the higher percentage of urban girls got the money in cash than the urban boys (Table-2.16).

Table-2.16: Mode of Payment of Scholarship Amount

Mode	Rural			Urban			Total		
	Boys	Girls	Total	Boys	Girls	Total	Boys	Girls	Total
Cash	43 (46.74)	51 (47.22)	94 (47.00)	7 (43.75)	11 (45.83)	18 (45.00)	47 (43.52)	62 (46.97)	109 (45.42)
Cheque	49 (53.26)	57 (52.78)	106 (53.00)	9 (56.25)	13 (54.17)	22 (55.00)	61 (56.48)	70 (53.03)	131 (54.58)
Total	92 (100.00)	108 (100.00)	200 (100.00)	16 (100.00)	24 (100.00)	40 (100.00)	108 (100.00)	132 (100.00)	240 (100.00)

Note: Figures in brackets indicate percentages.
Source: Primary data based

2.18 Scholarship Given by Different Persons:

The beneficiary students have reported they get scholarship money from three persons. On the top are their teachers from whom 57.08 per cent students reported to have got the money. Others are as shown in table-2.17.

Table-2.17: Scholarship Given by Different Persons

Particulars	Rural			Urban			Total		
	Boys	Girls	Total	Boys	Girls	Total	Boys	Girls	Total
By Teachers	55 (59.78)	72 (66.67)	127 (63.50)	9 (56.25)	12 (50.00)	21 (52.50)	72 (66.67)	65 (49.24)	137 (57.08)
By Pradhan/Sabhasad	24 (26.09)	28 (25.93)	52 (26.00)	5 (31.25)	8 (33.33)	13 (32.50)	23 (21.30)	35 (26.51)	58 (24.17)
By Secretary	13 (14.13)	8 (7.40)	21 (10.50)	2 (12.50)	4 (16.67)	6 (15.00)	13 (12.03)	32 (24.24)	45 (18.75)
Total	92 (100.00)	108 (100.00)	200 (100.00)	16 (100.00)	24 (100.00)	40 (100.00)	108 (100.00)	132 (100.00)	240 (100.00)

Note: Figures in brackets indicate percentages.
Source: Primary data based.

2.19 Expenses of Getting Pre-matric Scholarship:

The beneficiary students have reported that they spent around Rs. 339 on different formalities to get Pre-matric scholarship. Getting income certificate and affidavit are the two major items of expenditure. The rural beneficiary students spent more as against urban beneficiary students as table-2.18 shows.

Table-2.18: Item wise Expenditure for getting Pre-matric Scholarship

Items	Average Amount (in Rs.)								
	Rural			Urban			Total		
	Boys	Girls	Total	Boys	Girls	Total	Boys	Girls	Total
Income Certificate	154	158	156	146	149	148	150	154	152
On Making Affidavit	106	108	107	93	97	95	100	103	101
Photos, Travels etc.	82	95	89	79	90	85	81	92	85
Total	343	362	353	319	337	319	332	348	339

Source: Primary data based.

2.20 Utilization of Pre-matric Scholarship Amount: Students of Class 1-5:

The beneficiary students have reported that more than 46 percent amount of Pre-matric scholarship is spent on their education. It is slightly higher in case of girls than the boys. Besides, around 17 per cent is spent on medical expenses and around 10 per cent on food. In this way, Pre-matric scholarship has very positive impact on the education of children in particular and also on their health care and food needs (Table-2.19).

Table-2.19: Items wise Average Expenditure of Scholarship Amount: Students of Class-1-5

Items	Average Amount (in Rs.)								
	Rural			Urban			Total		
	Boys	Girls	Total	Boys	Girls	Total	Boys	Girls	Total
1- Books & Stationary	72	73	73	73	75	74	73	74	74
2- Learning Materials	90	85	88	92	86	89	91	86	89
3- Travel	39	41	40	42	45	44	41	43	42
4- Private Tuition Fee	73	68	76	76	69	73	75	69	72
5- Course Fee	198	198	198	203	203	203	201	201	201
6- Medical Expenses	162	156	160	164	158	161	163	157	160
7- Food Expenses	103	94	99	102	97	100	103	96	100
8- Non Food Expenses	190	182	186	193	184	189	192	183	188
9- Debt Return	10	5	8	15	-	8	13	3	8
Total	938	901	927	961	918	940	953	911	935

Source: Primary data based.

2.21 Utilization of Pre-matric Scholarship Amount: Students of Class 6-10:

The utilization pattern of beneficiary students of classes 1-10 as shown in table-2.20 indicates that Pre-matric scholarship has very positive impact on the education of minority students of classes 1- to 10. The money of scholarship spent on health and food is substantial. Certainly the scholarship is great help to minority studentsin meeting their educational and health needs.

Table-2.20: Items wise Average Expenditure of Scholarship Amount: Students of Class-6-10

Items	Average Amount (in Rs.)								
	Rural			Urban			Total		
	Boys	Girls	Total	Boys	Girls	Total	Boys	Girls	Total
1- Books & Stationary	87	89	88	91	95	93	89	92	96
2- Learning Materials	96	98	97	102	106	104	99	102	101
3- Travel	74	76	75	78	82	80	76	79	78
4- Private Tuition Fee	94	98	96	104	107	106	99	103	101
5- Course Fee	208	212	210	213	218	216	210	215	213
6- Medical Expenses	193	198	196	203	207	205	196	203	200
7- Food Expenses	136	139	138	146	149	148	141	144	143
8- Non Food Expenses	203	206	205	212	218	215	208	209	209
9- Debt Return	5	-	3	-	-	-	3	-	2
Total	1097	1117	1107	1149	1182	1166	1123	1150	1137

Source: Primary data based.

2.22 Effectiveness of Pre-matric Scholarship: Rural Students:

The effectiveness of Pre-matric scholarship is evident in table-2.21.The Pre-matric scholarship is very effective in overall educational development of rural students, their health care and family needs and in providing them a silver lining for higher studies and good job prospect.

Table-2.21: Effectiveness of Pre-matric Scholarship: Rural Students

Particulars	Boys	Girls	Total
1. Admission Taken due to Scholarship	2(2.17)	4 (3.70)	6 (3.00)
2. Attendance at the School Improved	17 (18.48)	19 (17.59)	36 (18.00)
3. Scholarship has Fulfilled Study Needs	82 (89.13)	98 (90.74)	180 (90.00)
4. Scholarship has Helped in Health Care Needs	82 (89.13)	98 (90.74)	180 (90.00)
5. Desire to Continue Studies after Getting Scholarship	70 (76.09)	91 (98.91)	161 (80.50)
6. Educational Skills has Improved	83 (90.22)	103 (95.37)	186 (93.00)
7. Involvement in the Household Activities has Reduced.	84 (91.30)	101 (93.52)	185 (92.50)
8. Scholarship has Helped in Family Needs	51 (55.43)	68 (73.91)	119 (59.50)
9. Chances to Continue Study in Higher Class and get a job increased	50 (54.35)	62 (57.41)	112 (56.00)

Note: Figures in brackets indicate percentages.
Source: Primary data based.

2.23 Effectiveness of Pre-matric Scholarship: Urban Students

The positive effectiveness of Pre-matric scholarship to urban students is also evident in table-2.22. The Pre-matric scholarship is very effective in overall educational development of urban students, their health care needs and in providing them a silver lining for higher studies and good job prospect in future.

Table-2.22: Effectiveness of Pre-matric Scholarship: Urban Students

Particulars	Boys	Girls	Total
1. Admission Taken due to Scholarship	0 (0.00)	1 (4.16)	1 (2.50)
2. Attendance at the School Improved	4 (25.00)	3 (12.5)	7 (17.50)
3. Scholarship has Fulfilled Study Needs	14 (87.50)	21 (87.50)	35 (87.50)
4. Scholarship has Helped in Health Care Needs	14 (87.50)	21 (87.50)	35 (87.50)
5. Desire to Continue Studies after Getting Scholarship	14 (87.50)	20 (83.34)	34 (85.00)
6. Educational Skills has Improved	15 (93.75)	24(100..00)	39 (97.50)
7. Involvement in the Household Activities has Reduced.	16(100.00)	24(100.00)	40(100.00)
8. Scholarship has Helped in Family Needs	5 (31.25)	14 (58.34)	19 (47.50)
9. Chances to Continue Study in Higher Class and get a job increased	9 (56.25)	15 (62.50)	24 (60.00)

Note: Figures in brackets indicate percentages.
Source: Primary data based.

2.24 Effectiveness of Pre-matric Scholarship: All Students

The positive effectiveness of Pre-matric scholarship is evident in table-2.23. The Pre-matric scholarship is effective in overall educational development of rural students, their health care and family needs and in providing them a silver lining for higher studies and good job prospect in future.

Table-2.23: Effectiveness of Pre-matric Scholarship: All Students

Particulars	Boys	Girls	Total
1. Admission Taken due to Scholarship	2 (1.85)	5 (3.79)	7 (2.92)
2. Attendance has Increased due to Scholarship	21 (19.44)	22 (16.67)	43(17.92)
3. Scholarship has Fulfilled study Needs	96 (88.89)	112(90.15)	215(89.58)
4. Scholarship have Helped in the Health Care Needs	96 (88.89)	119(90.15)	215(89.58)
5. Desire to Continue his Studies after Getting Scholarship	84 (77.78)	111(84.09)	195(81.25)
6. Educational Skills has Improved	98 (90.74)	127(96.21)	225(93.75)
7. Involvement in the Household Activities had Reduced.	100 (92.59)	125(94.70)	225(93.75)
8. Scholarship have Helped in Family Needs	56 (51.85)	82 (62.12)	138(57.50)
9. Improved the Chances to Continue Study in Higher Class or to Get a Job	59 (54.63)	77 (58.33)	136(56.67)

Note: Figures in brackets indicate percentages.
Source: Primary data based.

2.25 Perception of Rural Students about Pre-matric Scholarship:

The table-2.24 shows that more than 80 per cent rural students both beneficiary and non-beneficiaries feel that there is lack of awareness about the Pre-matric scholarship scheme and language of application form is problem and it is lengthy too. 60 to 71 per cent+ find documentation and income limit as problems. Untimely payment is an issue for less than half of the rural students.

Table-2.24: Views of Rural Students about Pre-matric Scholarship Scheme

Views	Rural								
	Beneficiary			Non-Beneficiary			Total		
	Boys	Girls	Total	Boys	Girls	Total	Boys	Girls	Total
Lack of Awareness about the Details of Scheme	77 (83.70)	92 (85.19)	169 (84.50)	42 (80.77)	39 (81.25)	81 (81.00)	119 (82.64)	131 (83.97)	250 (83.33)
Application Form is Lengthy& Language Problems	73 (79.35)	88 (81.48)	161 (80.50)	40 (76.92)	36 (75.00)	76 (76.00)	113 (78.47)	124 (79.48)	237 (79.00)
Too Much Documentation etc.	67 (72.83)	85 (78.70)	152 (76.00)	37 (71.15)	35 (72.92)	72 (72.00)	104 (72.22)	120 (76.92)	224 (74.67)
Income limit of 1 Lakh	62 (67.39)	83 (76.85)	145 (72.50)	34 (65.38)	33 (68.75)	67 (67.00)	96 (66.67)	116 (74.36)	212 (70.67)
50 Percent limit of Marks	51 (55.43)	70 (64.81)	121 (60.50)	31 (59.62)	32 (66.75)	63 (63.00)	82 (56.94)	102 (65.38)	184 (61.33)
Untimely Payment	45 (48.91)	53 (49.07)	98 (49.00)	25 (48.08)	23 (47.92)	48 (48.00)	70 (48.61)	76 (48.71)	146 (48.67)
Total	92 (100.00)	108 (100.00)	200 (100.00)	52 (100.00)	48 (100.00)	100 (100.00)	144 (100.00)	156 (100.00)	300 (100.00)

Note: Figures in brackets indicate percentages.
Source: Primary data based.

2.26 Perception of Urban Students about Pre-matric Scholarship:

The urban students find four major problems of Pre-matric scholarship as given in table-2.25. The lack of awareness is most serious drawback of Pre-matric scholarship experienced by around more than 85 per cent urban students. Boys and girls feel this problem alike. Lengthy application form and its language are the two other issues felt by more than 78 per cent of urban students. Similarly, too much document is another problem felt by more than 65 per cent urban students.

Table-2.25: Views of Urban Students about Pre-matric Scholarship Scheme

Views	Urban								
	Beneficiary			Non-Beneficiary			Total		
	Boys	Girls	Total	Boys	Girls	Total	Boys	Girls	Total
Lack of Awareness about the Detail of Scheme	14 (87.50)	20 (83.33)	34 (85.00)	13 (86.67)	4 (80.00)	17 (85.00)	27 (87.10)	24 (82.76)	51 (85.00)
Application Form is Lengthy & Language Problems	13 (81.25)	19 (79.17)	32 (80.00)	11 (73.33)	4 (80.00)	15 (75.00)	24 (77.42)	23 (79.31)	47 (78.33)
Too Much Documentation etc.	10 (62.50)	16 (66.67)	26 (65.00)	10 (66.67)	3 (60.00)	13 (65.00)	20 (64.52)	19 (65.52)	39 (65.00)
Income limit of 1 Lakh	9 (56.25)	15 (62.50)	24 (60.00)	9 (60.00)	3 (60.00)	12 (60.00)	18 (58.06)	18 (62.07)	36 (60.00)
50 Percent limit of Marks	8 (50.00)	14 (58.33)	22 (55.00)	8 (53.33)	2 (40.00)	10 (50.00)	16 (51.61)	16 (55.17)	32 (53.33)
6. Untimely Payment	7 (43.75)	11 (45.83)	18 (45.00)	7 (46.67)	2 (40.00)	9 (45.00)	14 (45.16)	13 (44.83)	27 (45.00)
Total	16 (100.00)	24 (100.00)	40 (100.00)	15 (100.00)	5 (100.00)	20 (100.00)	31 (100.00)	29 (100.00)	60 (100.00)

Note: Figures in brackets indicate percentages.
Source: Primary data based.

2.27 Perceptionof AllStudents about Pre-matric Scholarship:

All the above perceptions are expressed by all the students as evident in table-2.26.

Table-2.26: Views of All Students about Pre-matric Scholarship Scheme

Views	Total (Rural and Urban)								
	Beneficiary			Non-Beneficiary			Total		
	Boys	Girls	Total	Boys	Girls	Total	Boys	Girls	Total
Lack of Awareness about the Detail of Scheme	91 (84.26)	112 (84.85)	203 (84.58)	55 (82.09)	43 (81.13)	98 (81.67)	146 (83.43)	155 (83.78)	301 (83.61)
Application Form is Lengthy & Language Problems	86 (79.63)	107 (81.06)	193 (80.42)	51 (76.12)	40 (75.47)	91 (75.83)	137 (78.29)	147 (79.46)	284 (78.89)
Too Much Documentation etc.	77 (71.30)	101 (76.52)	178 (74.17)	47 (70.15)	48 (90.57)	85 (70.83)	124 (70.86)	139 (75.14)	263 (73.06)
Income limit of 1 Lakh	71 (65.74)	98 (74.24)	169 (70.42)	43 (64.18)	36 (67.92)	79 (65.83)	114 (65.14)	134 (72.43)	248 (68.89)
50 Percent limit of Marks	59 (54.63)	84 (63.64)	143 (59.58)	39 (58.21)	34 (64.15)	73 (60.83)	98 (56.00)	118 (63.78)	216 (60.00)
Untimely Payment	52 (48.15)	64 (48.48)	116 (48.33)	32 (47.76)	25 (47.17)	57 (47.50)	84 (48.00)	89 (48.11)	173 (48.06)
Total	108 (100.00)	132 (100.00)	240 (100.00)	67 (100.00)	53 (100.00)	120 (100.00)	175 (100.00)	185 (100.00)	360 (100.00)

Note: Figures in brackets indicate percentages.
Source: Primary data based.

2.28 Main Findings:

- On the whole, detail awareness about the Pre-matric scholarship among the students is found to be poor in general in Rampur district of Uttar Pradesh and among the girls of the district it is in particular worse than that of the boys. It is to be mentioned here that out of total students (240 students) who were getting Pre-matric scholarship, large number of them were unknown (138 students) that they are getting the Pre-matric scholarship.
- It is found that the school teachers are the most important source of awareness to students followed by the fellow students who got scholarship, representative of gram panchayats/ urban bodies and radio/TV. It is to be noted here that newspapers are the least important source of awareness of Pre-matric scholarship to students.
- When sample students were asked to report their knowledge about two basic conditions for getting Pre-matric scholarship, 70 per cent of them reported to be aware of these conditions of Pre-matric scholarship.
- Substantial percentages of sample students are aware of the first condition of getting Pre-matric scholarship. The same is about second and third conditions. Further, it is evident that the level of awareness about each of the three conditions of getting scholarship was higher in urban areas as against in rural areas of the district.
- Getting income certificate, affidavit and photo are the three major items of expenditure

while applying for the Pre-matric scholarship.

- Substantial percentage of students (46 per cent) get scholarship money in cash and majority of students receives it through their teachers.
- The lack of awareness, lengthy application form and its language and too much document are three problems felt by majority students.
- The Pre-matric scholarship is very effective in overall educational development of students, their health care and food needs and in providing them a silver lining for higher studies and good job prospect in future.

Problems in Getting Pre-matric Scholarship and Suggestions of Students

2.29 Students Facing Difficulties while Applying:

The number of students who faced difficulties during the process of application has been shown in table-2.27. The table shows that a high percentage of students faced difficulties. The percentage of students who experienced difficulties were found to be more or less same across rural, urban, boys and girls indicating thereby that most of the applicants of Pre-matric scholarship face difficulties while applying for the scholarship.

Table-2.27: Number of Students Facing difficulties while applying for Pre-matric Scholarship

Students	Rural	Urban	Total
		Beneficiary Students	
Boys	69(75.00)	12(75.00)	81(75.00)
Girls	82(75.00)	18(75.00)	100(75.76)
Total	151(75.50)	30(75.00)	181(75.42)
		Non-Beneficiary Students	
Boys	39(75.00)	11(73.33)	50(74.63)
Girls	36(75.00)	4(80.00)	40(75.47)
Total	75(75.00)	15(75.00)	90(75.00)
		All Students	
Boys	108(75.00)	23(74.19)	131(74.86)
Girls	118(75.64)	22(75.86)	140(75.68)
Total	226(75.33)	45(75.00)	271(75.28)

Note: Figures in brackets indicate percentages.
Source: Primary data based.

2.30 Level of Difficulty in Obtaining Application Form for Rural Students:

Around half of the rural students felt difficulty and one-fourth of them find somewhat difficulty in getting application form. Thus, obtaining application form for applying the Pre-matric scholarship has been difficult for majority of rural students (Table-2.28). The pattern did not differ much across boys and girls.

Table-2.28: Level of Difficulty in Obtaining Application Form: Response of Rural Students

Level of difficulty	Rural								
	Beneficiary			Non-Beneficiary			Total		
	Boys	Girls	Total	Boys	Girls	Total	Boys	Girls	Total
Highly difficulty	19(20.65)	13 (12.04)	32 (16.00)	6 (11.54)	5 (10.42)	11 (11.00)	25 (17.36)	18 (11.54)	43 (14.33)
Difficulty	42 (45.65)	52 (48.15)	94 (47.00)	27 (51.92)	24 (50.00)	51 (51.00)	69 (47.92)	76 (48.72)	145 (48.33)
Somewhat difficulty	23 (25.00)	31 (28.70)	54 (27.00)	16 (30.77)	13 (27.08)	29 (29.00)	39 (27.08)	44 (28.20)	83 (27.67)
No difficulty	8 (8.70)	12 (11.11)	20 (10.00)	3 (5.77)	6 (12.50)	9 (9.00)	11 (7.64)	18 (11.54)	29 (9.67)
Total	92 (100.00)	108 (100.00)	200 (100.00)	52 (100.00)	48 (100.00)	100 (100.00)	144 (100.00)	156 (100.00)	300 (100.00)

Note: Figures in brackets indicate percentages.

Source: Primary data based.

2.31 Level of Difficulty in Obtaining Application Form for Urban Students:

The large number of urban students' also reported difficulty in obtaining application form of Pre-matric scholarship as evident from table-2.29. 13.33 per cent of all urban students found obtaining of application form highly difficult. As high as 80 per cent of total urban students found obtaining of application form difficult and somewhat difficult. Thus, in urban areas of the district Rampur, obtaining application form for Pre-matric scholarshiphas has been difficult for majority of students. Noticeable difference between boys and girls was not evident in this regard.

Table-2.29: Level of Difficulty in Obtaining Application Form: Response of Urban Students

Level of difficulty	Urban								
	Beneficiary			Non-Beneficiary			Total		
	Boys	Girls	Total	Boys	Girls	Total	Boys	Girls	Total
Highly difficulty	2 (12.50)	3 (12.50)	5 (12.50)	2 (13.33)	1 (20.00)	3 (15.00)	4 (12.90)	4 (13.79)	8 (13.33)
Difficulty	9 (56.25)	14 (58.33)	23 (57.50)	7 (46.67)	2 (40.00)	9 (45.00)	16 (51.61)	16 (55.17)	32 (53.33)
Somewhat difficulty	4 (25.00)	6 (25.00)	10 (25.00)	5 (33.33)	1 (20.00)	6 (30.00)	9 (29.03)	7 (24.14)	16 (26.67)
No difficulty	1 (6.25)	1 (4.17)	2 (5.00)	1 (6.67)	1 (20.00)	2 (10.00)	2 (6.45)	2 (6.90)	4 (6.67)
Total	16 (100.00)	24 (100.00)	40 (100.00)	15 (100.00)	5 (100.00)	20 (100.00)	31 (100.00)	29 (100.00)	60 (100.00)

Note: Figures in brackets indicate percentages.

Source: Primary data based.

2.32 Level of Difficulty in Obtaining Application Form for All Students:

While considering all the sample students together who have been the beneficiary of Pre-matric scholarship scheme, it is found in table-2.30 that 14.17 per cent of them found obtaining the application highly difficult. 49.17 per cent and 27.50 per cent found obtaining the application form difficult and somewhat difficult respectively. Around 9.17 per cent of them found obtaining the application form no difficult at all. Such pattern is evident across boys and girls beneficiaries. Thus, what the sample beneficiary students have reported that most of them, irrespective of boys and girls, faced difficulty in obtaining the application form of the Pre-matric scholarship in Rampur district.

Table-2.30: Level of Difficulty in Obtaining Application Form: Response of Total Students

Level of difficulty	Total (Rural and Urban)								
	Beneficiary			Non-Beneficiary			Total		
	Boys	Girls	Total	Boys	Girls	Total	Boys	Girls	Total
Highly difficulty	21 (19.44)	16 (12.12)	37 (15.42)	8 (11.94)	6 (11.32)	14 (11.67)	29 (16.57)	22 (11.89)	51 (14.17)
Difficulty	51 (47.22)	66 (50.00)	117 (48.75)	34 (50.75)	26 (49.06)	60 (50.00)	85 (48.57)	92 (49.73)	177 (49.17)
Somewhat difficulty	27 (25.00)	37 (28.03)	64 (26.67)	21 (31.34)	14 (26.41)	35 (29.17)	48 (27.43)	51 (27.57)	99 (27.50)
Less difficulty	9 (8.33)	13 (9.85)	22 (9.17)	4 (5.97)	7 (13.21)	11 (9.17)	13 (7.43)	20 (10.81)	33 (9.17)
Total	108 (100.00)	132 (100.00)	240 (100.00)	67 (100.00)	53 (100.00)	120 (100.00)	175 (100.00)	185 (100.00)	360 (100.00)

Note: Figures in brackets indicate percentages.

Source: Primary data based.

2.33 Level of Difficulty in Filling Application Form for Rural Students:

Around 18.33 percent of all rural students felt high level of difficulty infilling the application form.The proportion of non-beneficiary students who felt high level of difficulty in filling the form has been higher than the beneficiary boys. The proportion of girls versus boys who felt high level of difficulty was higher. However, majority of them (66 per cent) reported that they felt normal difficulty while 6.34 per cent students felt no problem in filling the form. On the whole, 92 per cent of all rural students felt some sort of difficulty in filling the application form of Pre-matric scholarship. The position in this regards between boys and girls was not substantially apart from each other (Table-2.31).

Table-2.31: Level of Difficulty in filling the Application Form: Response of Rural Students

Level of difficulty	Rural								
	Beneficiary			Non-Beneficiary			Total		
	Boys	Girls	Total	Boys	Girls	Total	Boys	Girls	Total
High difficulty	11 (11.96)	21 (19.44)	32 (16.00)	12 (23.07)	11 (22.91)	23 (23.00)	23 (15.97)	32 (20.51)	55 (18.33)
Difficulty	70 (76.08)	77 (71.30)	147 (73.50)	28 (53.85)	23 (47.92)	51 (51.00)	98 (68.06)	100 (64.10)	198 (66.00)
Somewhat difficulty	7 (7.61)	6 (5.56)	13 (6.50)	6 (11.54)	9 (18.75)	15 (15.00)	13 (9.03)	15 (9.62)	28 (9.33)
No difficulty	4 (4.35)	4 (3.70)	8 (4.00)	6 (11.54)	5 (10.42)	11 (11.00)	10 (6.94)	9 (5.77)	19 (6.34)
Total	92 (100.00)	108 (100.00)	200 (100.00)	52 (100.00)	48 (100.00)	100 (100.00)	144 (100.00)	156 (100.00)	300 (100.00)

Note: Figures in brackets indicate percentages.

Source: Primary data based.

2.34 Level of Difficulty in Filling Application Form for Urban Students:

Out of total urban students, 28.33 per cent reported that they felt high level of difficulty while filling the application form. The percentage of such girls was higher (31.03) as against boys (25.81 per cent). However; majority of them reported difficulty and somewhat difficulty in filling the

Table-2.32: Level of Difficulty in filling the Application Form: Response of Urban Students

Level of difficulty	Urban								
	Beneficiary			Non-Beneficiary			Total		
	Boys	Girls	Total	Boys	Girls	Total	Boys	Girls	Total
High difficult	4 (25.00)	8 (33.33)	12 (30.00)	4 (26.67)	1 (20.00)	5 (25.00)	8 (25.81)	9 (31.03)	17 (28.33)
Difficult	9 (56.25)	13 (54.17)	22 (55.00)	7 (46.66)	3 (60.00)	10 (50.00)	16 (51.61)	16 (55.17)	32 (53.33)
Somewhat difficult	2 (12.5)	1 (4.16)	3 (7.50)	3 (20.00)	1 (20.00)	4 (20.00)	5 (16.13)	2 (6.90)	7 (11.67)
No difficult	1 (6.25)	2 (8.34)	3 (7.50)	1 (6.67)	-	1 (5.00)	2 (6.45)	2 (6.90)	4 (6.67)
Total	16 (100.00)	24 (100.00)	40 (100.00)	15 (100.00)	5 (100.00)	20 (100.00)	31 (100.00)	29 (100.00)	60 (100.00)

Note: Figures in brackets indicate percentages.

Source: Primary data based.

application form. Only around 6 per cent of students find no difficulty in filling the application form as the following table-2.32 shows. On the whole, it can be inferred that difficulty of different levels was encountered by the majority of students whether they were boys or girls in urban areas of Rampur district in filling the application form of Pre-matric scholarship.

2.35 Level of Difficulty in Filling Application Form for All Students:

It is further evident from the response analyzed at the combined level of all students in table-2.33 that 20 per cent of all students felt high difficulty in filling the application form. The proportion of girls finding difficulty is higher (22.16 per cent) than the boys (17.71 per cent). To be precise in other way, majority of boys and girls reported to have faced difficulty in filling the application form of Pre-matric scholarship whether they belong to rural or urban areas as only 6.39 per cent of students encountered no difficulty in filling the application.

Table-2.33: Level of Difficulty in filling the Application Form: Response of Total Students

Level of difficulty	Total (Rural and Urban)								
	Beneficiary			Non-Beneficiary			Total		
	Boys	Girls	Total	Boys	Girls	Total	Boys	Girls	Total
High difficulty	15 (13.88)	29 (21.97)	44 (18.34)	16 (23.88)	12 (22.64)	28 (23.33)	31 (17.71)	41 (22.16)	72 (20.00)
Difficulty	79 (73.15)	90 (68.18)	169 (70.41)	35 (52.24)	26 (49.06)	61 (50.84)	114 (65.14)	116 (62.70)	230 (63.89)
Somewhat difficulty	9 (8.34)	7 (5.30)	16 (6.67)	9 (13.43)	10 (18.87)	19 (15.83)	18 (10.29)	17 (9.19)	35 (9.72)
No difficulty	5 (4.63)	6 (4.55)	11 (4.58)	7 (10.45)	5 (9.43)	12 (10.00)	12 (6.86)	11 (5.95)	23 (6.39)
Total	108 (100.00)	132 (100.00)	240 (100.00)	67 (100.00)	53 (100.00)	120 (100.00)	175 (100.00)	185 (100.00)	360 (100.00)

Note: Figures in brackets indicate percentages.

Source: Primary data based.

2.36 Cooperation of Institution in getting Pre-matric Scholarship: Rural Students:

The table-2.34 shows that around 64 per cent students in rural areas of Rampur district find the role of institution where they study satisfactory in helping them to get Pre-matric scholarship. In this regard, the proportion of boys and girls are roughly the same. There is also no major difference among the beneficiary versus non beneficiary boys and girls.It is also to be noted here that those rural students who find the cooperation of their institutions unsatisfactory and highly unsatisfactory constitute around 36 per cent of rural students. These are the good number of rural students who find the cooperation of their institutions unsatisfactory.

Table-2.34: Level of Cooperation of Institutions in helping Students to get Scholarship: Perception of Rural Students

Items	Rural								
	Beneficiary			Non-Beneficiary			Total		
	Boys	Girls	Total	Boys	Girls	Total	Boys	Girls	Total
Highly Satisfactory	17 (18.48)	15 (13.89)	32 (16.00)	9 (17.31)	7 (14.58)	16 (16.00)	26 (18.05)	22 (14.10)	48 (16.00)
Satisfactory	41 (44.57)	59 (54.63)	100 (50.00)	24 (46.15)	21 (43.75)	45 (45.00)	65 (45.14)	80 (51.28)	145 (48.33)
Unsatisfactory	25 (27.17)	29 (26.85)	54 (27.00)	15 (28.85)	18 (37.50)	33 (33.00)	40 (27.78)	47 (30.13)	87 (29.00)
Highly Unsatisfactory	9 (9.78)	5 (4.63)	14 (7.00)	4 (7.69)	2 (4.17)	6 (6.00)	13 (9.03)	7 (4.49)	20 (6.67)
Total	92 (100.00)	108 (100.00)	200 (100.00)	52 (100.00)	48 (100.00)	100 (100.00)	144 (100.00)	156 (100.00)	300 (100.00)

Note: Figures in brackets indicate percentages.
Source: Primary data based.

2.37 Cooperation of Institution in getting Pre-matric Scholarship: Urban Students:

The students reported that 15 per cent of them were highly satisfied and 48.33 were satisfied with the cooperation of their institution in helping to them to get the Pre-matric scholarship (Table-3.35).

Table-2.35: Level of Cooperation of Institutions in helping Students to get Scholarship: Perception of Urban Students

Items	Urban								
	Beneficiary			Non-Beneficiary			Total		
	Boys	Girls	Total	Boys	Girls	Total	Boys	Girls	Total
Highly Satisfactory	2 (12.50)	4 (16.67)	6 (15.00)	2 (13.33)	1 (20.00)	3 (15.00)	4 (12.90)	5 (17.24)	9 (15.00)
Satisfactory	8 (50.00)	11 (45.83)	19 (47.50)	8 (53.34)	2 (40.00)	10 (50.00)	16 (51.61)	13 (44.83)	29 (48.33)
Unsatisfactory	5 (31.25)	6 (25.00)	11 (27.50)	3 (20.00)	1 (20.00)	4 (20.00)	8 (25.81)	7 (24.14)	15 (25.00)
Highly Unsatisfactory	1 (6.25)	3 (12.50)	4 (10.00)	2 (13.33)	1 (20.00)	3 (15.00)	3 (9.68)	4 (13.79)	7 (11.67)
Total	16 (100.00)	24 (100.00)	40 (100.00)	15 (100.00)	5 (100.00)	20 (100.00)	31 (100.00)	29 (100.00)	60 (100.00)

Note: Figures in brackets indicate percentages. Source: Primary data based.

2.38 Cooperation of Institution in getting Pre-matric Scholarship to All Students:

It reflects from the table-2.36 that majority of students whether boys and girls are found to be satisfied from their respective institutions which help them to get the Pre-matric scholarship. However, it is also evident that around 35 per cent of students are not satisfied with their institutions this regard.

Table-2.36: Level of Cooperation of Institutions in helping Students to get Scholarship: Perception of All Students

Items	Total (Rural and Urban)								
	Beneficiary			Non-Beneficiary			Total		
	Boys	Girls	Total	Boys	Girls	Total	Boys	Girls	Total
Highly Satisfactory	19 (17.59)	19 (14.39)	38 (15.84)	11 (16.42	8 (15.09)	19 (15.83)	30 (17.14)	27 (14.59)	57 (15.83)
Satisfactory	49 (45.37)	70 (53.03)	119 (49.58)	32 (47.76)	23 (43.40)	55 (45.83)	81 (46.29)	93 (50.27)	174 (48.34)
Unsatisfactory	30 (27.78)	35 (26.52)	65 (27.08)	18 (26.87)	19 (35.85)	37 (30.84)	48 (27.43)	54 (29.19)	102 (28.33)
Highly Unsatisfactory	10 (9.26)	8 (6.06)	18 (7.50)	6 (8.95)	3 (5.66)	9 (7.50)	16 (9.14)	11 (5.95)	27 (7.50)
Total	108 (100.00)	132 (100.00)	240 (100.00)	67 (100.00)	53 (100.00)	120 (100.00)	175 (100.00)	185 (100.00)	360 (100.00)

Note: Figures in brackets indicate percentages.
Source: Primary data based.

2.39 Role of State Government Officials: Perception of Rural Students

The table-2.37 indicates that around half of the rural students feel unsatisfied with the role of state government officials in the matter of Pre-matric scholarship. No difference among beneficiary and non-beneficiary students is evident in this regard.

Table-2.37: Role of State Government Officials: Response of Rural Students

Level of Satisfaction	Rural								
	Beneficiary			Non-Beneficiary			Total		
	Boys	Girls	Total	Boys	Girls	Total	Boys	Girls	Total
Highly Satisfactory	19 (20.65)	19 (17.59)	38 (19.00)	11 (21.15)	9 (18.75)	20 (20.00)	30 (20.83)	28 (17.95)	58 (19.33)
Satisfactory	31 (33.70)	33 (30.56)	64 (32.00)	16 (30.77)	15 (31.25)	31 (31.00)	47 (32.64)	48 (30.77)	95 (31.67)
Unsatisfactory	36 (39.13)	48 (44.44)	84 (42.00)	21 (40.39)	21 (43.75)	42 (42.00)	57 (39.58)	69 (44.23)	126 (42.00)
Highly Unsatisfactory	6 (6.52)	8 (7.41)	14 (7.00)	4 (7.69)	3 (6.25)	7 (7.00)	10 (6.95)	11 (7.05)	21 (7.00)
Total	92 (100.00)	108 (100.00)	200 (100.00)	52 (100.00)	48 (100.00)	100 (100.00)	144 (100.00)	156 (100.00)	300 (100.00)

Note: Figures in brackets indicate percentages.
Source: Primary data based.

2.40 Role of State Government Officials: Perception of Urban Students:

As far the urban students are concerned, around half of the students are found to be unsatisfied with the role of state government officials and around half of them feel otherwise (Table-2.38).

Table-2.38: Role of State Government Officials: Response of Urban Students

Level of Satisfaction	Urban								
	Beneficiary			Non-Beneficiary			Total		
	Boys	Girls	Total	Boys	Girls	Total	Boys	Girls	Total
Highly Satisfactory	3 (18.75)	5 (20.83)	8 (20.00)	3 (20.00)	1 (20.00)	4 (20.00)	6 (19.35)	6 (20.69)	12 (20.00)
Satisfactory	5 (31.25)	8 (33.33)	13 (32.50)	5 (33.33)	1 (20.00)	6 (30.00)	10 (32.26)	9 (31.03)	19 (31.67)
Unsatisfactory	7 (43.75)	10 (41.67)	17 (42.50)	6 (40.00)	2 (40.00)	8 (40.00)	13 (41.94)	12 (41.38)	25 (41.66)
Highly Unsatisfactory	1 (6.25)	1 (4.17)	2 (5.00)	1 (6.67)	1 (20.00)	2 (10.00)	2 (6.45)	2 (6.90)	4 (6.67)
Total	16 (100.00)	24 (100.00)	40 (100.00)	15 (100.00)	5 (100.00)	20 (100.00)	31 (100.00)	29 (100.00)	60 (100.00)

Note: Figures in brackets indicate percentages.
Source: Primary data based.

2.41 Role of State Government Officials: Perception of All Students:

It becomes evident from table-2.39 that around half of them were satisfied and within this group around 20 per cent were highly satisfied. Thus, around half of the students were also not satisfied with the role of state government officials in getting Pre-matric scholarship to them.

Table-2.39: Role of State Government Officials: Response of All Students

Level of Satisfaction	Total (Rural and Urban)								
	Beneficiary			Non-Beneficiary			Total		
	Boys	Girls	Total	Boys	Girls	Total	Boys	Girls	Total
Highly Satisfactory	22 (20.37)	24 (18.18)	46 (19.17)	14 (20.90)	10 (18.87)	24 (20.00)	36 (20.57)	34 (18.38)	70 (19.44)
Satisfactory	36 (33.34)	41 (31.06)	77 (32.08)	21 (31.34)	16 (30.19)	37 (30.83)	57 (32.57)	57 (30.81)	114 (31.67)
Unsatisfactory	43 (39.81)	58 (43.94)	101 (42.08)	27 (40.30)	23 (43.39)	50 (41.67)	70 (40.00)	81 (43.78)	151 (41.94)
Highly Unsatisfactory	7 (6.48)	9 (6.82)	16 (6.67)	5 (7.46)	4 (7.55)	9 (7.50)	12 (6.87)	13 (7.03)	25 (6.95)
Total	108 (100.00)	132 (100.00)	240 (100.00)	67 (100.00)	53 (100.00)	120 (100.00)	175 (100.00)	185 (100.00)	360 (100.00)

Note: Figures in brackets indicate percentages.
Source: Primary data based.

2.42 Suggestions of Students to Improve the Pre-matric Scholarship Scheme:

The following tables shows that five major suggestions have been given by rural, urban and all students. These suggestions are that (i) awareness Campaign at community, institutions and panchayatlevel should be launched, (ii) amount of scholarship should be increased, (iii) income certificate given by Pradhan/Sabhasad should be accepted, (iv) more than 2 children should be eligible for the scholarship from one family and (v) application form should be simplifiedand be made multilingual.

Table-2.40: Suggestions of Students in Improving the Scheme: Rural Students

Suggestions	No. of Students								
	Beneficiary			Non-Beneficiary			Total		
	Boys	Girls	Total	Boys	Girls	Total	Boys	Girls	Total
Awareness Campaign at Community, Institutions and Panchayat Level	76 (82.61)	91 (84.26)	167 (83.50)	43 (82.69)	40 (83.33)	83 (83.00)	119 (82.64)	131 (83.97)	250 (83.33)
Scholarship amount should be Increased.	72 (78.26)	90 (83.33)	162 (81.00)	39 (75.00)	37 (77.08)	76 (76.00)	111 (77.08)	127 (81.41)	238 (79.33)
Income certificate given by Pradhan/Sabhasad should be accepted	67 (72.83)	86 (79.63)	153 (76.50)	31 (59.62)	30 (62.50)	61 (61.00)	98 (68.06)	116 (74.36)	214 (71.33)
More than 2 children should be eligible from onle Family	61 (66.30)	82 (75.93)	143 (71.50)	28 (53.85)	27 (56.25)	55 (55.00)	89 (61.81)	109 (69.87)	198 (66.00)
Application form should be simple and multilingual.	59 (64.13)	71 (65.74)	130 (65.00)	22 (42.31)	23 (47.92)	45 (45.00)	81 (56.25)	94 (60.26)	175 (58.33)
No criteria of percentage of marks	48 (52.17)	59 (54.63)	107 (53.50)	18 (34.62)	17 (35.42)	35 (35.00)	66 (45.83)	76 (48.72)	142 (47.33)
Total	92 (100.00)	108 (100.00)	200 (100.00)	52 (100.00)	48 (100.00)	100 (100.00)	144 (100.00)	156 (100.00)	300 (100.00)

Note: Figures in brackets indicate percentages.
Source: Primary data based.

Table-2.41: Suggestions of Students in Improving the Scheme: Urban Students

Suggestions	No. of Students								
	Beneficiary			Non-Beneficiary			Total		
	Boys	Girls	Total	Boys	Girls	Total	Boys	Girls	Total
Awareness Campaign at Community, Institutions and Panchayat Level	13 (81.25)	19 (79.17)	32 (80.00)	12 (80.00)	4 (80.00)	16 (80.00)	25 (80.65)	23 (79.31)	48 (80.00)
Scholarship amount should be increased.	12 (75.00)	18 (75.00)	30 (75.00)	11 (73.33)	4 (80.00)	15 (75.00)	23 (74.19)	22 (75.86)	45 (75.00)
Income certificate given by Pradhan/Sabhasad should be accepted	10 (62.50)	16 (66.67)	26 (65.00)	9 (60.00)	3 (60.00)	12 (60.00)	19 (61.29)	19 (65.52)	38 (63.33)
More than 2 children should be eligible from one family	10 (62.50)	15 (62.50)	25 (62.50)	8 (53.33)	3 (60.00)	11 (55.00)	18 (58.06)	18 (62.07)	36 (60.00)
Application form should be simple and multilingual.	9 (56.25)	14 (58.33)	23 (57.50)	7 (46.67)	2 (40.00)	9 (45.00)	16 (51.61)	16 (55.17)	32 (53.33)
No criteria of Percentage of marks	8 (50.00)	12 (50.00)	20 (50.00)	6 (40.00)	2 (40.00)	8 (40.00)	14 (45.16)	14 (48.28)	28 (46.67)
Total	16 (100.00)	24 (100.00)	40 (100.00)	15 (100.00)	5 (100.00)	20 (100.00)	31 (100.00)	29 (100.00)	60 (100.00)

Note: Figures in brackets indicate percentages.
Source: Primary data based

Table-2.42: Suggestions of Students in Improving the Scheme: All Students

Suggestions	No. of Students								
	Beneficiary			Non-Beneficiary			Total		
	Boys	Girls	Total	Boys	Girls	Total	Boys	Girls	Total
Awareness Campaign at Community, Institutions and Panchayat Level	89 (82.40)	110 (83.33)	199 (82.92)	55 (82.09)	44 (83.02)	99 (82.50)	144 (82.28)	154 (83.24)	298 (82.78)
Scholarship amount should be Increased.	84 (77.78)	108 (81.82)	192 (80.00)	50 (74.63)	41 (77.36)	91 (75.83)	134 (76.57)	149 (80.54)	283 (78.61)
Income certificate given by Pradhan/Sabhasad should be accepted	77 (71.30)	102 (77.27)	179 (74.58)	40 (59.70)	33 (62.26)	73 (60.83)	117 (66.86)	135 (72.97)	252 (70.00)
More than 2 children should be eligible from one family	71 (65.74)	97 (73.48)	168 (70.00)	36 (53.73)	30 (56.60)	66 (55.00)	107 (61.14)	127 (68.65)	234 (65.00)
Application Form should be simple and multilingual.	68 (62.96)	85 (64.39)	153 (63.75)	29 (43.28)	25 (47.17)	54 (45.00)	97 (55.43)	110 (59.46)	207 (57.50)
No Criteria of Percentage of marks	56 (51.85)	71 (53.79)	127 (52.92)	24 (35.82)	19 (35.85)	43 (35.83)	80 (45.71)	90 (48.65)	170 (47.22)
Total	108 (100.00)	132 (100.00)	240 (100.00)	67 (100.00)	53 (100.00)	120 (100.00)	175 (100.00)	185 (100.00)	360 (100.00)

Note: Figures in brackets indicate percentages.
Source: Primary data based.

2.43 Main Findings:

- A very high percentage of students faced difficulties while applying for the Pre-matric scholarship. The percentage of students who experienced difficulty were found to be more or less same across rural, urban, boys and girls and beneficiaries versus non-beneficiaries.
- The obtaining of application form for applying the Pre-matric scholarship has been difficult for majority of students. The pattern did not differ much across rural, urban, boys and girls and beneficiaries and non-beneficiaries.
- The majority of boys and girls, beneficiaries and non-beneficiaries, rural and urban students faced difficulties in filling the application form of Pre-matric scholarship.
- The majority of students were satisfied with cooperation of their intuitions in helping them to get the Pre-matric scholarship but around 35 per cent of them were found to be unsatisfied too.
- Around half of the students were satisfied and half unsatisfied with the role of state government officials in helping them to get the Pre-matric scholarship. Marginally higher percentage of beneficiary students was dissatisfied than the non-beneficiary students. Similarly, more girls were dissatisfied than the boys.

- The five suggestions were given by the students to make the Pre-matric scholarship more students friendly. These are that awareness Campaign at community, institutions and panchayat level should be launched, amount of scholarship should be increased, income certificate given by Pradhan/Sabhasad should be accepted, more than 2 children should be eligible for the scholarship from one family and application form should be simplified and be made multilingual

Parents of Beneficiary and Non-Beneficiary Students, Institutions and Officials

2.44 Sample Parents:

The total sample of parents was 180 which included 150 parents from rural areas and 30 from urban areas of Rampur district. The beneficiary parents were 120 and non-beneficiary parents were 60 as shown in the following table-2.43.

Table-2.43 Sample of the Parents

Particular	Location	No. of Parents
Beneficiary Parents	Rural	100 (83.33)
	Urban	20 (16.67)
	Total	120 (100.0)
Non-beneficiary Parents	Rural	50 (83.33)
	Urban	10 (16.67)
	Total	60 (100.0)
Total	Rural	150 (83.33)
	Urban	30 (16.67)
	Total	180 (100.0)

Note: Figures in brackets indicate percentages.
Source: Primary data based.

2.45 Housing and Family Features:

Housing and family features have been shown in table-2.44. Houses are generally pucca or semi-pucca, having 3 and 2 rooms in houses of beneficiary and non-beneficiary parents respectively. The family size is 6 persons in both cases. Around 30 per cent houses have no electricity and all of them hold ration card.

Table-2.44: Housing and Family Conditions of Sample Parents

Particular	Beneficiary	Non-beneficiary Parents
Type of House		
Katchcha	20 (16.67)	11 (18.34)
Pucca	53 (44.16)	26 (43.33)
Semi Pucca	47 (39.17)	23 (38.33)
Average Value of House (Rs.)	4,75000	4,50000
Average No. of Rooms	3	2
Average Family Size	6	6
Average Earning Members in the family	2	2
House Electrified (Yes)	83 (69.17)	41(68.33)
Ration Card Holders		
BPL	62 (51.67)	25 (41.67)
APL	53 (44.16)	32 (53.33)
Other	5 (4.17)	3 (5.00)

Note: Figures in brackets indicate percentages.
Source: Primary data based.

2.46 Land Size and Income of Beneficiary Parents:

Beneficiary parents are mostly the marginal and small land owners and around 60 per cent of them have average annual income in the range of Rs. 20-50 thousand (Table-2.45).

Table-2.45: Land Size and Income of Beneficiary Parents

Land Holding	Number-120	HH Income	Number-120
Less than 0.5 acre	89 (74.16)	Less than Rs. 20,000	--
0.5 to 1.00 acre	18 (15.00)	20-50,000	76 (63.33)
More than 1.00 acre	13 (10.84)	50,000 +	44 (36.67)
Average	0.6	Average	48,900
Min	0.3	Min	36,000
Max	6	Max	72,000

Note: Figures in brackets indicate percentages.
Source: Primary data based.

2.47 Land Size and Income of Non-beneficiary Parents:

The non-beneficiary parents are also the marginal and small land owners but 67 per cent of them have average annual income of Rs. 50,000 and more (Table-2.46).

Table-2.46: Land Size and Income of Non-beneficiary Parents

Land Holding	Number-60	HH Income	Number-60
Less than 0.5 acre	12 (20.00)	Less than Rs. 20,000	-
0.5 to 1.00 acre	28 (46.67)	20-50,000	20 (33.33)
More than 1.00 acre	20 (33.33)	50,000 +	40 (66.67)
Average	0.66	Average	57467
Min	0.5	Min	36000
Max	4	Max	90000

Note: Figures in brackets indicate percentages.
Source: Primary data based.

2.48 Awareness about Pre-matric Scholarship:

The awareness about the Pre-matric scholarship is found to limited among the beneficiary, non-beneficiary, rural and urban parents as evident from the following table.

Table-2.47: Parents Knowing the Pre-matric Scholarship Scheme

Particulars	Number of Parents		
	Beneficiary	Non Beneficiary	Total
Rural	50 (50.00)	25 (50.00)	75 (50.00)
Urban	11 (55.00)	5 (50.00)	16 (53.33)
Total	61 (50.83)	30 (50.00)	91 (50.56)

Note: Figures in brackets indicate percentages.
Source: Primary data based.

2.49 Sources of Awareness of Pre-matric Scholarship:

For majority of parents of rural, urban, beneficiary and non-beneficiary students, major sources of awareness of Pre-matric scholarship are teachers, relatives and radio/TV (Table-2.48).

Table-2.48: Sources of Awareness of Pre-matric Scholarship Scheme

Source	Number of Parents								
	Rural			Urban			Total		
	B	NB	Total	B	NB	Total	B	NB	Total
Teachers	21 (42.00)	12 (48.00)	33 (44.00)	6 (54.54)	3 (60.00)	9 (56.25)	27 (44.26)	15 (50.00)	42 (46.15)
Radio/T.V	6 (12.00)	3 (12.00)	9 (12.00)	1 (9.10)	-	1 (6.25)	7 (11.48)	3 (10.00)	10 (10.99)
News Papers	3 (6.00)	1 (4.00)	4 (5.33)	1 (9.10)	-	1 (6.25)	4 (6.56)	1 (3.33)	5 (5.49)
Other Students who have Previously received the scholarship	1 (2.00)	-	1 (1.33)	-	-	-	1 (1.64)	-	1 (1.10)
Relatives	15 (30.00)	6 (24.00)	21 (28.00)	3 (27.26)	2 (40.00)	5 (31.25)	18 (29.50)	8 (26.68)	26 (28.57)
Local Community	2 (4.00)	1 (4.00)	3 (4.00)	-	-	-	2 (3.28)	1 (3.33)	3 (3.30)
Informal Chatting	1 (2.00)	1 (4.00)	2 (2.67)	-	-	-	1 (1.64)	1 (3.33)	2 (2.20)
Private Tutors	1 (2.00)	1 (4.00)	2 (2.67)	-	-	-	1 (1.64)	1 (3.33)	2 (2.20)
Total Responses	50 (100.00)	25 (100.00)	75 (100.00)	11 (100.00)	5 (100.00)	16 (100.00)	61 (100.00)	30 (100.00)	91 (100.00)

Note: Figures in brackets indicate percentages.
Source: Primary data based.

2.50 Reasons of untimely payment of Pre-matric Scholarship:

The beneficiary parents have given three reasons of untimely payment of Pre-matric scholarship which are as shown in table-2.49.

Table-2.49: Reasons of Pre-matric Scholarship not getting Timely

Reasons	Number of Parents		
	Rural	Urban	Total
Delay by MOMA	23 (27.38)	3 (21.43)	26 (26.53)
Delay by District Authorities	36 (42.86)	7 (50.00)	43 (43.88)
Delay by the Institutions	25 (29.76)	4 (28.57)	29 (29.59)
Total	84 (100.00)	14 (100.00)	98 (100.00)

Note: Figures in brackets indicate percentages.
Source: Primary data based.

2.51 Problems Faced by Beneficiary Students: Perception of their Parents:

70 per cent parents of beneficiary students felt that their ward faced problems in getting the Pre-matric scholarship (Table-2.50).

Table-2.50: problems Faced by Students in getting the Pre-matric Scholarship: Parents Responses

Particulars	Number of Parents		
	Yes	No	Total
Rural	70 (70.00)	30 (30.00)	100 (100.00)
Urban	14 (70.00)	6 (30.00)	20 (100.00)
Total	84 (70.00)	36 (30.00)	120 (100.00)

Note: Figures in brackets indicate percentages.
Source: Primary data based.

2.52 Level of Difficulty Faced in Filling the Application Form: Perception of their Parents:

All 180 Parents are faced difficulties at different levels in filling the application form as evident in following table-2.51.

Table-2.51: Level of Difficulty in Filling the Application Form

Level of Difficulty	Rural			Urban			Total (Rural and Urban)		
	Beneficiary	Non Beneficiary	Total	Beneficiary	Non Beneficiary	Total	Beneficiary	Non Beneficiary	Total
High Difficulty	29 (29.00)	13 (26.00)	42 (28.00)	4 (20.00)	2 (20.00)	6 (20.00)	33 (27.50)	15 (25.00)	48 (26.67)
Difficulty	46 (46.00)	20 (40.00)	66 (44.00)	12 (60.00)	5 (50.00)	17 (56.67)	58 (48.33)	25 (41.67)	83 (46.11)
Some What Difficulty	15 (15.00)	12 (24.00)	27 (18.00)	2 (10.00)	2 (20.00)	4 (13.33)	17 (14.17)	14 (23.33)	31 (17.22)
Less Difficult	10 (10.00)	5 (10.00)	15 (10.00)	2 (10.00)	1 (10.00)	3 (10.00)	12 (10.00)	6 (10.00)	18 (10.00)
Total	100 (100.00)	50 (100.00)	150 (100.00)	20 (100.00)	10 (100.00)	30 (100.00)	120 (100.00)	60 (100.00)	180 (100.00)

Note: Figures in brackets indicate percentages.
Source: Primary data based.

2.53 Rating of Various Processes of Pre-matric Scholarship: Beneficiary Parents:

The rating of various processes of Pre-matric Scholarship by the beneficiary rural, urban and all parents has been given in tables-2.52, 2.53 and 2.54. To the six aspects of Pre-matric scholarship, four has been given average rating while renewal process has been given poor rating and support of school administration as good rating.

Table-2.52: Perception of Beneficiary Parents about various Aspects of Pre-matric Scholarship Scheme: Rural Parents

Particulars	Number of Parents					
	Poor	Average	Good	Very good	Excellent	Total
Scholarship Amount	4 (2.67)	63 (42.00)	42 (28.00)	26 (17.33)	15 (10.00)	150 (100.00)
Documentation	47 (31.33)	71 (47.33)	32 (21.34)	0 (0.00)	0 (0.00)	150 (100.00)
Renewal Process	98 (65.33)	52 (34.67)	0 (0.00)	0 (0.00)	0 (0.00)	150 (100.00)
Availability of Application Form	1 (0.67)	67 (44.67)	41 (27.33)	24 (16.00)	17 (11.33)	150 (100.00)
Timeliness of Processing	39 (26.00)	71 (47.33)	34 (22.67)	6 (4.00)	0 (0.00)	150 (100.00)
Support of School Administration	2 (1.33)	46 (30.67)	69 (46.00)	29 (19.33)	4 (2.67)	150 (100.00)

Note: Figures in brackets indicate percentages.
Source: Primary data based.

Table-2.53: Perception of Beneficiary Parents about various Aspects of Pre-matric Scholarship Scheme: Urban Parents

Particulars	Number of Parents					
	Poor	Average	Good	Very good	Excellent	Total
Scholarship Amount	2 (6.67)	11 (36.66)	7 (23.33)	5 (16.67)	5 (16.67)	30 (100.00)
Documentation	7 (23.34)	19 (63.33)	4 (13.33)	0 (0.00)	0 (0.00)	30 (100.00)
Renewal Process	19 (63.33)	11 (36.67)	0 (0.00)	0 (0.00)	0 (0.00)	30 (100.00)
Availability of Application Form	2 (6.67)	14 (46.67)	7 (23.33)	5 (16.66)	2 (6.67)	30 (100.00)
Timeliness of Processing	9 (30.00)	16 (53.33)	3 (10.00)	2 (6.67)	0 (0.00)	30(100.00)
Support of School Administration	2 (6.67)	7 (23.33)	14 (46.66)	5 (16.67)	2 (6.67)	30 (100.00)

Note: Figures in brackets indicate percentages.
Source: Primary data based.

Table-2.54: Perception of Beneficiary Parents about various Aspects of Pre-matric Scholarship Scheme: All Parents

Particulars	Number of Parents					
	Poor	Average	Good	Very good	Excellent	Total
Scholarship Amount	6 (3.34)	74 (41.11)	49 (27.22)	31 (17.22)	20 (11.11)	180(100.00)
Documentation	54 (30.00)	90 (50.00)	36 (20.00)	0 (0.00)	0 (0.00)	180(100.00)
Renewal Process	117(65.00)	63 (35.00)	0 (0.00)	0 (0.00)	0 (0.00)	180(100.00)
Availability of Application Form	3 (1.67)	81 (45.00)	48 (26.67)	29 (16.11)	19 (10.55)	180(100.00)
Timeliness of Processing	48 (26.67)	87 (48.33)	37 (20.56)	8 (4.44)	0 (0.00)	180(100.00)
Support of School Administration	4(2.22)	53(29.44)	83(46.11)	34(18.89)	6(3.34)	180(100.00)

Note: Figures in brackets indicate percentages.
Source: Primary data based.

2.54 Parents Perceptions on Scholarship:

The following views were expressed by the parents about the Pre-matric Scholarship Scheme:

1. Scholarship is helpful for education of Children.
2. Lack of Awareness about Pre-matric Scholarship Scheme implemented by MOMA Government of India.
3. Lack of Knowledge about important dates of Scheme.
4. Non-Corporative attitude of government educational Institutions.
5. Application form is in English and also lengthy.
6. Applying process is costly due to need of income certificate and Affidavit by Court.
7. Delay processing and late distribution of Scholarship.
8. Conditions of only two children from a family, income and 50 marks of last examination should be relaxed.
9. Scholarship Amount should be increased for girls' students.
10. Regular checking of Scheme at community and institution level should be encouraged.

2.55 Sample Institutions:

The sample institutions are located mainly in rural areas of the district as per following table-5.55.

Table-2.55: Location of Sample Institution

Location	Number of Institution
Rural	8 (61.54)
Urban	5 (38.46)
Total	13 (100.00)

2.56: Type of Sample Institutions

The sample institutions are mainly of primary level and private (Table-2.56 and Table-2.57).

Table-2.56: Type of Institutions

Particulars	No. of Institutions
Primary	7 (53.84)
Middle	3 (23.08)
Secondary	-
Higher Secondary	3 (23.08)
Total	13 (100.00)

Table-2.57: Type of Institutions

S. No.	Particulars	No. of Institutions
1	Government	-
2	Private	12 (92.31)
3	Aided	1 (7.69)
	Total	13 (100.00)

Source: Primary data based

2.57: Enrolment, Applied and Award of Pre-matric Scholarship: Rural Areas:

Among the total enrolled students, 52 per cent applied for Pre-matric Scholarship and 42 per cent succeeded in getting it. The percentage of applied and awarded boys was higher than girls in rural areas.

Table-2.58: Year-wise Enrolment, Applied and Pre-matric Scholarship Awarded to Students in Sample Institutions of Rampur District (Rural)

Year	Enrolled			Applied			Awarded		
	Boys	Girls	Total	Boys	Girls	Total	Boys	Girls	Total
2009-10	186 (100.00)	133 (100.00)	319 (100.00)	95 (51.07)	53 (39.85)	148 (46.39)	27 (28.32)	23 (43.40)	50 (33.78)
2010-11	188 (100.00)	131 (100.00)	319 (100.00)	112 (59.57	72 (54.96)	184 (57.68)	52 (46.42)	38 (52.77)	90 (48.91)
Total	374 (100.00)	264 (264.00)	638 (100.00)	207 (55.34)	125 (47.34)	332 (52.03)	79 (38.16)	61 (48.8)	140 (42.16)

Source: Records of Sample Institutions.

2.58: Enrolment, Applied and Award of Pre-matric Scholarship: Urban Areas

In urban areas of the district, only 31 per cent applied for Pre-matric Scholarship and out of those who applied, 66 per cent succeeded in getting it. In urban areas, though the percentage of girl's applicants in their Enrolment was lower than of the boys but the success rate of girls (75 per cent) was far higher than of the boys (2.60 per cent).

Table-2.59: Year-wise Enrolment, Applied and Pre-matric Scholarship Awarded to Students in Sample Institutions of Rampur District (Urban)

Year	Enrolled			Applied			Awarded		
	Boys	Girls	Total	Boys	Girls	Total	Boys	Girls	Total
2009-10	114 (100.00)	67 (100.00)	181 (100.00)	44 (38.59)	35 (52.23)	79 (43.64)	27 (61.36)	27 (77.14)	54 (68.35)
2010-11	113 (100.00)	236 (100.00)	349 (100.00)	34 (30.08)	53 (22.45)	87 (24.92)	17 (50.00)	39 (73.58)	56 (64.36)
Total	227 (100.00)	303 (100.00)	530 (100.00)	78 (34.36)	88 (29.04)	166 (31.32)	44 (56.4)	66 (75.00)	110 (66.26)

Source: Records of Sample Institutions

2.59: Enrolment, Applied andAward of Pre-matric Scholarship: All District

Considering all the sample institutions of rural and urban areas of the district together, it became evident that out of total enrolled students, 42.63 per cent of them applied for Pre-matric Scholarship and out of those who applied, 50.20 per cent succeeded in getting it. Though, the percentage of applicant's girls in their total enrolment was lower than of the boys but higher percentage of girls than boys succeeded in getting it (Table-2.60).

Table-2.60: Year-wise Enrolment, Applied and Pre-matric Scholarship Awarded to Students in Sample Institutions of Rampur District (Rural and Urban)

Year	Enrolled			Applied			Awarded		
	Boys	Girls	Total	Boys	Girls	Total	Boys	Girls	Total
2009-10	300 (100.00)	200 (100.00)	500 (100.00)	139 (46.34)	88 (44.00)	227 (45.40)	54 (38.85)	50 (56.82)	104 (45.81)
2010-11	301 (100.00)	367 (100.00)	668 (100.00)	146 (48.50)	125 (34.06)	271 (40.57)	69 (47.26)	77 (61.60)	146 (53.87)
Total	601 (100.00)	567 (100.00)	1168 (100.00)	285 (47.42)	213 (37.56)	498 (42.63)	123 (43.15)	127 (59.62)	250 (50.20)

Source: Records of Sample Institutions.

2.60 Reasons of not getting Scholarship: Perspective of Institutions:

The sample institutions have given the following reasons due to which the Pre-matric scholarship could not be given to all its applicants. The main reason is the lack of awareness in the Muslim community about the Pre-matric scholarship.

Table-2.61: Reasons of not getting Scholarship

Reasons	Rural	Urban	Total
Lack of awareness in the community	8 (100.00)	5 (100.00)	13 (100.00)
Lengthy and expensive paper work	6 (75.00)	4 (80.00)	10 (76.92)
Language problem in filling the application form	7 (87.5)	2 (40.00)	9 (69.23)
Follow up of application is not easily accessible	6 (75.00)	5 (100.00)	11 (84.61)
Lack of monitoring about the scholarship	7 (87.5)	4 (80.00)	11 (84.61)

Source: Staff of the Institutions.

2.61 Mode of Payment of Scholarship Amount:

The mode of payment of scholarship money was found to be in cash in 61.54 per cent institutions. The cash payment was done in 87.50 per cent institutions in rural areas in the district as against 20 per cent in urban areas of the district (Table-2.62).

Table-2.62: Mode of Payment of Scholarship Amount

Mode	Number of Institutions		
	Rural	Urban	Total
Cash	7 (87.50)	1 (20.00)	8 (61.54)
Cheque	1 (12.50)	4 (80.00)	5 (38.46)
Total	8 (100.00)	5 (100.00)	13 (100.00)

Source: Record of the Institutions

2.62 Time taken in Processing:

Around 76.92 per cent institutions reported that entire processing of application takes more than 15 days.

Table-2.63: Average Time Taken in Processing of Application

Time Taken	Number of Institutions		
	Rural	Urban	Total
10-15 Days	-	3 (60.00)	3 (23.08)
More than 15 Days	8 (100.00)	2 (40.00)	10 (76.92)
Total	8 (100.00)	5 (100.00)	13 (100.00)

Source: Staff of the Institutions.

2.63 Level of Difficulty in Processing:

69 per cent of sample institutions reported difficulty in processing of application while only 15 per cent found no difficulty in processing.

Table-2.64: Level of Difficulty in Processing the Application

Level of Difficulty	Number of Institutions		
	Rural	Urban	Total
Difficult	7 (87.5)	2 (40.00)	9 (69.24)
Somewhat Difficult	1 (12.5)	1 (20.00)	2 (15.38)
Not Difficult	-	2 (40.00)	2 (15.38)
Total	8 (100.00)	5 (100.00)	13 (100.00)

Source: Staff of the Institutions.

2.64 Time taken from Proposal to Disbursement of Pre-matric Scholarship:

The sample institutions have reported that considerable time (3-4 months) is taken in the sanction of the scholarship. The entire time duration is as given in table-2.65.

Table-2.65: Duration of Pre-matric Scholarship Distribution

Proposal sent to MOMA:	September 2009
Sectioned:	December to January 2009, 2010
Scholarship reached the District:	February to March 2010
Scholarship Disbursed:	March to April 2010

2.65 Improvement in Enrolment and Drop out:

The records of sample institutions showed that there was overall growth of around 18 per cent in the Enrolment of minority students and there was no drop out of minority students during the last years.

2.66 Level of Satisfaction of Institutions with State and Central Government Agencies:

In timely processing and approval and timely release of fund, the majority of institutions were dissatisfied with the state and central government agencies (Table-2.66).

Table-2.66: Level of Satisfaction with State and Central Government Agencies

Heads	Level of Satisfaction: State Government				
	Highly Satisfied	Very Satisfied	Satisfied	Dissatisfied	Total No. of Institutions
Timely Processing and Approval	-	-	5 (38.46)	8 (61.54)	13 (100.00)
Timely Release of Funds	-	-	6 (46.15)	7 (53.85)	13 (100.00)
Staff Behavior	1 (7.69)	9 (69.24)	2 (15.38)	1 (7.69)	13 (100.00)

Heads	Level of Satisfaction: Central Government				
	Highly Satisfied	Very Satisfied	Satisfied	Dissatisfied	Total No. of Institutions
Timely Processing and Approval	-	-	5 (38.46)	8 (61.54)	13 (100.00)
Timely Release of Funds	-	-	6 (46.15)	7 (53.85)	13 (100.00)
Staff Behavior	-	9 (69.23)	4 (30.77)	-	13(100.00)

Source: Staff of the Institutions

2.67 Data Management:

In 61.54 per cent of institutions, data management of Pre-matric scholarship is manual (Table-2.67).

Table-2.67: System of Data Management of Pre-matric Scholarship

Procedure	No. of Institutions
Manual	8 (61.54)
Semi- Computerized	5 (38.46)
Fully Computer	-
Number of Institution	13 (100.00)

2.68 Impact of Pre-matric Scholarship Scheme:

The staff of the sample institutions reported that the beneficiary students have become more regular in attending their classes and the interest of the beneficiary students in their studies has increased. On account of Pre-matric scholarship more and more minority students are taking admission in schools.

2.69 Most Important Problems and Overall Assessment of Pre-matric Scholarship Scheme:

The sample institutions have reported the following three most important problems of Pre-matric Scholarship Scheme:

- Lengthy paper work and application form in English.
- Lack of awareness in Parents, panchayats and community.
- Non-cooperative attitudes of concerning officials.

Around 60 per cent institutions are reported to be satisfied with Pre-matric Scholarship Scheme

Table-2.68: Overall Assessment of Pre-matric Scholarship Scheme

Level of Satisfaction	No. of Institution
Highly Satisfied	-
Very Satisfied	1(7.69)
Satisfied	8 (61.54)
Dissatisfied	4 (30.77)
Number of Institution	13 (100.00)

2.70 Main Suggestions of Institutions for Improvement of Scheme:

- Mass awareness campaign should be launched in the community about the scheme.
- Separate staff should be provided at the district level for management of scheme.
- Service charges should be also provided to the institution for management of scheme.
- Application forms should be made available in Hindi.

2.71 District Official:

2.72 On the Guidelines:

The District Minority Welfare Officer, Rampur District reported that guidelines of the Pre-matric Scholarship are available with him and the scheme is implemented as per guidelines.

2.73 Selection Criteria:

The official reported that in selection process, apart from the marks obtained in the previous examination, poverty and girls students are given the preference.

2.74 Awardees of Pre-matric Scholarship:

Data of only two years were available with the Minority Welfare Officer of Rampur district about the awardee students of Pre-matric Scholarship as shown in table-2.69. It reflects from the table that the number of awardee students declined by 44.41 per cent in 2010-11 as compared with the 2009-10. The Muslim awardee were 94.33 per cent in 2009-10 which declined to 89.05 per cent while the percentage of Sikh and Christian awardees increased from 3.99 per cent and 1.68 per cent in 2009-10 to 7.74 per cent and 3.21 per cent in 2010-11 respectively. No reason for decline in awardees could be given by the official.

Table-2.69: Year and Religion wise Number of Awardees Students of Pre-matric Scholarship in Rampur District

Year	Religion	Number of Awardees Students		
		Male	Female	Total
2009-10	Muslim	1691	106	1797
	Sikh	50	26	76
	Christian	20	12	32
	Total	1761	144	1905
2010-11	Muslim	681	262	943
	Sikh	37	45	82
	Christian	18	16	34
	Total	736	323	1059

Source: District Minority Welfare Department, Rampur District.

2.75 Grants of Pre-matric Scholarship:

The grant of Rs. 23.06 lakh allocated in the year 2009-10 was utilized but despite decrease in the number of awardees in 2010-11 from 2009-10, the amount of grant was increased to Rs. 25.90 lakhs but Rs. I lakh remained unutilized during 2010-11.

Table-2.70: Grant Allocation, Approval and Utilization (Rs. Lakhs)

Year	Amount allocated	Grants Approved/ Sanctioned	Grants Utilized
2009-10	23.06	23.06	23.06
2010-11	25.90	25.90	25.89

Source: District Minority Welfare Department, Rampur District.

2.76 Strategy of Community Awareness Adopted:

1. Advertisement in local newspapers
2. Meetings with representatives of district, block and village panchayats
3. head of Educational institutions in the districts
4. Publication of pamphlets and booklets

2.77 Time Spent in Disbursement of Pre-matric Scholarship

Details are given in Table 2.71

Table-2.71: Time Spent in Disbursement of Pre-matric Scholarship

Proposal sent to MOMA	: September
Sanctioned	: January
Scholarship reached the District	: February
Scholarship Disbursed	: March

2.78 Impact of Pre-matric Scholarship Scheme: Officer's Views

- Scholarship scheme enhanced Enrolment of student belonging to minority communities.
- Scholarship amount provided adequate cover to students in their study needs.
- Improved the educational achievement level of students.

2.79 Problems in Implementation of Scheme: Officer's Views

- Staff Shortage
- Lack of Awareness
- Too much Volume of Application forms
- Delay in processing of Central Government Scholarship Schemes as compared with the State Government schemes.

2.80 Suggestions for Improvement:

- Funds should be provided for mass awareness campaign in the community.
- Separate staff should be provided.
- Application form should be easy and in Hindi.

2.81 Main Findings:

- More than half of the houses are katchcha or semi-pucca.
- The family size is of 6 persons in which 2 are working.
- 70 per cent houses are electrified.
- Majority of parents owned marginal and small land and majority of them also earned average annual income of Rs. 50,000 in case of beneficiary parents.
- Generally, the same pattern is in case of non-beneficiary parents.
- Only 50 per cent parents are aware of Pre-matric scholarship and their main source of awareness is the teachers of the schools where their wards study.
- Three reasons of delay in getting the Pre-matric scholarship are given by the parents in whom delay by the district officials is the main.
- The parents have given mostly the average rating to various aspects of Pre-matric Scholarship of the district.
- The sample institutions are mainly from rural area, private and up to primary level.
- Among the total enrolled students, 52 per cent applied for Pre-matric Scholarship and 42

per cent succeeded in getting it. The percentage of applied and awarded boys is higher than girls in rural areas.

- In urban areas of the district, only 31 per cent applied for Pre-matric Scholarship and out of those who applied, 66 per cent succeeded in getting it. In urban areas, though the percentage of girl's applicants in their Enrolment is lower than of the boys but the success rate of girls (75 per cent) is far higher than of the boys (56.4 per cent).
- Considering all the sample institutions of rural and urban areas of the district together, it became evident that out of total enrolled students, 42.63 per cent of them applied for Pre-matric Scholarship and out of those who applied, 50.20 per cent succeeded in getting it. Though, the percentage of applicant's girls in their total enrolment is lower than of the boys but higher percentage of girls than boys succeeded in getting it.
- The main reason of not getting the scholarship is the lack of awareness in the Muslim community about the Pre-matric scholarship.
- The mode of payment of scholarship money is found to be in cash in 61.54 per cent institutions. The cash payment is done in 87.50 per cent institutions in rural areas in the district as against 20 per cent in urban areas of the district.
- Around 76.92 per cent institutions reported that entire processing of application takes more than 15 days.
- The sample institutions have reported that considerable time (3-4 months) is taken in the sanction of the scholarship.
- The records of sample institutions showed that there is overall growth of around 18 per cent in the Enrolment of minority students and there is no drop out of minority students during the last year.
- In timely processing and approval and timely release of fund, the majority of institutions are dissatisfied with the state and central government agencies.
- In 61.54 per cent of institutions, data management of Pre-matric scholarship is manual.
- The staff of the sample institutions reported that the beneficiary students have become more regular in attending their classes and the interest of the beneficiary students in their studies has increased. On account of Pre-matric scholarship more and more minority students are taking admission in schools.

Field Observations, Key Issues and Suggestions: Pre-matric Scholarship

2.82 Field Observations:

During the field work of this evaluation, extensive discussions were held with each of the stakeholders of the Pre-matric Scholarship Scheme in Rampur district of Uttar Pradesh. On the basis of these discussions, we have reached to the conclusion that the implementation of this scheme has been very poor in the district. The inefficiency and corruption in the implementation of the scheme in the district can be gauged from the fact that one of the concerned officials is still in jail because of the massive embezzlement of the scholarship money in Rampur district. The vested interests that are to be termed as intermediaries or middlemen have got involved in the award of Pre-matric Scholarship. The students and their parents have little idea that how and from where to procure the application form. At this stage, the management of private schools comes to their rescue that obtains form in bulk and fills it and gets it signed by the students. They also do other formalities like obtaining income certificate and affidavit on behalf of students. After completing the applications, they go to the office of District Minority Welfare Officer. The Minority Welfare Officer has appointed a private data entry firm. After checking and signing the applications, the Minority Welfare Officer sends all forms to data entry firm. The data entry firm charges around Rs. 10-20 per application for entryof their application from the students. After the applications are entered, a CD is prepared by the data entry firm which it gives to the Minority Welfare Officer who sends this CD for onward processing. Many data entry firms approached our field staff in Rampur district during field work of this to arrange the contract to them and in turn offered money to us. When the sanctioned money is received by the District Minority Welfare Officer from the state, his office makes a consolidated cheque of all awardee students' institution wise. In this way, an institution receives a cheque of all its students who are studying there and applied from the institution. After getting the cheque, the school deposits it in its account. The schools deduct their entire annual fee of the students from the money the school received in the form of cheque of Pre-matric Scholarship and gives only Rs. 300 to 400 to each awardee students. In this way, every party remains in win situation. The students need not to bother about the formalities of applying, students have no botheration to pay annual fee to their schools, schools administration get assured fee, data entry firm do a good business and there is possibility that many more may be profiting. But ultimately the students are losers as they get only marginal part of money of the Pre-matric scholarship. We have found little interest among the teachers of government schools about the Pre-matric Scholarship Scheme. The private schools get involved because the payment of their annual fee is ensured from the Pre-matric Scholarship Money. This practice has been going on since the beginning of the scheme but recently appointed District Minority Welfare Officer is trying his best to change the situation. He is known as honest officer in the district and if he continues there, all round efficiency in the implementation of the scheme is expected. It was also known that in a similar inefficient and corrupt pattern the Pre-matric Scholarship is being implemented in entire Uttar Pradesh. We can well understand the inefficiency and lethargy of the concerned officials right from state level to district in implementation of the Scholarship Schemes of the Ministry of Minority Welfare, Government of India from the fact that the Free Coaching and Allied Scheme has not been implemented in Rampur district as yet though the district Rampur is the second largest minority concentrated district in Uttar Pradesh. However, these observations are difficult to capture in quantitative data form.

2.33 Key Issues of Pre-matric Scholarship:

- The important fact has emerged from this evaluation that the Pre-matric scholarship has been very effective in overall development of students which included their educational needs, their health care needs and in providing them a silver lining for higher studies and good job prospect in future.
- It is also the fact that there is a great demand of Pre-matric Scholarship among the minority communities but roughly 40-50 per cent of them manage to get it. This has been proved from the primary as well as district level secondary data.
- Considering the present income level of parents and level of expenditure on education, the income limit of parents and the amount of Pre-matric Scholarship require upward revision.

- The detail awareness about the Pre-matric scholarship among the students was found to be very poor in general in Rampur district. This has been told by the students, parents, institutions and officials.
- Substantial percentages of awardee students are being paid their scholarship money in cash.
- Substantial number of students felt difficulty in obtaining application form, filling it and submitting it.
- Considerable time is also spent during application to award of scholarship.
- Most of the students feel that the state government officials are mainly responsible for the delay of scholarship.
- The private schools are playing the role of middlemen in the award of Pre-matric scholarship which could be known during the filed investigation.
- On the whole, it can be concluded that the implementation of Pre-matric Scholarship Scheme is poor and inefficient in Rampur district in particular and in entire Uttar Pradesh in general.

2.84 Suggestions:

- There is need of rigorous orientation training of state and district level officials who oversee the scheme.
- Simultaneously need is to generate awareness among the minority community about the scholarship scheme.
- The teachers of government schools should be made aware of the scheme and they should be made to encourage their students to apply for the Pre-matric scholarship. The state officials may also be asked to involve village panchayats in this matter.
- The income limit of parents should be raised to Rs. 1,50,000/. The amount of Pre-matric Scholarship should reasonably be increased.
- The application form should be in Hindi and be simplified.
- The private data entry firms should not be engaged in processing of application. One computer literate staff may be appointed on contact basis at the office of District Minority Welfare Officer to see the entire process of Pre-matric Scholarship.
- The payment of scholarship in cash must be stopped and bulk payment to schools should be prohibited. All students should be asked to open an account in the bank and scholarship money should be electronically transferred in their account directly from the state level.
- In some way accountability clause should be added in the scheme and District Magistrates should be held responsible if poor and inefficient implementation is found.

Chapter III

Introduction : Post-matric Scholarship—Rampur District

3.1 Sample of the Study:

It has been mentioned in the sampling methodology of Pre-matric Scholarship that institution based sampling technique was adopted in the selection of beneficiary and non-beneficiary students. Following the same methodology, beneficiary and non-beneficiary students of Post-matric Scholarship were also selected from the same villages and urban areas from where the sample was taken for the Pre-matric Scholarship. It was decided that 10 per cent of all beneficiary and non-beneficiary students of Post-matric scholarship will be taken as sample if the number of such students exceeds 50 but in our sample villages, the number was found to be less than 50. Therefore, all the beneficiary and non-beneficiary students of Post-matric Scholarship were selected as sample which is as follows:

Table-3.1 Sample Size of the Post-matric Scholarship: Students

Gender	Rural	Urban	Total
	Beneficiary Students		
Boys	5	2	7
Girls	7	12	19
Total	12	14	26
	Non-Beneficiary Students		
Boys	5	1	6
Girls	3	5	8
Total	8	6	14
	All Students		
Boys	10	3	13
Girls	10	17	27
Total	20	20	40

Characteristics of Sample Students-Post-matric Scholarship

3.2 Age of Students:

There are two age-groups of beneficiary and non-beneficiary students as shown in table-3.2. The beneficiary students are 50 per cent in age group of 16-18 years and 50 per cent in age group of 19-21 years while majority (64.29 per cent) of non-beneficiaries is in the age group of 16-18 years. The boys of both groups are mostly in the age group of 16-18 years while the percentage of non-beneficiary girls is higher (62.50 per cent) in the age group of 16-18 years as against the beneficiary girls (47.37 per cent) in the same age group. On the whole, more than half of the sample students are in the first age group of 16-18 years.

Table-3.2: Age-wise Number of Sample Students

Sex	Students	16-18 Years	19-21Years	Total
Boys	Beneficiaries	4 (57.14)	3 (42.86)	7 (100.00)
	Non-Beneficiaries	4 (66.67)	2 (33.33)	6 (100.00)
	Total	8 (61.54)	5 (38.46)	13 (100.00)
Girls	Beneficiaries	9 (47.37)	10 (52.63)	19 (100.00)
	Non-Beneficiaries	5 (62.50)	3 (37.50)	8 (100.00)
	Total	14 (51.85)	13 (48.15)	27 (100.00)
Total	Beneficiaries	13 (50.00)	13 (50.00)	26 (100.00)
	Non-Beneficiaries	9 (64.29)	5 (35.71)	14 (100.00)
	All	22 (55.00)	18 (45.00)	40 (100.00)

Note: Figures in brackets indicate percentages.
Source: Primary data based.

3.3 Level of Schools:

The sample students are mostly (95 per cent) studying in intermediate while 2.5 per cent each are in graduation and post-graduation. Those who are studying above intermediate are the girls (Table-3.3).

Table-3.3: Institutions Where Sample Students are Studying

Sex	Students	Intermediate	Graduation	Post-Graduation	Total
Boys	Beneficiaries	7 (100.00)	-	-	7 (100.00)
	Non-Beneficiaries	6 (100.00)	-	-	6 (100.00)
	Total	13 (100.00)	-	-	13 (100.00)
Girls	Beneficiaries	19 (100.00)	-	-	19 (100.00)
	Non-Beneficiaries	6 (75.00)	1 (12.50)	1 (12.50)	8 (100.00)
	Total	25 (92.60)	1 (3.70)	1 (3.70)	27 (100.00)
Total	Beneficiaries	26 (100.00)	-	-	26 (100.00)
	Non-Beneficiaries	12 (85.72)	1 (7.14)	1 (7.14)	14 (100.00)
	All Total	38 (95.00)	1 (2.50)	1 (2.50)	40 (100.00)

Note: Figures in brackets indicate percentages.
Source: Primary data based.

3.4 Type of Institutions:

Out of totals sample students, 90 per cent are studying in government institutions. The same pattern is at the intermediate level but at the graduate level, 50 percent are studying in government institutions and rest in private and aided institutions (Table-3.4).

Table-3.4: Type of Institutions of Sample Students

Type of Institution	Type Of Institution			
	Government	Private	Aided	Total
Intermediate	33 (94.28)	1 (2.86)	1 (2.86)	35 (100.00)
Graduation	2 (50.00)	1 (25.00)	1 (25.00)	4 (100.00)
Post-Graduation	1 (100.00)	0	0	1 (100.00)
Total Students	36 (90.00)	2 (5.00)	2 (5.00)	40 (100.00)

Note: Figures in brackets indicate percentages.
Source: Primary data based.

3.5 Sources of Income:

Despite different sources of income, majority of sample students (65 per cent) have reported to be studying in government institutions (Table-3.5).

Table-3.5: Sources of Income of Sample households: Students Response

S.No.	Source	Type of Institution			
		Government	Private	Aided	Total
1	Casual Labour	4 (66.66)	1 (16.67)	1 (16.67)	6 (100.00)
2	Small Farmer	6 (66.67)	2 (22.22)	1 (11.11)	9 (100.00)
3	Cultivator	7 (77.78)	1 (11.11)	1 (11.11)	9 (100.00)
4	Artisan	3 (60.00)	1 (20.00)	1 (20.00)	5 (100.00)
5	Salaried (Government /Private)	4 (57.14)	2 (28.57)	1 (14.29)	7 (100.00)
6	Small Business/Trade	2 (50.00)	1 (25.00)	1 (25.00)	4 (100.00)
Total		26 (65.00)	8 (20.00)	6 (15.00)	40 (100.00)

Note: Figures in brackets indicate percentages.
Source: Primary data based.

3.6 Income of Students:

All the students of Post-matric Scholarship which included beneficiary and non-beneficiary both are classified according their income in table-3.6 which indicated that 50 per cent in rural areas and 60 per cent in urban areas have average annual income in the range of Rs. 50,000 to 100,000.

Table-3.6: Classification of Students According to their Income

Income	Number of Students		
	Rural	Urban	Total
Less than 20,000	1 (5.00)	-	1 (2.50)
20,001 to 50,000	8 (40.00)	7 (35.00)	15 (37.50)
50,001 to 1,00,000	10 (50.00)	12 (60.00)	22 (55.00)
1,00,001 to 1,50,000	1 (5.00)	1 (5.00)	2 (5.00)
Total	20 (100.00)	20 (100.00)	40 (100.00)

Note: Figures in brackets indicate percentages.
Source: Primary data based.

3.7 Expenditure on Education:

The average expenditure per student on Post-matric education has been calculated in table-3.7 which shows that more than 10 thousands are spent per students and there is no major difference between the beneficiary and non-beneficiary students.

Table-3.7: Average Annual Expenditure of Education per Student on Different Items

Item	Amounts (in Rs.)		
	Beneficiary	Non-Beneficiary	Total
Course Fee	2080	1950	2016
Teaching Learning Materials	1604	1560	1583
Travel	1980	1940	1960
Tuition	2700	2700	2700
Others	1960	1950	1956
Total	10324	10100	10215

Source: Primary data based.

3.8 Attending Schools, Getting Scholarship and Family Features:

In the families of students getting Post-matric scholarship, roughly 60 per cent of eligible adults are found to be going for study. The percentage of females is higher than the males and only 45.61 per cent of them could get Post-matric Scholarship. In urban areas of Rampur district, proportion of Post-matric Scholarship holders are higher their counterparts in rural areas of the district. The younger age populations is very high and near about one-fourth of total family members are working and highest qualification of one member in majority of families is intermediate (Table-3.8).

Table-3.8: Going to Schools, Getting Scholarships and Family Structure

Item	Number of Students		
	Rural	Urban	Total
Going to School			
Boys	16 (55.17)	13 (59.09)	29 (56.86)
Girls	14 (63.64)	14 (66.67)	28 (65.12)
Total	30 (58.82)	27 (62.79)	57 (60.64)
Getting Scholarships			
Boys	5 (31.25)	2 (15.38)	7 (24.14)
Girls	7 (50.00)	12 (85.71)	19 (67.86)
Total	12 (40.00)	14 (51.85)	26 (45.61)
Age Structure of Family Members			
Less than 5 Years	80 (51.28)	64 (52.89)	144 (52.55)
5-14 Years	19 (12.18)	15 (12.40)	34 (12.41)
15-23 Years	17 (10.90)	13 (10.74)	27 (9.86)
24-35 Years	9 (5.77)	7(5.79)	16(5.84)
36-59 years	6(3.85)	3(2.48)	9(3.28)
60 + years	25(16.02)	19(15.70)	44(16.06)
All Members	156(100.00)	121(100.00)	274(100.00)
No. of Earning Members in the Family	32 (20.51)	29 (23.97)	61 (22.26)
Highest Educational Status of a Member in Family			
Intermediate	15 (75.00)	12 (60.00)	27 (67.50)
Graduate	5 (25.00)	4 (20.00)	9 (22.50)
Post Graduate	-	3 (15.00)	3 (7.50)
Technical/Professional	-	1 (5.00)	1 (2.50)
Total	20 (100.00)	20 (100.00)	40 (100.00)

Note: Figures in brackets indicate percentages.
Source: Primary data based.

3.9 Housing:

Housing condition is not good. Even in urban areas of Rampur district, 75 per cent houses are Pucca. Electrified houses are only 45 per cent in rural areas and only 70 per cent of households have ration cards (Table-3.9).

Table-3.9: Housing and other Conditions of Sample Students

Housing Type	Rural	Urban	Total
Kachcha	2 (10.00)	-	2 (5.00)
Pucca	10 (50.00)	15 (75.00)	25 (62.50)
Mix	8 (40.00)	5 (25.00)	13 (32.50)
Total	20 (100.00)	20 (100.00)	40 (100.00)
Ownership of the House			
Owned	19	15	34
Rented	1	3	4
Given by Employer	-	2	2
Value of the House, if owned (Average)	192645	261182	226913
Average Number of Rooms	4	2	3
Houses with Electricity (Yes)	9 (45.00)	20 (100.00)	29 (72.50)
No. of Households with Ration Cards	16 (95.00)	12 (60.00)	28 (70.00)
Percentage of Marginal and Small Land owning Households	16 (80.00)	14 (70.00)	30 (75.00)

Note: Figures in brackets indicate percentages.
Source: Primary data based.

3.10 Main Findings:

- It has been found that more than half of the sample students are in the first age group of 16-18 years.
- The sample students are mostly (95 per cent) studying in intermediate while 2.5 per cent each are in studying in graduation and post-graduation.
- Out of totals sample students, 90 per cent are studying in government institutions.
- Despite different sources of income, majority of sample students (65 per cent) have reported to be studying in government institutions.
- It is found that out of total sample families, 50 per cent in rural areas and 60 per cent in urban areas has average annual income in the range of Rs. 50,000 to 100,000.
- The expenditure pattern on Post-matric education shows that more than 10 thousands rupees are spent per students per annum and there is no major difference between the beneficiary and non-beneficiary students.
- In the families of students getting Post-matric scholarship, roughly 60 per cent of eligible adults are found to be going for study. The percentage of females is higher than the males and only 45.61 per cent of them could get Post-matric Scholarship. In urban areas of Rampur district, proportion of Post-matric Scholarship holders are higher than their counterparts in rural areas of the district.
- The younger age populations is very high and near about one-fourth of total family members are working and highest qualification of one member in majority of families is intermediate.
- Housing condition is not good. Even in urban areas of Rampur district, 75 per cent houses are Pucca. Electrified houses are only 45 per cent in rural areas and only 70 per cent of households have ration cards.

Awareness, Utilization and Impact of Post-matric Scholarship

3.11 Complete Awareness about Post-matric Scholarship:

The complete awareness about the details of Post-matric Scholarship is limited to less than half of the sample students (Table-3.10).

Table-3.10: Students who are Completely Aware of the Post -matric Scholarship Scheme

Students	Number of Students		
	Rural	Urban	Total
	Beneficiary		
Boys	2(40.00)	1(50.00)	3(42.86)
Girls	3(42.86)	5(41.67)	8(42.10)
Total	5(41.67)	6(42.86)	11(42.31)
	Non- Beneficiary		
Boys	2(40.00)	1(100.00)	3(50.00)
Girls	2(66.67)	2(40.00)	4(50.00)
Total	4(50.00)	3(60.00)	7(50.00)
	All		
Boys	4(40.00)	2(66.67)	6(46.15)
Girls	5(50.00)	7(41.18)	12(44.44)
Total	9(45.00)	9(45.00)	18(45.00)

Note: Figures in brackets indicate percentage.
Source: Primary data based.

3.12 Sources of Awareness of Post-matric Scholarship to Rural Students:

The main source of awareness of Post-matric scholarship to rural students is the teachers of the institutions where the students study (Table-3.11).

Table-3.11: Source of Awareness of Post- matric Scholarship among Rural Students

Source	Rural (Students)								
	Beneficiary			Non-Beneficiary			Total		
	Boys	Girls	Total	Boys	Girls	Total	Boys	Girls	Total
Teachers	2 (40.00)	3 (42.85)	5 (41.67)	3 (60.00)	2 (66.67)	5 (62.50)	4 (40.00)	5 (50.00)	9 (45.00)
Students who got Scholarship	1 (20.00)	2 (28.57)	3 (25.00)	1 (20.00)	1 (33.33)	2 (25.00)	3 (30.00)	3 (30.00)	6 (30.00)
Sabhasad	-	1 (14.29)	1 (8.33)	1 (20.00)	-	1 (12.50)	1 (10.00)	1 (10.00)	2 (10.00)
Radio/TV	1 (20.00)	1 (14.29)	2 (16.67)	-	-	-	1 (10.00)	1 (10.00)	2 (10.00)
News Paper	1 (20.00)	-	1 (8.33)	-	-	-	1 (10.00)	-	1 (5.00)
Total	5 (100.00)	7 (100.00)	12 (100.00)	5 (100.00)	3 (100.00)	8 (100.00)	10 (100.00)	10 (100.00)	20 (100.00)

Note: Figures in brackets indicate percentage.
Source: Primary data based.

3.13 Sources of Awareness of Post-matric Scholarship to Urban Students:

The main source of awareness of Post-matric scholarship to urban students is the teachers of the institutions where the students study (Table-3.12).

Table-3.12: Source of Awareness of Post -matric Scholarship among Urban Students

Source	Urban (Students)								
	Beneficiary			Non-Beneficiary			Total		
	Boys	Girls	Total	Boys	Girls	Total	Boys	Girls	Total
Teachers	2 (100.00)	5 (41.67)	7 (50.00)	1 (100.00)	2 (40.00)	3 (50.00)	3 (50.00)	7 (41.18)	10 (50.00)
Students who got Scholarship	-	3 (25.00)	3 (21.43)	-	1 (20.00)	1 (16.67)	-	4 (23.53)	4 (20.00)
Sabhasads	-	2 (16.67)	2 (14.29)	-	1 (20.00)	1 (16.67)	-	3 (17.65)	3 (15.00)
Radio/TV	-	1 (8.33)	1 (7.14)	-	1 (20.00)	1 (16.66)	-	2 (11.76)	2 (10.00)
News Paper	-	1 (8.33)	1 (7.14)	-	-	-	-	1 (5.88)	1 (5.00)
Total	2 (100.00)	12 (100.00)	14 (100.00)	1 (100.00)	5 (100.00)	6 (100.00)	3 (100.00	17 (100.00)	20 (100.00)

Note: Figures in brackets indicate percentage.
Source: Primary data based.

3.14 Sources of Awareness of Post-matric Scholarship to All Students:

The main source of awareness of Post-matric scholarship to all students is the teachers of the institutions where the students study (Table-3.13).

Table-3.13: Source of Awareness of Post -matric Scholarship among All Students

Source	Number of Students								
	Beneficiary			Non-Beneficiary			Total		
	Boys	Girls	Total	Boys	Girls	Total	Boys	Girls	Total
Teachers	4 (57.13)	8 (42.11)	12 (46.15)	4 (66.66)	4 (50.00)	8 (57.14)	7 (53.85)	12 (44.44)	19 (47.50)
Students who got Scholarship	1 (14.29)	5 (26.31)	6 (23.08)	1 (16.67)	2 (25.00)	3 (21.43)	3 (23.08)	7 (25.93)	10 (25.00)
Sabhasads	-	3 (15.79)	3 (11.54)	1 (16.67)	1 (12.50)	2 (14.29)	1 (7.69)	4 (14.82)	5 (12.50)
Radio/TV	1 (14.29)	2 (10.53)	3 (11.54)	-	1 (12.50)	1 (7.14)	1 (7.69)	3 (11.11)	4 (10.00)
News Papers	1 (14.29)	1 (5.26)	2 (7.69)	-	-	-	1 (7.69)	1 (3.70)	2 (5.00)
Total	7 (100.00)	19 (100.00)	26 (100.00)	6 (100.00)	8 (100.00)	14 (100.00)	13 (100.00	27 (100.00)	40 (100.00)

Note: Figures in brackets indicate percentage.
Source: Primary data based.

3.15 Detailed Knowledge of Post-matric Scholarship:

The sample students have reported that 72.50 per cent of them are aware of the eligibility conditions of Post-matric Scholarship. The proportion of rural students knowing eligibility conditions are less (58.33 per cent) in rural areas versus (85 per cent) in urban areas of the district.

Table-3.14: Detail Knowledge of Post-matric Scholarship Scheme: Students Response

Students	Number of Students		
	Rural	Urban	Total
	Beneficiary		
Boys	3 (60.00)	2 (100.00)	5 (71.43)
Girls	4 (57.14)	10 (83.33)	14 (73.68)
Total	7 (58.33)	12 (85.71)	19 (73.08)
	Non- Beneficiary		
Boys	3 (60.00)	1 (100.00)	4 (66.67)
Girls	2 (66.67)	4 (80.00)	6 (75.00)
Total	5 (62.50)	5 (83.33)	10 (71.43)
	All		
Boys	6 (60.00)	3 (100.00)	9 (69.23)
Girls	6 (60.00)	14 (82.35)	20 (74.07)
Total	12 (60.00)	17 (85.00)	29 (72.50)

Note: Figures in brackets indicate percentage.
Source: Primary data based.

3.16 Knowledge of Eligibility Conditions:

There are 3 main eligibility conditions for getting the Post-matric Scholarship. The sample students were enquired about each of these conditions. The answers given by them have been shown

Table-3.15: Knowledge of Sample Students about Each of the Eligibility Conditions of Post-matric Scholarship

Conditions	Number of Students								
	Rural			Urban			Total		
	B.	NB.	Total	B.	NB.	Total	B.	NB.	Total
Household Income not more than Rs. 2 Lakh	5 (71.43)	1 (20.00)	6 (50.00)	2 (16.67)	3 (60.00)	5 (29.41)	7 (36.84)	4 (40.00)	11 (37.93)
Marks not less than 50 per cent in last exam	7 (100.00)	5 (100.00)	12 (100.00)	10 (83.33)	5 (100.00)	15 (88.24)	17 (89.47)	10 (100.00)	27 (93.10)
Only 2 Student from one household	3 (42.86)	1 (20.00)	4 (33.33)	1 (8.33)	1 (20.00)	2 (11.76)	4 (21.05)	2 (20.00)	6 (20.69)
Total	7 (100.00)	5 (100.00)	12 (100.00)	12 (100.00)	5 (100.00)	17 (100.00)	19 (100.00)	10 (100.00)	29 (100.00)

Note: B- Beneficiary
NB – Non Beneficiary
Note: Figures in brackets indicate percentage.
Source: Primary data based

in table-3.15 which indicates that among the 3 conditions, the condition of marks not less than 50 per cent in last examination is known to all most all of them (93.10 per cent of studnents).

3.17 Students Receiving Different Amount of Post-matric Scholarship:

The sample students have reported that 65.38 per cent of them received the Post-matric Scholarship of Rs.3000 to 4000. The proportion of such students is higher in rural areas (75 per cent) as against in urban areas (57.14 per cent).

Table-3.16: Classification of Beneficiary students According to amount of Scholarship

Amount (Rs.)	Number of Beneficiary Students		
	Rural	Urban	Total
2000-3000	1(8.33)		1 (3.85)
3000-4000	9 (75.00)	8 (57.14)	17 (65.38)
4000-5000	2 (16.67)	6 (42.86)	8 (30.77)
Total	12 (100.00)	14 (100.00)-	26 (100.00)

Note: Figures in brackets indicate percentage.
Source: Primary data based

3.18 Mode of Payment:

The mode of payment of Post-matric Scholarship is through cheque only as all the sample students have reported it.

3.19 Scholarship Given by Different Persons:

The majority of students have reported that they are given their Post-matric Scholarships by their teachers (Table-3.17). The percentage of such students is higher in rural areas (83.33 per cent) as against the urban areas (64.29 per cent) of the district.

Table-3.17: Scholarship Given by Different Persons

Particulars	Rural	Urban	Total
By Teachers	10 (83.33)	9 (64.29)	19 (73.08)
By Pradhan/Sabhasad	2 (16.67)	5 (35.71)	7 (26.92)
Total Beneficiaries	12 (100.00)	14 (100.00)	26 (100.00)

Note: Figures in brackets indicate percentages.
Source: Primary data based.

3.20 Expenses for Applying the Post-matric Scholarship:

The total expenditure of Rs. 172 is required to apply for the Post-matric Scholarship. There are two main items of expenditure. These are on obtaining income certificate and getting affidavit. The expenditure is higher in rural areas and for the girl students (Table 3.18).

Table-3.18: Item wise Expenses for Applying the Post-matric Scholarship

Items	Average Amount (in Rs.)								
	Rural			Urban			Total		
	Boys	Girls	Total	Boys	Girls	Total	Boys	Girls	Total
Income Certificate	82	96	90	55	76	73	74	83	81
On Making Affidavit	68	59	62	62	57	58	66	58	60
Photos and Travel etc	30	29	29	25	32	31	28	31	30
Total	182	187	185	143	166	163	169	175	172

Source: Primary data based.

3.21 Utilization of Pre-matric Scholarship Money: Students of Class 11-12:

The students have reported that most part of the money they get as Post-matric Scholarship is spent on the items related to their education (Table-3.19). In this way, the role of Post-matric Scholarship in the educational development of minority students of classes 11-12 is paramount.

Table-3.19: Items wise Average Expenditure of Scholarship Amount : Students of Class-11-12

Items	Average Amount (In Rs)
Books & Stationary	815
Learning Materials	552
Travel	268
Private Tuition Fee	504
Course Fee	1000
Medical Expenses	205
Food Expenses	294
Non Food Expenses	203
Debt Return	12
Total	3853

Source: Primary data based.

3.22 Utilization of Pre-matric Scholarship Money:Graduation and above:

The role of Post-matric Scholarship in the educational development of minority students in graduation and above is paramount as major part of the Post-matric Scholarship money is reported to be spent on their education related needs (Table 3.20).

Table-3.20: Items wise Average Expenditure of Scholarship Amount: Graduation and above

Items	Average Amount (In Rs)
Books & Stationary	918
Learning Materials	645
Travel	280
Private Tuition Fee	605
Course Fee	1500
Medical Expenses	203
Food Expenses	385
Non Food Expenses	304
Debt Return	15
Total	4855

Source: Primary data based.

3.23 Effectiveness of Post-matric Scholarship:

The students have been very straight forth in replying about the effectiveness of Post-matric Scholarship. All of them said that they did not take the admission due to Post-matric Scholarship. There has been no improvement in their school attendance but all them reported that the Post-matric Scholarship has been useful to them in meeting their educational, family and health care needs (Table-3.21).

Table-3.21: Response of Students on the Effectiveness of Post-matric Scholarship

Particulars	Yes	No	Total
Admission Taken due to Scholarship	-	26(100.00)	26(100.00)
Attendance at the School Improved	-	26(100.00)	26(100.00)
Scholarship has Fulfilled Study Needs	26(100.00)	-	26(100.00)
Scholarship has Helped in Health Care Needs	21(80.77)	05(19.23)	26(100.00)
Desire to Continue Studies after Getting Scholarship	26(100.00)	-	26(100.00)
Educational Skills has Improved	26(100.00)	-	26(100.00)
Involvement in the Household Activities has Reduced.	20(76.92)	6(23.08)	26(100.00)
Scholarship has Helped in Family Needs	18(69.23)	8(30.77)	26(100.00)
Chances to Continue Study in Higher Class and get a job increased	24(92.31)	2(7.64)	26(100.00)

Note: Figures in brackets indicate percentages.
Source: Primary data based.

3.24 Perception of Rural Students about Pre-matric Scholarship:

The students feel that too much documentation and income limit of Rs. 2 lakh are the two major problem of the Post-matric Scholarship. Some other problems are also viewed by majority of the respondents as shown in table-3.22.

Table-3.22: Views of Students about Post-matric Scholarship Scheme

Views	Number of Students		
	Beneficiary	Non-Beneficiary	Total
Lack of Awareness about the Detail of Scheme	22 (84.62)	12 (85.71)	34 (85.00)
Application Form is Lengthy & Language Problems	24 (92.31)	11 (78.57)	35 (87.50)
Too Much Documentation etc.	26 (100.00)	14 (100.00)	40 (100.00)
Income limit of Rs. 2 Lakh	26 (100.00)	14 (100.00)	40 (100.00)
50 Percent limit of Marks	26 (100.00)	12 (85.71)	38 (95.00)
Untimely Payment	23 (88.46)	14 (100.00)	37 (92.50)
Total Students	26 (100.00)	14 (100.00)	40 (100.00)

Note: Figures in brackets indicate percentages.
Source: Primary data based.

3.25 Main Findings:

- The complete awareness about the Post-matric Scholarship is limited to less than half of the sample students.
- The main source of awareness of Post-matric scholarship to students is the teachers of the institutions where the students study.
- The sample students have reported that 72.50 per cent of them are aware of the eligibility conditions of Post-matric Scholarship. The proportion of rural students knowing eligibility conditions are less (58.33 per cent) in rural areas versus in urban areas (85 per cent) of the district.
- The sample students have reported that 65.38 per cent of them received the Post-matric Scholarship of Rs.3000 to 4000. The proportion of such students is higher in rural areas (75 per cent) as against in urban areas (57.14 per cent).
- The majority of students have reported that they are given their Post-matric Scholarships by their teachers. The percentage of such students is higher in rural areas (80 per cent) as against the urban areas (65 per cent) of the district.
- The total expenditure of Rs. 172 is required to apply for the Post-matric Scholarship. There are two main items of expenditure. These are on obtaining income certificate and getting affidavit. The expenditure is higher in rural areas and for the girl students.
- The students have reported that most part of the money they get as Post-matric Scholarship is spent on the items related to their education (Table-3.10). In this way, the role of Post-matric Scholarship in the educational development of minority students of classes 11-12 is paramount.
- The role of Post-matric Scholarship in the educational development of minority students in graduation and above is paramount as major part of the Post-matric Scholarship money is reported to be spent on their education related needs.
- The students have been very straight forth in replying about the effectiveness of Post-

matric Scholarship. All of them said that they did not take the admission due to Post-matric Scholarship. There has been no improvement in their school attendance but all reported that the Post-matric Scholarship has been very useful to them in meeting their educational, family and health care needs.

- The students feel that too much documentation and income limit of Rs. 2 lakh are the two major problems of the Post-matric Scholarship.

Problems in Getting Post-matric Scholarship and Suggestions of Students

3.26 Students Facing Difficulties while Applying:

Around 65 per cent of the sample students face problems while applying for the Post-matric Scholarship (Table-3.23).

Table-3.23: Number of Students Facing problems while applying for Post-matric Scholarship

Students	Number
Beneficiary	17 (65.38)
Non-Beneficiary	9 (64.29)
Total	26 (65.00)

Note: Figures in brackets indicate percentages.
Source: Primary data based.

3.27 Level of Difficulty in Obtaining Application Form:

The students have reported that half of them face difficulty while obtaining the application form of Post—matric Scholarship. Around 12 per cent of them also reported high level of difficulty in obtaining the application form of Post—matric Scholarship (Table-3.24).

Table-3.24: Level of Difficulty in Obtaining Application Form: Response of Students

Level of difficulty	Number of Students		
	Beneficiary	Non-Beneficiary	Total
Highly difficulty	3 (11.54)	2 (14.29)	5 (12.50)
Difficulty	13 (50.00)	7 (50.00)	20 (50.00)
Somewhat difficulty	8 (30.77)	4 (28.57)	12 (30.00)
No difficulty	2 (7.69)	1 (7.14)	3 (7.50)
Total	26 (100.00)	14 (100.00)	40 (100.00)

Note: Figures in brackets indicate percentages.
Source: Primary data based.

3.28 Level of Difficulty in Filling Application Form:

In filling the application form, more than 50 per cent felt difficulty. Around 10 per cent of sample students reported high level of difficulty in filling the application form (Table-3.25).

Table-3.25: Level of Difficulty in Filling the Application Form: Response of Students

Level of difficulty	Number of Students		
	Beneficiary	Non-Beneficiary	Total
Highly difficulty	3 (11.54)	1 (7.14)	4 (10.00)
Difficulty	13 (50.00)	8 (57.14)	21 (52.50)
Somewhat difficulty	8 (30.77)	3 (21.43)	11 (27.50)
No difficulty	2 (7.69)	2 (14.29)	4 (10.00)
Total	26 (100.00)	14 (100.00)	40 (100.00)

Note: Figures in brackets indicate percentages.
Source: Primary data based.

3.29 Level of Cooperation of Institutions:

The majority of beneficiary as well as non-beneficiary students are reported to be satisfied with the cooperation of their institutions in getting Post-matric Scholarship to them.

Table-3.26: Level of Cooperation of Institutions in helping Students to get Scholarship : Perception of Students

Level of Satisfaction	Number of Students		
	Beneficiary	Non-Beneficiary	Total
Highly Satisfactory	3 (11.54)	2 (14.29)	5 (12.50)
Satisfactory	18 (69.23)	10 (71.43)	28 (70.00)
Unsatisfactory	3 (11.54)	1 (7.14)	4 (10.00)
Highly Unsatisfactory	2 (7.69)	1 (7.14)	3 (7.50)
Total	26 (100.00)	14 (100.00)	40 (100.00)

Note: Figures in brackets indicate percentages.
Source: Primary data based.

3.30 Role of State Government Officials:

More than 80 per cent of sample students are reported to be satisfied with the role of state government officials in getting the Post-matric Scholarship.

Table-3.27: Role of State Government Officials: Perception of Students

Level of Satisfaction	Number of Students		
	Beneficiary	Non-Beneficiary	Total
Highly Satisfactory	3 (11.54)	2 (14.29)	5 (12.50)
Satisfactory	18 (69.23)	10 (71.43)	28 (70.00)
Unsatisfactory	3 (11.54)	1 (7.14)	4 (10.00)
Highly Unsatisfactory	2 (7.69)	1 (7.14)	3 (7.50)
Total	26 (100.00)	14 (100.00)	40 (100.00)

Note: Figures in brackets indicate percentages.
Source: Primary data based.

3.31 Suggestions of Students for Improving the Post-matric Scholarship Scheme:

Six suggestions to improve the Post-matric Scholarship have been given by the students. These have been shown in Table-3.28. The most important is that the income certificate given by the Pradhans/Sabhasads should be acceptable.

Table-3.28: Suggestions of Students in Improving the Scheme

Suggestions	Number of Students		
	Beneficiary	Non-Beneficiary	Total
Awareness Campaign at Community, Institutions and Panchayat Level	21 (80.77)	14 (100.00)	35 (87.50)
Scholarship amount should be Increased.	26 (100.00)	11 (78.57)	37 (92.50)
Income certificate given by Pradhan/Sabhasad should be accepted	26 (100.00)	14 (100.00)	40 (100.00)
More than 2 children should be eligible from one Family	18 (69.23)	9 (64.29)	27 (67.50)
Application form should be simple and multilingual.	22 (84.62)	12 (85.71)	34 (85.00)
No criteria of percentage of marks	18 (69.23)	8 (57.14)	26 (65.00)
Total	26 (100.00)	14 (100.00)	40 (100.00)

Note: Figures in brackets indicate percentages.
Source: Primary data based.

3.32 Main Findings:

- Around 65 per cent of the sample students face problems while applying for the Post-matric Scholarship.
- The students have reported that half of them face difficulty while obtaining the application form of Post-matric Scholarship. Around 12 per cent of them also reported high level of difficulty in obtaining the application form of Post—matric Scholarship.
- In filling the application form, more than 50 per cent felt difficulty. Around 10 per cent of sample students reported high level of difficulty in filling the application form.
- The majority of beneficiary as well as non-beneficiary students are reported to be satisfied with the cooperation of their institutions in getting Post-matric Scholarship to them.
- More than 80 per cent of sample students are reported to be satisfied with the role of state government officials in getting the Post-matric Scholarship.
- Six suggestions to improve the Post-matric Scholarship have been given by the students. The most important is that the income certificate given by the Pradhans/Sabhasads should be acceptable.

Parents of Beneficiary and Non-Beneficiary Students, Institutions and Officials Parents :

3.33 Sample Size:

The sample size of beneficiary and non-beneficiary parents of the study is as follows:

Table-3.29: Sample Parents of Students of Post-matric Scholarship

Particulars	Location	No. of Parents
Beneficiary Parents	Rural	5 (45.45)
	Urban	6 (54.55)
	Total	11 (100.00)
Non-Beneficiary Parents	Rural	5 (55.56)
	Urban	4 (44.44)
	Total	9 (100.00)
Total	Rural	10 (50.00)
	Urban	10 (50.00)
	Total	20 (100.00)

Note: Figures in brackets indicate percentages.
Source: Primary data based.

3.34 Housing and Family Features:

72.73 per cent houses of beneficiaries and 77.78 per cent houses of non-beneficiaries parents are pucca. There are 3 rooms per house in both cases and family size is of 6 persons. 72.73 per cent houses of beneficiary and 77.78 per cent houses of non-beneficiary parents are electrified. On an average 2 persons are working in a family. 63.64 per cent beneficiary households and 66.67 per cent non-beneficiary households have ration cards.

Table-3.30: Housing and Family Features of Sample Parents

Parents	Beneficiary	Non-beneficiary
Type of House		
Katcha	1 (9.09)	-
Pucca	8 (72.73)	7 (77.78)
Semi Pucca	2 (18.18)	2 (22.22)
Average Value of House	240615	255467
Average No. of Rooms	3	3
Average Family Size	6	6
Average Earning Members in the family	2	2
Houses Electrified	8 (72.73)	7 (77.78)
Ration Card Holders	7 (63.64)	6 (66.67)
BPL	2 (28.57)	2 (33.33)
APL	4 (57.14)	3 (50.00)
Others	1 (14.29)	1 (16.67)

Note: Figures in brackets indicate percentages.
Source: Primary data based.

3.35 Land Size of Parents:

The beneficiary as well as non-beneficiary parents have small size of land. The minimum size of land is 1 acre and maximum size is 2 acres (Table-3.31).

Table-3.31: Land Size of Parents

Land Holding	Beneficiary	Non-beneficiary	Total
Less than 0.5 acre	-	-	-
0.5 to 1.00 acre	-	2 (22.22)	2 (10.00)
More than 1.00 acre	5 (45.45)	1 (11.11)	6 (30.00)
Average	2	1	2
Min	1.00	1.00	1.00
Max	2.00	2.00	2.00

Note: Figures in brackets indicate percentages.
Source: Primary data based.

3.36 Annual Income of parents:

The table-3.32 shows that 55 per cent of sample parents earn annual income in the range of Rs. 1, 00001 to 1, 50,000.

Table-3.32: Classification of Parents According to their Annual Income

Income	No. of Students		
	Beneficiary	Non-Beneficiary	Total
20,000 to 50,000	1 (9.09)	1 (11.11)	2 (10.00)
50,001 to 100,000	4 (36.36)	3 (33.33)	7 (35.00)
1,00001 to 1,50,000	6 (54.55)	5 (55.56)	11 (55.00)
Total	11 (100.00)	9 (100.00)	20 (100.00)

Note: Figures in brackets indicate percentages.
Source: Primary data based.

3.37 Parents Knowledge of Post-matric Scholarship:

Though 55 per cent of all parents are aware of the Post-matric Scholarship Scheme but 45 per cent of them are unaware also which is quite high percentage (Table-3.33).

Table-3.33: Parents Knowledge of the Post-Matric Scholarship Scheme

Particulars	Number of Parents		
	Beneficiary	Non Beneficiary	Total
Rural	3 (60.00)	3 (60.00)	6 (60.00)
Urban	3 (50.00)	2 (50.00)	5 (50.00)
Total	6 (54.55)	5 (55.56)	11 (55.00)

Note: Figures in brackets indicate percentages.
Source: Primary data based.

3.38 Sources of Awareness of Post-matric Scholarship:

The teachers of the schools where the wards of the parents study are the main source of information of the Post-matric Scholarship to the parents (Table-3.34)

Table-3.34: Sources of Awareness of Post-Matric Scholarship Scheme

Source	Beneficiary	Non Beneficiary	Total
Teachers	4 (66.66)	3 (60.00)	7 (63.64)
Radio/T.V	1 (16.67)	1 (20.00)	2 (18.18)
News Paper	1 (16.67)	1 (20.00)	2 (18.18)
Total Responses	6 (100.00)	5 (100.00)	11 (100.00)

Note: Figures in brackets indicate percentages.
Source: Primary data based.

3.39 Reasons of Untimely Payment of Post-matric Scholarship:

The parents have told 3 reasons for the delay in timely payment of Post-matric Scholarship as shown in table-3.35. But two are the prominent reasons. These are the delay from the MOMA and district officials.

Table-3.35: Reasons of Post matric Scholarship not getting Timely: Beneficiary Responses

Reasons	Number of Parents		
	Rural	Urban	Total
Delay by MOMA	2 (40.00)	1 (16.67)	3 (27.27)
Delay by District Authorities	1 (20.00)	1 (16.67)	2 (18.18)
Delay by the Institutions	-	1 (16.66)	1 (9.10)
Total	3 (60.00)	3 (50.00)	6 (54.55)

Note: Figures in brackets indicate percentages.
Source: Primary data based.

3.40 Problems faced by Beneficiary Students: Parents Response

36.36 per cent of sample parents feel their wards faced problems in getting the Post-matric Scholarship (Table-3.36). In other words, 63.64 per cent felt their wards faced no problem in getting the Post-matric Scholarship which indicates that majority of parents find that their wards faced no problem in getting the Post-matric Scholarship.

Table-3.36: Problem Faced by Students in Getting the Post Matric Scholarship: Parents Response

Particulars	Number of Parents		
	Yes	No	Total
Rural	2 (40.00)	3 (60.00)	5 (50.00)
Urban	2 (33.33)	4 (66.67)	6 (60.00)
Total	4 (36.36)	7 (63.64)	11 (55.00)

Note: Figures in brackets indicate percentages.
Source: Primary data based.

3.41 Level of Difficulties:

The parents feel that their wards feel not much difficulty in filling the application form as evident from following table-3.37.

Table-3.37: Level of Difficulty in Filling the Application Form: Parent Response

Level of Difficulty	Beneficiary	Non Beneficiary	Total
High Difficulty	-	-	-
Difficulty	5 (45.46)	5 (55.56)	10 (50.00)
Some What Difficulty	4 (36.36)	3 (33.33)	7 (35.00)
Less Difficult	2 (18.18)	1 (11.11)	3 (15.00)
Total	11 (100.00)	9 (100.00)	20 (100.00)

Note: Figures in brackets indicate percentages.
Source: Primary data based.

3.42 Perception of Beneficiary Parents about various Aspects of Post-matric Scholarship:

The perception of beneficiary parents is generally poor or average about different aspects of Post-matric scholarship (Table-3.38). They feel that documentation, renewal, and timely availability of application forms are poor while scholarship amount, timeliness of processing and support of school administration are at average level.

Table-3.38: Perception of Beneficiary Parents about various Aspects of Post-Matric Scholarship Scheme

Particulars	Number of Parents					
	Poor	Average	Good	Very good	Excellent	Total
Scholarship Amount	3 (27.27)	6 (54.55)	1 (9.09)	1 (9.09)	-	11 (100.00)
Documentation	5 (45.46)	3 (27.27)	2 (18.18)	1 (9.09)	-	11 (100.00)
Renewal Process	11 (100.00)	-	-	-	-	11 (100.00)
Availability of Application Form	4 (36.37)	3 (27.27)	2 (18.18)	1 (9.09)	1 (9.09)	11 (100.00)
Timeliness of Processing	2 (18.19)	5 (45.45)	4 (36.36)	-	-	11 (100.00)
Support of School Administration	3 (27.27)	6 (54.55)	1 (9.09)	1 (9.09)	-	11 (100.00)

Note: Figures in brackets indicate percentages.
Source: Primary data based.

3.43 Perception of Non-beneficiary Parents about various Aspects of Post-matric Scholarship:

The perception of non-beneficiary parents about various aspects of Post-matric Scholarship is generally poor or average as evident in following table-3.39.

Table-3.39: Perception of Non Beneficiary Parents about various Aspects of Post-matric Scholarship Scheme: Non Beneficiary

Particulars	Number of Parents					
	Poor	Average	Good	Very good	Excellent	Total
Scholarship Amount	2 (22.22)	5 (55.56)	1 (11.11)	1 (11.11)	-	9 (100.00)
Documentation	4 (44.45)	3 (33.33)	1 (11.11)	1 (11.11)	-	9 (100.00)
Renewal Process	9 (100.00)	-	-	-	-	9 (100.00)
Availability of Application Form	3 (33.34)	2 (22.22)	2 (22.22)	1 (11.11)	1 (11.11)	9 (100.00)
Timeliness of Processing	3 (33.34)	3 (33.33)	3 (33.33)	-	-	9 (100.00)
Support of School Administration	2 (22.22)	6 (66.67)	1 (11.11)	-	-	9 (100.00)

Note: Figures in brackets indicate percentages.
Source: Primary data based.

3.44 Perception of All Parents about various Aspects of Post-matric Scholarship:

Considering the perception of all parents of beneficiary and non-beneficiary students, it becomes

Table-3.40: Perception of All Parents (Beneficiary and Non Beneficiary) about various Aspects of Post-Matric Scholarship Scheme

Particulars	Number of Parents					
	Poor	Average	Good	Very good	Excellent	Total
Scholarship Amount	5 (25.00)	11 (55.00)	2 (10.00)	2 (10.00)	-	20 (100.00)
Documentation	9 (45.00)	6 (30.00)	3 (15.00)	2 (10.00)	-	20 (100.00)
Renewal Process	20 (100.00)	-	-	-	-	20 (100.00)
Availability of Application Form	7 (35.00)	5 (25.00)	4 (20.00)	2 (10.00)	2 (10.00)	20 (100.00)
Timeliness of Processing	5 (25.00)	8 (40.00)	7 (35.00)	-	-	20 (100.00)
Support of School Administration	5 (25.00)	12 (60.00)	2 (10.00)	1 (5.00)	-	20 (100.00)

Note: Figures in brackets indicate percentages.
Source: Primary data based.

evident that most of them give poor or average rating to the various aspects of Post-matric Scholarship as evident in table-3.40.

3.45 Observations of Parents

The parents have given 8 observations about the Post-matric Scholarship Scheme which have been shown as following table-3.41. These observations have been put in descending order of ranking. It appears that parents feel that the importance of Post-matric Scholarship is most in the education of their wards. The lack of awareness about the scheme is the other most important observation of the parents.

Table-3.41: Observations of Sample Parents about Post-matric Scholarship Scheme

1.	Scholarship is helpful for students in their education.
2.	Lack of Awareness about Post-Matric Scholarship Scheme implemented by MOMA Government of India.
3.	Lack of Knowledge about important dates of Scheme.
4.	Non-Corporative attitude of Government educational Institutions.
5.	Application Form is lengthy.
6.	Applying process is costly due to arrangement of various types of certificates like Income Certificate, Affidavit etc.
7.	Delay processing and late distribution of Scholarship.
8.	Regular checking of Scheme at community and Institution level should be encouraged.

3.46 Main Findings:

- Majority of beneficiary and non-beneficiary parents have pucca houses. The family size is large but there are 3 rooms per house in both cases. On an average 2 persons are working in a family.
- The beneficiary as well as non-beneficiary parents has small size of land. The minimum size of land is 1 acre and maximum size is 2 acres.
- 55 per cent of sample parents earn annual income in the range of Rs. 1, 00001 to 1, 50,000.
- Though 55 per cent of all parents are aware of the Post-matric Scholarship Scheme but 45 per cent of them are unaware also which is quite high percentage.
- The parents find the teachers of the schools where their wards study as the main source of information of the Post-matric Scholarship.
- The parents have told 3 reasons for the delay in timely payment of Post-matric Scholarship. But 2 are the prominent reasons. These are the delay from the MOMA and district officials.
- 36.36 per cent of sample parents feel their wards faced problems in getting the Post-matric Scholarship. In other words, 63.64 per cent felt their wards faced no problem in getting the Post-matric Scholarship which indicates that majority of parents find that their wards faced no problem in getting the Post-matric Scholarship.
- The parents feel that their wards feel not much difficulty in filling the application form.

- The parents observe that the Post-matric Scholarship is most important in the education of their wards. The lack of awareness about the scheme is the other most important observation of the parents.

Educational Institutions :

3.47 Enrolment, Applicants and Scholarship Award:

The basic information relating to these institutions are presented in Table-3.42. Out of five, three are inter colleges, one degree and one postgraduate college. Three of these represent rural areas and remaining two are from urban part of the district, representing the disbursement of highest percentage of post- matric scholarship among Muslim minority students. Two of these institutions are private and three are government run colleges. The maximum level of teachers' qualification has been up to PH. D. and M. Phil. levels in four colleges. The maximum teachers' qualification turned out to be at PG level only in one of the sample inters college.

Table-3.42: Basic Information on Surveyed Institutions

Name of School	Category of the Institutions	Type	Maxium Level of Teachers's Qualification
Government Inter College, Swar	Inter College	Government	M.Phil
GovernementRaza P.G. College	P.G. College	Government	Ph.D
Government Inter College, Shahabad	Inter College	Government	M.Phil
Shamsi Girls Inter College	Inter College	Private	Master Dgree
Ramrata Degree College	Degree College	Private	Ph.D

The information relating to enrolled students applied for Post- Matric Scholarship and awarded in all the five sample institutes are presented in Table-3.43 (a to e) . Out of total sample institutions the highest 52.92 percent enrolled Muslim students have applied for post-Matric Scholarship from Raza PG College during the year 2009-10. The highest more than 93 percent of the applicants were awarded scholarship in the same college. In other colleges the applicants out of total enrolled Muslim students ranged from around 3 percent to 11 percent during the same year. The minimum 15 percent of the total application, awarded for Post-matric Scholarship was recorded in Ramtara degree college, Shahabad of the district during this year. In subsequent year under consideration (2010-11) also, more than 5 percent to 66 percent of the total enrolled students applied for the scholarship. However, the awarded scholarship out of total applicants ranged from a low of more than 12 percent to 93 percent across the sample institutions during the year 2010-11.

Table-3.43 (a): Information on Students Enrolled Applied and Awarded Scholarship in the Surveyed Institutions

1-Government Inter College, Swar

Year	Muslim Students								
	Enrolled			Applied			Awarded		
	Male	Female	Total	Male	Female	Total	Male	Female	Total
2009-10	Not Available								
2010-11	198 (100.00)	152 (100.00)	350 (100.00)	15(7.58) (100.00)	7(4.61) (100.00)	21(6.00) (100.00)	2 (13.33)	1 (14.29)	3 (14.29)

Source: Records of the Institution.

Table-3.43 (b): Government Raza Post Graduate College

Years	Muslim Students								
	Enrolled			Applied			Awarded		
	Male	Female	Total	Male	Female	Total	Male	Female	Total
2009-10	3214 (100.00)	1083 (100.00)	4297 (100.00)	1432(42.44) (100.00)	842(77.75) (100.00)	2274(52.92) (100.00)	1391 (97.14)	725 (86.10)	2116 (93.05)
2010-11	3381 (100.00)	1201 (100.00)	4582 (100.00)	1672(49.45) (100.00)	894(74.44) (100.00)	2566(56.00) (100.00)	1555 (93.00)	781 (87.36)	2336 (91.04)

Source: Records of the Institution

Table-3.43 ©: Government Inter College Shahabad

Years	Muslim Students								
	Enrolled			Applied			Awarded		
	Male	Female	Total	Male	Female	Total	Male	Female	Total
2009-10	153 (100.00)	105 (100.00)	258 (100.00)	6(3.92) (100.00)	2(1.90) (100.00)	8(3.10) (100.00)	1 (16.67)	1 (50.00)	2 (25.00)
2010-11	185 (100.00)	121 (100.00)	306 (100.00)	11(5.95) (100.00)	5(4.13) (100.00)	16(5.29) (100.00)	2 (18.19)	- (0.00)	2 (12.50)

Source: Records of the Institution.

Table-3.43 (d): Shamsi Girls Inter College

Years	Muslim Students								
	Enrolled			Applied			Awarded		
	Male	Female	Total	Male	Female	Total	Male	Female	Total
2009-10	-	126 (100.00)	126 (100.00)	-	14(11.11) (100.00)	14(11.11) (100.00)	-	6 (42.86)	6 (42.86)
2010-11	-	291 (100.00)	291 (100.00)	-	193(66.32) (100.00)	193(66.33) (100.00)	-	114 (59.07)	114 (59.07)

Source: Records of the Institution.

Table-3.43 (e): Ramrata Degree College, Zahidpur : Shahabad

Years	Muslim Students								
	Enrolled			Applied			Awarded		
	Male	Female	Total	Male	Female	Total	Male	Female	Total
2009-10	236 (100.00)	132 (100.00)	368 (100.00)	15(6.35) (100.00)	5(3.78) (100.00)	20(5.43) (100.00)	2 (13.33)	1 (20.00)	3 (15.00)
2010-11	237 (100.00)	151 (100.00)	389 (100.00)	20(8.44) (100.00)	4(2.65) (100.00)	24(15.00) (100.00)	3 (15.00)	1 (25.00)	4 (16.67)

Source: Records of the Institution

A perusal of information regarding number of enrolled Muslim students, percentage change in the total applicants and percentage of total awarded to total applicants for Post-matric Scholarship over the years indicated increment in enrolment and also marginal improvement in the number of applicants and awarded students. The rise in enrolment, application and award of Post- Matric Scholarship among Muslin female students was also noticed in institutions during this period.

3.48 Reasons for Non- Award of Scholarship:

Out of five-sample institution, four have reported lack of awareness among students and their parents about the provisions of Post-matric Scholarship in the colleges they are studying. The lengthy application form and language problem was reported by the institutional authorities, including head of the institutes in almost all the sample colleges. Three out five institutions have also reported problems in documentation owing to the involvement of formality in this process. The processing of scholarship form involves distribution, collection, scrutiny preparation of the list and finally sending it to district administration. After obtaining the sanction from the district authority the new process of preparing cheques, transferring it to the beneficiary bank account, maintaining the ledger is a tedious job and needs skilled man power. Almost all the colleges suffer from the shortage of clerical staff which causes problem in the processing of the scholarship forms. This leads to delay and ultimately inconvenience to the recipient students. All the heads of the institutions have reported for the delay in the disbursement of the Post-matric Scholrship due to this reason. Apart from this, there is delay involved in the final payment of the scholarship due to other procedural delays and problems at the state and centre levels.

Table-3.44: Important Reasons for Students Not Being Awarded Scholarship

Reasons	No of Institution
Lack of Awarness About the Scheme	4 (80.00)
Lenthy Application Form And Language Problem	5(100.00)
To Much Formilatiy For Documentation	3 (60.00)
Delay Payment of Schlorship	5(100.00)

Source: Staff of the Institution.

3.49 Method of Scholarship Payment and Processing of Application:

The payment of post- matric scholarship was found to be made through Cheques in all the five sample institutions of district Rampur. As per information provided by the institutions, the average time taken for processing the duly completed post- matric scholarship applications is more than 15 days. 40 percent institutions faced the difficulty in processing of application but processing was not found to be very difficult by any of the sample institutions. Remaining 40 and 20 percent institutions found processing somewhat difficult and less difficult respectively. All this is realised by the college management due to lack of trained staff in the colleges.

After processing the post- matric scholarship applications, proposals are sent to MoMA in the month of September. These are usually sanctioned by the months of December- January. After getting sanction, amount reaches at the district level during the months of February and March and the scholarship in disbursed between March to April. Thus, the whole process takes around six to seven months. As compared to other state government run scholarship schemes, this involves a very time consuming procedure. This is found to be causing inconvenience to institutions as well as scholarship holding students. Due to this delay the scholars get impatient and lose their interest in the scheme by the time scholarship is finalised.

3.50 Institutions' Satisfaction Level with Govt. agencies Involved:

Only 40 percent institutions were found to be satisfied with the time involved in the processing for the approval for post- matric scholarship by the state government agencies. 60 percent institutions were not satisfied with this system. It was the same response for timely release of scholarship funds. Only 40 percent institutions were satisfied with the time taken for the release of the funds. Rest of the 60 percent were dissatisfied due to excessive time involved in the release of funds from the state government agencies. However, the behaviour of the staff of state government official agencies was reported to be far better as presented in Table-3.45.

Table-3.45: Institutions' Level of Satisfaction with State Government Agencies

Heads	Level of Satisfaction (Code)			
	1	2	3	4
Timely Processing of Approval	-	-	2(40.00)	3(60.00)
Timely Release of Funds	-	-	2(40.00)	3(60.00)
Staff Behaviour	-	3(60.00)	2(40.00)	-

1- Highly Satisfied, 2- Very Satisfied, 3-Satisfied, 4-Dissatisfied

The institutions' response with respect to their satisfaction level with the central governmental agencies involved in the processing of approval are found to be the same as in case of state government agencies as presented in Table-3.46.

Table-3.46: Institutions' Level of Satisfaction with Central Government Agencies

S.N	Heads	Level of Satisfaction (Code)			
		1	2	3	4
1.	Timely Processing of Approval	-	-	2(40.00)	3(60.00)
2.	Timely Release of Funds	-	-	2(40.00)	3(60.00)
3.	Staff Behaviour	-	3(60.00)	2(40.00)	-
Number of Institutions		5(100.00)			

1- Highly Satisfied, 2- Very Satisfied, 3-Satisfied, 4-Dissatisfied

3.51 Bottlenecks Faced in the Teaching process and Education System:

There is much inefficiency found to be prevailing in the existing teaching process and education system, which are hindering the dissemination of benefits emanating from educational scholarship schemes according to the sample institutions. Out of five-sample institution, one has reported for inefficient teaching methods. Four of these found the dearth of qualified teachers in their institutions. However, institutions have reported their satisfaction with the teaching process. Factors like Improvement in attendance, good student results and students' participation in co- curricular activities have served the purpose of scholarship scheme to a reasonable extent.

Table-3.47: Bottlenecks Faced in the Education System

Bottlenecks	No of Institution
Inefficient Teaching Methods	1(20.00)
Lack of Qualified Teachers	4(80.00)
Number of Institution	5 (100.00)

Institutions are lacking computerized data management system. Forty percent of the sample institutions are using manual data processing/ management system. Sixty percent institutions are using only semi- computerized system for data management.

Table-3.48: Procedure of Data Management

Procedure	No of Institution
Manual	2 (40.00)
Semi- Computerized	3(60.00)
Fully Computer	-
Number of Institution	5 (100.00)

3.52 Selection of Beneficiary Students:

The target beneficiaries among the students are identified through discussion in the classroom through exploring their eligibility. For ensuring the percolation of scholarship benefits to the deserving students, some important mechanisms are adopted. These include, preparation of check list of needy students, seeking feedbacks from parents and interaction with concerned district officials. The most important changes that are found after the award of scholarship among beneficiaries included, increased enrolment and regular attendance. Despite these achievements, there are some important problems, which are faced by students in the availing of post-matric scholarship. These include involvement of excessive and clumsy documentation and too much expenditure.

3.53 Main Findings:

- A mass awareness campaign regarding whereabouts of the scheme, eligibility and selection criteria should be launched among the community and institutions.
- The lengthy application format for scholarship should be simplified and possibly be made available to the students in Hindi/ Urdu language..
- Funds should be provided by MOMA to form a separate cell for the processing the scholarship application forms and maintenance of related records in institutions.

District Officials

3.54 On the Guidelines:

The District Minority Welfare Officer, Rampur District reported that guidelines of the Post-matric Scholarship are available with him and the scheme is implemented as per guidelines.

Table-3.49: Availability of Guidelines of Post-matric Scholarship

Particular	Responses	
	Yes	No
Guidelines Available about the Scheme with District Minority Welfare Officer	√	—
Scheme Implemented as per Guidelines	√	—
Guidelines Followed Easily	√	—

Source: Response of District Minority Welfare Officer, Rampur

3.55 Selection Criteria:

The official reported that in selection process, apart from the marks obtained in the previous examination, poverty and girls students are given the preference.

3.56 Problems Regarding Implementations of the Scheme:

The following problems were found to be faced in course of implementation of scheme in the district

Application Form Lengthy and Complicated.
Language Problem
No Fund Allotted From MOMA for Advertisement and Monitoring the Scheme
Separate Staff not Available for Maintaining/Monitoring the Scheme
Required Computers also not provided by MOMA regarding documentation/application form

3.57 Awardees of Post-matric Scholarship:

Out of total Post- matric scholarship awardees,' the share of Muslim students was found to be the highest (96.41 percent).

Table-3.50: Year and Religion wise Number of Awardee Students

Year	Religion	Number of Awardee Students		
		Male	Female	Total
2010-11	Muslim	258 (95.91)	602 (96.63)	860 (96.41)
	Sikh	6 (2.23)	14 (2.25)	20 (2.24)
	Christian	5 (1.86)	7 (1.12)	12 (1.35)
	Total	269 (100.00)	623 (100.00)	892 (100.00)

Source : District Minority Welfare Department, Rampur.

3.58 Criteria for Selecting Institutions:

Priority was given to minority institutions and majority of minority students enrolled.

3.59 Grants of Post-matric Scholarship:

As per information provided by District Minority Welfare Officer, Rampur, the grant of Rs. 34.31 lakh allocated in the year 2010-11 was fully utilized. The amount was utilized only under the head of scholarship distribution (Table-3.51).

Table-3.51: Grant Approval and utilization

Year	Grants Approved/Sanctioned (In Rs. Lakh)	Grants Utilized
2010-11	34,31078	34,31078

Source: District Minority Welfare Department, Rampur

3.60 Mechanisms for Community Awareness :

5. Advertisement in local newspapers
6. Meetings with representatives of district, block and village panchayats
7. Meeting with Head of Educational Institutions in the districts
8. Publication of Pamphlets and Booklets

3.61 Availability and Accessibility of the Scheme:

District Minority Welfare Officer was reported to be satisfied with respect to timely processing of approval and release of funds along with staff behavior.

3.62 Satisfaction Level with MOMA for the Following Heads: Response of DMWO

Major Head	Satisfaction Level
Timely Processing of approval	Satisfied
Timely Release of Funds	Very Satisfied
Staff Behaviour	Very Satisfied

Source: Response of District Minorty Welfare Officer, Rampur

Table-3.52: Time Spent in Disbursement of Post- matric Scholarship

Proposal sent to MOMA:	September
Sanctioned: January	
Scholarship reached the District:	February
Scholarship Disbursed:	March

3.63 Impact of Post-matric Scholarship:

A .Scholarship scheme has enhanced Enrolment of student belonging to minority communities.

B. Scholarship amount provided adequate cover to the student to meet their study needs.

C. Improving the educational achievement level of students.

3.64 Suggestions for Improvement of Post-matric Scholarship

1. Funds for awareness of the Scheme should be allotted by MOMA
2. Staff should be recruited under the scholarship scheme
3. Availability of application form in Hindi version.

3.65 Main Findings:

- The District Minority Welfare Officer, Rampur District reported that guidelines of the Post- matric Scholarship are available with him and the scheme is implemented as per guidelines.
- The official reported that in selection process, apart from the marks obtained in the previous examination, poverty and girls students are given the preference.
- Out of total Post- matric scholarship awardees,' the share of Muslim students was found to be the highest (96.41 percent).
- Priority was given to minority institutions and majority of minority students enrolled.
- The District Minority Welfare Officer feels that the Post-matric Scholarship has been very helpful to the students in their educational achievements.

Field Observations, Key Issues and Suggestions: Post-matric Scholarship

3.66 Field Observations:

It was observed during the survey of this evaluation in Rampur district of Uttar Pradesh that the implementation of the Post-matric Scholarship Scheme in the district is not as poor and inefficient as was observed in case of Pre-matric Scholarship. In the Post-matric Scholarship, the awardees are the adults. So they encounter all the problems and are not exploited easily. But one point was noticed that there is great reluctance on the part of institutions in encouraging minority students to apply for the Post-matric Scholarship. The institutions were found to be reluctant to forward the applications of the students.When this matter was discussed with them, they pretended to be overloaded with other works and pleaded the problem of lack of staff. The management expressed their feeling that when they are not paid for it why they should do it. Moreover, they said that they have not received any instruction from their affiliated universities to help minority students to get the scholarship. We found a great degree of reluctance on the part of institutions officials to implement the Post-matric Scholarship in their respective colleges.The reluctance is also on the part of district officials like District Magistrates who do little or no follow up or monitoring of the Scholarship Schemes of minorities.

3.67 Key Issues of Post-matric Scholarship:

- The important fact has emerged from this evaluation that the post-matric scholarship has been very effective in overall educational development of students.
- It is also the fact that there is a great demand of Post-matric Scholarship among the minority communities but support system is not adequately supportive to their demand.
- Considering the present income level of parents and level of expenditure on education, the income limit of parents and the amount of Post-matric Scholarship require upward revision.
- The detail awareness about the post-matric scholarship among the students was found to be very in general in Rampur district.
- Substantial number of students felt difficulty in obtaining application form, filling it and submitting it.
- Considerable time is also spent during application to award of scholarship.
- On the whole, it can be concluded that the implementation of Post-matric Scholarship Scheme in Rampur district is not as efficient as it should have been and there is great reluctance on the part of colleges/institution officials to help minority students in getting the Post-matric Scholarship.

3.68 Suggestions:

- There is need of rigorous orientation training of state and district level officials who oversee the scheme.
- Simultaneously need is to generate awareness among the minority community about the scholarship scheme.
- The management of colleges/institutions should be made accountable for the proper implementation of the scheme and instruction in this regard may be issued by the affiliating universities.

- Action should be taken against those colleges/institutions against whom complaint from the minority students/parents are received by the District Minority Welfare Officer for reluctance or not extending adequate support in the matter of scholarships.
- The income limit of parents and amount of Post-matric Scholarship should reasonably be increased.
- The application form should be in Hindi and be simplified.
- In some way accountability clause should be added in the scheme and District Magistrates should be held responsible if poor and inefficient implementation is found.

Chapter IV

Characteristics of Sample Students-Merit cum Means based Scholarship—Rampur District

4.1 Age of Students:

The classification of sample students as per their age indicated that majority of them (beneficiaries as well non-beneficiaries) is in the age group of 18-21 years (Table-4.1).

Table-4.1: Classification of Sample Students according to their Age

Age-Group	Beneficiary	Non-Beneficiary	Total
18-21 Years	12 (80.00)	3 (75.00)	15 (78.95)
22-23 Years	3 (20.00)	1 (25.00)	4 (21.05)
Total	15 (100.00)	4 (100.00)	19 (100.00)

Note: Figures in brackets indicate percentages.
Source: Primary data based.

4.2 Occupations:

Trade and salaried jobs are the two main occupations of the families of sample students.

Table-4.2: Classification of Sample Students according to their Family Occupations

Occupation	Beneficiary	Non-Beneficiary	Total
Agricultiture	3 (20.00)	–	3 (15.78)
Trade	7 (46.67)	1 (25.00)	8 (42.11)
Salaried (Private/ Government)	5 (33.33)	3 (75.00)	8 (42.11)
Total	15 (100.00)	4 (100.00)	19 (100.00)

Note: Figures in brackets indicate percentages.
Source: Primary data based.

4.3 Location of Previous Institutions :

More than half of the sample students were studying in government institutions prior to joining the present institutions and sizeable numbers of them were studying in private institutions (Table-4.3).

Table-4.3: Type and Location of Institutions of Students

Type of Institution	Rural	Urban	Total
Government	6 (40.0o)	4 (100.00)	10 (52.63)
Private	9 (60.00)	-	9 (47.37)
Total	15 (100.00)	4 (100.00)	19 (100.00)

Note: Figures in brackets indicate percentages.
Source: Primary data based.

4.4 Family Income of Students:

The average annual income of around half of the students families is between Rs. 1,50,000 to Rs. 2,00,000 while near about half of them have annual income of above Rs. 2,00,000.

Table-4.4: Annual Income of Student Households

Category of Income (Rs.)	Beneficiary	Non-Beneficiary	Total
150000-200000	7 (46.67)	3 (75.00)	10 (52.63)
Above 200000	8 (53.33)	1 (25.00)	9 (47.37)
Total	15 (100.00)	4 (100.00)	19 (100.00)

Note: Figures in brackets indicate percentages.
Source: Primary data based.

4.5 Courses of Study of Students:

It reflects from table-4.5 that students are studying in various types of technical/professional courses. But around 58 per cent of them are studying engineering.

Table- 4.5: Students Studying in Different Courses

Course	Beneficiary	Non-Beneficiary	Total
BUMS	2 (13.33)	-	2 (10.53)
B. Phama	3 (20.00)	-	3 (15.79)
B. Tech/BE	7 (46.66)	4 (100.00)	11 (57.89)
P.G.D.M	1 (6.67)	-	1 (5.26)
M.B.A	2 (13.33)	-	2 (10.53)
Total	15 (100.00)	4 (100.00)	19 (100.00)

Note: Figures in brackets indicate percentages.

Source: Primary data based.

4.6 Main Findings:

- The classification of sample students as per their age indicated that majority of them is in the age group of 18-21 years.
- Trade and salaried jobs are the two main occupations of the families of sample students.
- More than half of the sample students are studying in government institutions but sizeable numbers of them are also studying in private institutions.
- The average annual income of around half of the students families is between Rs. 1,50,000 to Rs. 2,00,000 while near about half of them have annual income of above Rs. 2,00,000
- The students are studying in various types of technical/professional courses. But around 58 per cent of them are studying engineering.

Merit cum Means based Scholarship: Views of Students

4.7 Scholarship Amount Received:

The average amount of Merit cum Means based Scholarship received by the students has been shown in table 4.6 which is Rs. 25, 867.

Table-4.6: Amount of Scholarship Received

Sex	Amount (in Rs.)		
	Course Fee	Mentainece Fee	Total
Boys	15083	12000	27083
Girls	12000	9000	21000
Total	14467	11400	25867

Source: Primary data based.

4.8 Expenditure of Scholarship Amount:

Most part of the scholarship amount is spent by the beneficiary students on their education related expenses and major item is course fee on which 41.48 per cent of entire scholarship amount is spent as shown in table- 4.7.

Table- 4.7: Item wise Average Expenditure of Scholorship Amout: Beneficiary Students

Item	Average Amount (Rs.)
Book & Stationary etc.	3233
School Dress	1433
Learning Materials	3086
Travelling Expenditure	2066
Course Fees	8733
Medical Expenditure	2500
Total	21051

Source: Primary data based.

4.9 Sources of Information of the Scheme:

Most of the students could get information about the scheme from their institutions and class teachers where they were studying.

Table-4.8: Sources of Information about the Scheme to Students

Source	Number of Student		
	Beneficiary	Non Beneficiary	Total
Institution	7 (46.67)	2 (50.00)	9 (47.37)
Class Teachers	4 (26.67)		4 (21.05)
Friends	1 (6.66)	1 (25.00)	2 (10.53)
Television	2 (13.33)	-	2 (10.53)
News Paper	1 (6.67)	1 (25.00)	2 (10.52)
Total	15 (100.00)	4 (100.00)	19 (100.00)

Note: Figures in brackets indicate percentages.
Source: Primary data based.

4.10 Level of Difficulty in Receiving the Scholarship: Students Perception

The level of difficulty faced by the students has been shown in table- 4.9. It appears that most of them face some sort of difficulty in this regard.

Table-4.9: Level of Difficulty Faced by Students in receiving the Scholarship

Level of Difficulty	Number of Students
High Difficulty	3 (20.00)
Difficulty	5 (33.33)
Somewhat Difficulty	6 (40.00)
No Difficulty	1 (6.67)
Total	15 (100.00)

Note: Figures in brackets indicate percentages.
Source: Primary data based.

4.11 Students Satisfied with the Amount of Scholarship:

It appears from the table-4.10 that more than half (53.33 per cent) of the students are not satisfied with the amount of Scholarship.

Table-4.10: Response of Beneficiary Students on the Satisfaction with Scholarship Amount

Particular	Number of Response		
	Yes	No	Total
Boys	6 (50.00)	6 (50.00)	12 (100.00)
Girls	1 (33.33)	2 (66.67)	3 (100.00)
Total	7 (46.67)	8 (53.33)	15 (100.00)

Note: Figures in brackets indicate percentages.
Source: Primary data based.

4.12 Level of Satisfaction with Reimbursement of Course Fee:

60 per cent students have reported average level of satisfaction for the reimbursement of course fee by their institutions after getting course fee amount from the scholarship. The percentage of boys and girls is the same who reported average level of satisfaction.

Table- 4.11: Level of Satisfaction with Method of Reimbursement of Course Fee: Beneficiary Students

Items	Boys	Girls	Total
Satisfaction	2 (16.67)	1 (33.33)	3 (26.67)
Average	8 (66.66)	2 (66.67)	10 (60.00)
Poor	2 (16.67)	-	2 (13.33)
Total	12 (100.00)	3 (100.00)	15 (100.00)

Note: Figures in brackets indicate percentages.
Source: Primary data based.

4.13 Perception of Students about Various Aspects of Scholarship:

It is evident from table-4.12 that students have average level of perception about various aspects of Merit cum Means based Scholarship. For the eligibility, more than half of the students (52.63 Per cent) have poor opinion.

Table-4.12: Perception about various Aspects of Merit Cum Means Scholorship

Particular	Good	Average	Poor	Total
Documentation	1 (5.26)	14 (73.69)	4(21.05)	19(100.00)
Eligibility	-	9 (47.37)	10 (52.63)	19 (100.00)
Scholarship Amount	3 (15.79)	11 (57.89)	5 (26.32)	19 (100.00)
Mode of Payement	1 (5.26)	12 (63.16)	6 (31.58)	19 (100.00)
Time of Reimbussment of Schlorship	-	6 (31.58)	13 (68.42)	19 (100.00)

Note: Figures in brackets indicate percentages.
Source: Primary data based.

4.14 Future Plan of Students:

Majority of students want to search job after completing their course but more than one-fourth of them want to start the self-employment (Table-4.13).

Table-4.13: Future Plans of Students

Plans	Beneficiary			Non-Beneficiary			Total		
	Boys	Girls	Total	Boys	Girls	Total	Boys	Girls	Total
Get High Education	1 (8.33)	2 (66.67)	3 (20.00)	-	-	-	1 (6.67)	2 (50.00)	3 (15.79)
Search of Employment	5 (41.67)	1 (33.33)	6 (40.00)	2 (66.67)	1 (100.00)	3 (75.00)	7 (46.67)	2 (50.00)	9 (47.37)
Foreign Visit	2 (16.67)	-	2 (13.33)	-	-	-	2 (13.33)	-	2 (10.53)
Start Self Employment	4 (33.33)	-	4 (26.67)	1 (33.33)	-	1 (25.00)	5 (33.33)	-	5 (26.31)
Total	12 (100.00)	3 (100.00)	15 (100.00)	3 (100.00)	1 (100.00)	4 (100.00)	15 (100.00)	4 (100.00)	19 (100.00)

Note: Figures in brackets indicate percentages.
Source: Primary data based.

4.15 Satisfaction of Students with their Institutions:

Only 26 per cent of all sample students have been found to be dissatisfied with their institutions. The remaining is either satisfied or very satisfied. This shows that majority of students are satisfied with their institutions.

Table-4.14: Level of Satisfaction with Institutions

Level of Satisfaction	Beneficiary	Non-Beneficiary	Total
Highly Satisfied	-	-	-
Very Satisfied	5(33.33)	-	5 (26.32)
Satisfied	7 (46.67)	2 (50.00)	9 (47.36)
Dissatisfied	3 (20.00)	2 (50.00)	5 (26.32)
Total	15 (100.00)	4 (100.00)	19 (100.00)

Note: Figures in brackets indicate percentages.
Source: Primary data based.

4.16 Satisfaction with the State Government:

The table-4.15 shows that despite very satisfaction and satisfaction of more than half of the students about state government, 42 per cent of them are dissatisfied too.

Table-4.15: Level of Satisfaction with State Government

Level of Satisfaction	Beneficiary	Non-Beneficiary	Total
Highly Satisfaction	-	-	-
Very Satisfaction	3(20.00)	-	3 (15.78)
Satisfaction	8 (53.33)	-	8 (42.11)
Dissatisfaction	4 (26.67)	4 (100.00)	8 (42.11)
Total	15 (100.00)	4 (100.00)	19 (100.00)

Note: Figures in brackets indicate percentages.
Source: Primary data based.

4.17 Satisfaction with the Central Government:

It reflects from the table-4.16 that majority of students are satisfied with Ministry of Minority Affairs, Government of India.

Table-4.16: Level of Satisfaction with Central Government

Level of Satisfaction	Beneficiary	Non-Beneficiary	Total
Highly Satisfactory	-	-	-
Very Satisfactory	2 (13.33)	-	2 (10.53)
Satisfactory	10 (66.67)		10(52.63)
Dissatisfactory	3 (20.00)	4 (100.00)	7 (36.84)
Total	15 (100.00)	4 (100.00)	19 (100.00)

Note: Figures in brackets indicate percentages.
Source: Primary data based.

4.18 Impact of Merit cum Means Scholarship: Perception of Students

There is no doubt to the fact the Merit cum Means Based Scholarship has very positive impact on the education of beneficiary students as revealed from their views as shown in table-4.17.

Table-4.17: Impact of Scholarship: Students Views

Particular	No. of Beneficiary		
	Boys	Girls	Total
Great help in continuation of education	8 (66.67)	1 (33.33)	9 (60.00)
Scholarship helped them to get higher education	5(41.67)	2(66.67)	7 (46.67)
Improvement in quality of education	2 (66.67)	-	2 (13.33)
Total Sample Beneficiaries	12 (100.00)	3 (100.00)	15 (100.00)

Note: Figures in brackets indicate percentages.
Source: Primary data based.

4.19 Suggestions of Students to Improve the Scheme:

The following suggestions have been given by the students to improve the Merit cum Mean Based Scholarship.

Table-4.18: Suggestions for Improvement of Merit cum Means Based Scholarship-Students Views

Suggestions
Distribution of Scholarship should be timely.
50 percent mark should not be compelsory for getting schlorship.
Easy Processes for scholarship Scheme
The scholarship should be distributed at the time of admission.
Scholarship Scheme should be for all students of Minorities.

4.20 Main Findings:

- Most part of the scholarship amount is spent by the beneficiary students on their education related expenses.
- Most of the students could get information about the scheme from their institutions and class teachers where they were studying.
- It became known that most of them face some sort of difficulty in getting the scholorship.
- It appeared that more than half (53.33 per cent) of the students are not satisfied with the amount of Scholarship.

- 60 per cent students have reported average level of satisfaction for the reimbursement of course fee by their institutions after getting course fee amount from the scholarship.
- For the eligibility conditions, more than half of the students (52.63 Per cent) had poor opinion.
- The Merit cum Means Based Scholarship has very positive impact on the education of beneficiary students.

Educational Institutions

4.21 About the Educational Institutions:

Two institutes namely-Swami Kalyan Deo Management & Technology Institute and Apex Institute of Technology & Management has been taken to acquire feedback on the Merit cum Means Scholarship Scheme. Both the institutes are private located in Rampur district of Uttar Pradesh. These Institutes are well aware about the Merit cum Means Scholarship Scheme. Table-4.19 indicates that a total number of 810 students were enrolled in these two technical institutes, out of which 77 (9.50 per cent) were minority students. Out of these total minority students 30 were studying in Swami Kalyan Deo Management & Technical Institute and 47 were studying in Apex Institute of Technology & Management. 22 students applied for Merit cum Means Scholarship in the year 2009-10 and 26 students applied for this Scholarship in the year 2010-11 from both the institutes. All these application had been forwarded by the institutes to the state department for further processing.

Table-4.19: Enrolment of Minority Students and their Application for MCM

Name of Institute	Knowledge of MCM		Total Students Enrolled	No. & % of Total Minority Students	No. of Students applied for Scholarship		Application Forwarded to State Department	
	Yes	No			2009-10	2010-11	2009-10	2010-11
Swami Kalyan Deo Management & Tech. Institute	1	-	385	30 (7.80)	7	9	7	9
Apex Institute of Tech. & Management	1	-	425	47 (11.05)	15	17	15	17
Total			810	77 (9.50)	22	26	22	26

4.22 Trend in Enrolment and Processing of Applications for Scholarship:

In these two institutes of higher education a few (9.50 per cent) minority community students are enrolled. Above table depicts, that during two academic years of 2009-10 and 2010-11, enrolment of minority students has increased a bit. The method of processing of application was computerized which has been done by the employees of the institutes without any severe difficulty. Two computers in each institute have been used to process all information regarding the scholarship of the students. On an average around 30 days were involved in the processing of application. It has been found that both the institutes were satisfied with the level of cooperation of the state department and were also satisfied with the state department for time taken in reimbursement of course fee (Table-4.20).

Table-4.20: Processing of Applications

Name of Institute	Difficulty in the Process of Application	Method of Processing of Application	If through Computer, By whom	No. of computer used	Ave. no. of days involved in processing of Applica.	Time taken in reimbursement of course fee after getting state dept.	Are you satisfied with the co-operation of state dept.
Swami Kalyan Deo Management & Tech. Institute	Least difficulty	Computer	Institute Employee	2	30	Satisfied	Satisfied
Apex Institute of Tech. & Management	Least difficulty	Computer	Institute Employee	2	30	Satisfied	Satisfied

Source: Officials of the Institutions, District Rampur.

4.23 Impact of MCM Scheme:

It has been found that usually 30 days took to reimburse the course fee to minority students from state department after the release of funds by Government of India. It has also been observed

Table-4.21: Impact of Merit cum Means Scholorship

Name of Institute	Time taken for reimbursement of course fee to students	Any student dropout from course		Improvement in level of education	Impact of MCM scheme
		Yes	No		
Swami Kalyan Deo Management & Tech. Institute	30 days	-	✓	Very good	Improvement in admission of Minority Student
Apex Institute of Tech. & Management	30 days	-	✓	Good	Improvement in continuity and reduction in dropout of minority student

Source: Officials of the Institutions, District Rampur.

that the entire students those who received the course fee through the MCM scheme were continuing their studies in these institutions and no student was found dropout during the course. Institutions informed us that due to MCM schemes the availability of minority students has slightly increased and improvement in the level of education of minority student was also good (Table-4.21)

4.24 Assessment of Merit cum Means Scheme:

There is no dropout case from either of the institute. Both the institutes are performing well in case of Merit cum Means Scheme. The overall feedback given by the institutes regarding the Merit cum Means Scheme was satisfactory.

Table-4.22: Assessment of MCM Scheme

Very Satisfied	Satisfied	Little Satisfied	Unsatisfied
-	✓	-	-
-	✓	-	-

4.25 Suggestions for Improvement in MCM Scheme:

The institute officials were found satisfed with the level of performance of the students and their continuity during the course but not satisfied with the complexity of the application form. They suggested that application form should be shortened and made easy. Also processing of application should be quicker and issuing money should not be delayed.

4.26 Response of District official (Implementing Agency):

Mr. Krishn Murari (DMWO) has been recently appointed by the State Government as Nodal Officer (In charge) for the implementation of Merit cum Means Scholarship Scheme in Rampur district. The Nodal officer responded that sufficient time has been provided for all minority students to apply for the scheme. Selection of the candidates for the scholarship has not been done on the basis of the minority candidates available in the state. 92 students applied for the Merit cum Means Scholarship scheme in the year 2010-11, out of which only 8 students were awarded this scholarship (Table-4.23).

Table-4.23: Selection of Candidates

Particulars	Responses	
	Yes	No
Appointment of Nodal Officer by State Govt. for implementation of the scheme	✓	
Sufficient time has been given for applying the scheme	✓	
Number of student applied for the scholarship	92	
Number of awardees students of scholarship	8	
Scholarship provided to Girls student	-	
Selection of candidate on the basis of minority of the State.		✓

4.27 Scholarship Application and Grant:

It has been found that Institutes are forwarding all the applications of the minority candidates well in time. State Government has issued the guideline/directive to the Minority Welfare Department about the minority candidate scholarship scheme. It has been informed by the district officials that after receiving scholarship amount from Central Government, State level department releases scholarship amount within a period of one month (Table 4.24).

Table-4.24: Scholarship Application and Grant

Particulars	Responses	
	Yes	No
Department forward Applications timely	✓	
State Govt. has issued any Guideline/directive to the Minority Welfare Department	✓	
Consolidated proposal has been sent by the institute to the Central Govt. for scholarship amount.		✓
After receiving scholarship amount from Central Govt., State level department releases scholarship amount within a month.	✓	

4.28 Selection Process of Candidates:

The guidelines provided by the Ministry of Minority Affairs are followed. The list of selected candidates has been put on the website and website is hyperlinked with the Ministry of Minority Affairs'. All the applications of scholarship have been invited online through website. It was reported that all applications are processed manually as well as through computers. The status of data management in fully computerized (Table-4.25).

Table-4.25: Process of Selection

Particulars	Responses	
	Yes	No
The list of selected candidate has been float on website	✓	
Website hyperlinked with the Ministry of Minority Affairs' Website	✓	
Application has been invited online for scholarship	✓	
Process of sorting of application form is manually		✓
Status of computerization in data management	Fully computerized	

4.29 Distribution Method of Scholarship Amount:

The scholarship amount has been disbursed through cheques and the progress report has been sent to the Central Government. The implementing agency is fully satisfied with the cooperation of Central Government. Status of computerization of data management in College/Institutions is found manual. Implementing agencies are keeping separate bank account and records for receiving and disbursing of Merit cum Means scholarship amount (Table-4.26).

Table-4.26: Distribution Method of Scholarship Amount

Sl. No.	Particulars	Responses	
		Yes	No
1.	Mode of Scholarship Amount	Through Cheque	
2.	Progress Report sent to Central Govt.	✓	
3.	Satisfaction level of cooperation of Central Govt.	Satisfied	
4.	Status of computerization of data management in College/Institutions	Manually	
5.	Any separate bank account and record available	✓	

4.30 Number of Male and Female Candidates received Scholarship:

A total number of 18 candidates were found eligible to avail Merit cum Means scholarship in last two years (2009-10 and 2010-11). In the year 2009-10 there were 10 candidates who got the scholarship, out of which 7 candidates were Boys and 3 were Girls. Next year in 2010-11 the number of candidates those received this scholarship was 8 and all were Boys (Table-4.27).

Table-4.27: Year-wise Number of Male and Female candidates

Sl. No.	Year	Boys	Girls	Total
1.	2009-10	7	3	10
2.	2010-11	8	-	8
	Total	15	3	18

4.31 Suggestions for Better Implementation of the Scheme:

District officials feel that application form should be easier and scholarship amount should be released timely to the students. Selection of the candidate for the scholarship should be done on the basis of the minority candidates available in the state so that more students would be able to avail the benefit of the scheme.

Field Observations, Key Issues and Suggestions: Merit cum Means Based Scholarship

4.32 Field Observations:

It was observed during the field investigation that the implementation of Merit cum Means Based Scholarship has been better in comparison with the Pre-matric and Post-matric Scholarships in Rampur district of Uttar Pradesh. The reason is that the economic condition of parents of students eligible for Merit cum Means Based Scholarship is generally found to be better than of earlier cases. The other factor is that the fee and other expenses in technical and professional courses are quite higher and the mount of scholarship given under Merit cum Means Based Scholarship is quite inadequate. So neither the students nor their parents consider Merit cum Means Based Scholarship as means for them to get technical/professional education. This is the reason that all the sample students have reported that they have not taken admission due to the Merit cum Means Based Scholarship. However, the discussion with the students, their parents and officials of the institutions have revealed that there are certain issues related with the Merit cum Means Based Scholarship which need to be taken care of in view of the fact that this scholarship has helped them to continue their education. The great problem is that the amount of Merit cum Means Based Scholarship is quite meager in view of high course fee and other expenses involved. Therefore, the general sentiment was observed that there is need to make realistic upward revision in the amount of Merit cum Means Based Scholarship. The second observation is that the students receive Merit cum Means Based Scholarship very late during the year while they pay fee in beginning of the course, generally in April-July. The scholarship comes to their institutions who take considerable time in payment to students. The students were in view that when the scholarships do not cover their entire expenses of course so there should be direct payment to them not to their intuitions. The income limit is another serious problem which debars many needy students to benefit of Merit cum Means Based Scholarship. Therefore, income limit of parents needs to be raised. The documentation process is also cumbersome. What is the sense of asking for an affidavit in the application when any type of affidavit can be procured from the advocate by paying the fee? This needs to be looked into and needs modification.

4.33 Key Issues of Merit cum Means Bases Scholarship:

- Lack of awareness about the scheme.
- Meager amount of scholarship.
- Unnecessary formalities in filling the application form.
- Too much time is spent while scholarship reaches to students.
- Income limit is not realistic.

4.34 Suggestions:

- The amount of Merit cum Means Based Scholarship should reasonably be raised in view of expenses involved in technical/professional courses.
- The payment of scholarship should be made directly in the bank account of students not to the institutions who take lot of time in reimbursement of scholarships amount to the students.
- The application formalities need simplification like requirement of affidavit should be

done away as it is totally bogus. On the whole, simplification of application formalities is required.

- The income limit of parents needs revision.
- There is need that awareness campaign for the scholarships schemes should be launched so that the minority should be made aware of the schemes. The state and district level officials should also be given orientation training.
- The district level official should be made accountable for improper or poor implementation of the scheme. The responsibility should somehow be fixed on the District Magistrates. In the Rampur district, official inefficiency is visible in the implementation of the scholarship schemes. This has to be removed at the earliest.
- The number of Merit cum Means Based Scholarship given at the state level is too few taking the fact into consideration that Uttar Pradesh is a large state with sizeable population of minorities and demand of technical/professional courses has also picked up among the minorities.

Chapter-V

Characteristics of Sample Students-Pre-matric Scholarship : Indore District

5.1 Age of Students:

The data as shown in table-5.1 showed that majority of students (52.33 per cent) are in age group of 6-11 years. The share of beneficiary students is 54 per cent versus 49 per cent of non-beneficiary students. More than 50 per cent of the beneficiary boys and beneficiary and non-beneficiary girls are the age group of 6-11 years while in case of non-beneficiary boys more than half of them are in the age group of 11-14 years. The pattern indicates that more than half of the sample students are found to be in primary school going age and thereafter in upper primary schooling age. Only 3 per cent of them are in the high school going age.

Table-5.1: Age wise Number of Sample Students

Sex	Students	6-11	11-14	14-17	Total
Boys	Beneficiaries	59 (50.86)	56 (48.28)	1 (0.86)	116 (100.00)
	Non-Beneficiaries	31 (46.27)	35 (52.24)	1 (1.49)	67 (100.00)
	Total	90 (49.18)	91 (49.73)	2 (1.09)	183 (100.00)
Girls	Beneficiaries	49 (58.33)	31 (36.90)	4 (4.77)	84 (100.00)
	Non-Beneficiaries	18 (54.55)	12 (36.36)	3 (9.09)	33 (100.00)
	Total	67 (57.26)	43 (36.76)	7 (5.98)	117 (100.00)
Total	Beneficiaries	108 (54.00)	87 (43.50)	5 (2.50)	200 (100.00)
	Non-Beneficiaries	49 (49.00)	47 (47.00)	4 (4.00)	100 (100.00)
	All	157 (52.33)	134 (44.67)	9 (3.00)	300 (100.00)

Note: Figures in brackets indicate percentages.

Source: Primary data based.

5.2 Level of Schools:

Table-5.2 showed that majority of students (96.67 per cent) is studying in primary schools. There is no major difference between beneficiary and non-beneficiary and boys versus girls. When correlated with the age, it indicates that there is tendency on the part of Muslim children to start their education late.

Table-5.2: Schools Where Sample Students are Studying

Sex	Students	Primary School	Upper Primary School	High School	Total
Boys	Beneficiaries	112 (96.56)	2 (1.72)	2 (1.72)	116 (100.00)
	Non-Beneficiaries	64 (95.52)	3 (4.48)	-	67 (100.00)
	Total	176 (96.18)	5 (2.73)	2 (1.09)	183 (100.00)
Girls	Beneficiaries	83 (98.81)	1 (1.19)	-	84 (100.00)
	Non-Beneficiaries	31 (93.94)	2 (6.06)	-	33 (100.00)
	Total	114 (97.44)	3 (2.56)	-	117 (100.00)
Total	Beneficiaries	195 (97.50)	3 (1.50)	2 (1.00)	200 (100.00)
	Non-Beneficiaries	95 (95.00)	5 (5.00)	-	100 (100.00)
	All	290 (96.67)	8 (2.67)	2 (0.66)	300 (100.00)

Note: Figures in brackets indicate percentages.

Source: Primary data based.

5.3 Type of Schools:

It is evident from the table-5.3 that all most all the sample students are found to be going to private institutions at all levels of their education.

Table-5.3: Type of Institutions of Sample Students

Type of Institutions	Type Of Institutions		
	Government	Private	Total
Primary	-	290 (100.00)	290 (100.00)
Upper Primary	-	8 (100.00)	8 (100.00)
High School	1 (50.00)	1 (50.00)	2 (100.00)
Total	1 (0.33)	299 (99.67)	300 (100.00)

Note: Figures in brackets indicate percentages.

Source: Primary data based

5.4 Sources of Income and Schooling:

There are two major sources of income of the families of sample students. The first is small business/trade about which 60.34 per cent of total sample students have reported as their main source of income followed by the salaried jobs (34.33 per cent). The pattern is same for the beneficiary as well as non-beneficiary students.

Table-5.4: Sources of Income of Sample Students

	Beneficiary	Non-beneficiary	Total
Casual Labour	2 (1.00)	0	2 (0.67)
Small Farmer	7 (3.50)	3 (3.00)	10 (3.33)
Artisan	4 (2.00)	0	4 (1.33)
Salaried (Government /Private)	67 (33.50)	36 (36.00)	103 (34.33)
Small Business/Trade	120 (60.00)	61 (61.00)	181 (60.34)
Total	200 (100.00)	100 (100.00)	300 (100.00)

Note: Figures in brackets indicate percentages.
Source: Primary data based.

5.5 Income of Families:

The students were asked to report the estimated average annual income of their families and accordingly all of them have been classified according to different income slabs in table-5.5. It is evident from the table that 82 per cent of them have average annual income in the range of Rs. 20,000 to Rs. 50,000. The proportion of such families is higher (91 per cent) in case of non-beneficiary students versus beneficiary students (77.50 per cent).

Table-5.5: Classification of Students According to their Income

Income (Rs.)	Number of Students		
	Beneficiary	Non-beneficiary	Total
Less than 20,000	10 (5.00)	3 (3.00)	13 (4.33)
20,001 to 50,000	155 (77.50)	91 (91.00)	246 (82.00)
50,001 to 1,00,000	32 (16.00)	3 (3.00)	35 (11.67)
1,00,001 to 1,50,000	3 (1.50)	3 (3.00)	6 (2.00)
Total	200 (100.00)	100 (100.00)	300 (100.00)

Note: Figures in brackets indicate percentages.
Source: Primary data based.

5.6 Expenditure on Pre-matric Education:

The Pre-matric education may be classified in two parts. The first part is from class 1-5 and the other is from class 6-10. The average expenditure incurred by a family on first and second part has been calculated and presented in table-5.6. The average expenditure during class 1- 5 has been estimated to be Rs. 1970 which is Rs. 2012 in case of beneficiary students and Rs. 1927 of non-beneficiary students. In the entire expenses on education, course fee and other expenses like clothing and teaching learning materials are the major items of expenditure. The average expenditure for study during classes 6-10 comes around Rs. 3493 which is slightly higher for beneficiary students than for the non-beneficiary students. In these classes, private coaching, travel and course fee are the major components of expenses. The amount of Pre-matric scholarship being given at present needs upward revision in view of the current level of expenses incurred by the families on the education at Pre-matric level.

Table-5.6: Average Expenditure of Education per Student on Different Items

Item	Amounts (in Rs.)		
	Beneficiary	Non- Beneficiary	Total
	For Class 1-5		
Course Fee	485	428	457
Teaching Learning Materials	372	362	368
Travel	359	350	355
Tuition	251	248	250
Others	545	539	542
Total	2012	1927	1970
	For Class 6-10		
Course Fee	731	719	725
Teaching Learning Materials	485	471	478
Travel	715	708	712
Tuition	851	845	848
Others	735	726	731
Total	3517	3469	3493

Source: Primary data based.

5.7 Children Attending Schools, Getting Scholarship and Family Features:

It was to be assessed that how many children out of total children are going to schools that are in the age group of 6 to 14 years. It was found that at the aggregate level; around 64.05 per cent of them are attending the schools regularly. There is no major difference in the proportion of boys and girls in this regard.

It was also assessed that out of total children who applied for the Pre-matric scholarship, how many of them succeeded in getting this scholarship. As evident in table-2.7 that out of those children who applied for the Pre-matric scholarship, 43.57 per cent of them got it. The percentage of boys getting Pre-matric scholarship is higher than the girls.

The families have largely the younger population and on an average 2 persons are working per family. The highest education of a family member is high schools in majority of households (Table-5.7).

Table-5.7: Children Going to Schools, Getting Scholarships and Family Structure

Children Going to School			
Item	Beneficiary	Non-beneficiary	Total
Boys	152 (64.56)	98 (63.66)	250 (64.12)
Girls	120 (64.10)	88 (63.78)	208 (63.94)
Total	272 (64.25)	186 (63.74)	458 (64.05)
Students Getting Scholarships (Beneficiary)			
Item	Number of Students		
Boys	116 (46.40)		
Girls	84 (40.19)		
Total	200 (43.57)		
Age Structure of Family Members			
Less than 5 Years	598 (35.44)		
5-14 Years	191 (11.32)		
15-23 Years	208 (12.33)		
24-35 Years	161 (9.54)		
36-59 years	319 (18.92)		
60 + years	210 (12.45)		
All Members	1687 (100.00)		
Average No. of Earning Members per Family	2		
Highest Educational Status of a Member in Family			
High School	175 (44.98)		
Intermediate	134 (34.45)		
Graduate	72 (18.51)		
Post Graduate	6 (1.54)		
Technical/Professional	2 (0.52)		
Total	389 (100.00)		

Note: Figures in brackets indicate percentages.
Source: Primary data based.

5.8 Housing:

The housing condition appears to be better of minorities in Indore district as 90 per cent houses of sample families are pucca. Most of the houses are owned. The average rooms per house are 3 and 98 per cent houses are electrified. The ration card holders are 94.67 per cent.

Table-5.8: Housing and other Conditions of Sample Students

Housing Type	No. of Response
1. Kachcha	9 (3.00)
2. Pucca	270 (90.00)
3. Mix	21 (7.00)
Total	300 (100.00)
Ownership of the House	
1. Owned	277 (92.33)
2. Rented	14 (4.67)
3. Given by Employer	9 (3.00)
Value of the House, if owned (Average)	410813
Average Number of Rooms	3
House with Electricity (Yes)	294 (98.00)
No. of Households with Ration Cards	284 (94.67)
Percentage of Marginal and Small Land owning Households	22 (7.33)

Note: Figures in brackets indicate percentages.

Source: Primary data based.

5.9 Main Findings:

- It was found that more than half of the sample students were in primary school going age and thereafter in upper primary schooling age. Only 3 per cent of them were in the high school going age.
- The majority of students (96.67 per cent) were studying in primary schools. There was no major difference between beneficiary and non-beneficiary and boys versus girls. When correlated with the age, it appeared that there was tendency on the part of Muslim children to start their education late.
- All the sample students were found to be going to private institutions at all levels of their education.
- There were two major sources of income of the families of sample students. The first was the small business/trade followed by the salaried jobs. The pattern was same for the beneficiary as well as non-beneficiary students.
- It was evident that 82 per cent families had average annual income in the range of Rs. 20,000 to Rs. 50,000. The proportion of such families was higher (91 per cent) in case of non-beneficiary students versus beneficiary students (77.50 per cent).
- The average expenditure during class 1- 5 was estimated to be Rs. 1970. The average expenditure for study during classes 6-10 came around Rs. 3493.
- It was found that at the aggregate level around 64.05 per cent of school age children were attending the schools regularly. There was no major difference in the proportion of boys and girls in this regard.
- Out of those children who applied for the Pre-matric scholarship, 43.57 per cent of them

got it. The percentage of boys getting Pre-matric scholarship was higher than the girls.

- The housing condition of minorities appeared to be better in Indore district as 90 per cent of their houses were pucca. Most of the houses were owned. The average rooms per house were 3 and 98 per cent houses were electrified.

Awareness, Utilization and Impact of Pre-matric Scholarship\

5.10 Complete Awareness about Pre-matric Scholarship:

The awareness among the sample students about the Pre-matric scholarship was examined and the result has been shown in table-5.9. It is to be mentioned here that the awareness here means complete knowledge of details of Pre-matric scholarship scheme like the name of the scheme, source of availability of its application form, eligibility criteria, knowledge of filling of application form, submission of the form and the date on which the award of the scholarship is known. On the basis of wholesome knowledge of the Pre-matric scholarship scheme, number of beneficiary and non-beneficiary students is not much. There is no major difference between beneficiary and non-beneficiary and boys and girls students in this regard.

Table-5.9: Students who are Completely Aware of the Pre-matric Scholarship Scheme

Students	Beneficiary	Non- beneficiary	Total
Boys	46 (39.66)	26 (38.81)	72 (39.34)
Girls	32 (38.10)	12 (36.36)	44 (37.61)
Total	78 (39.00)	38 (38.00)	116 (38.67)

Note: Figures in brackets indicate percentages.
Source: Primary data based.

5.11 Sources of Awareness of Pre-matric Scholarship to Rural Students:

The sources of awareness of the beneficiary as well as non-beneficiary students and boys and girls were obtained from sample students. It is found in table-5.10 that the school teachers are the most important source of awareness to students followed by the fellow students who got scholarship, representative of gram panchayats/urban bodies and radio. It is to be noted here that newspaper is the least important source of awareness of Pre-matric scholarship to students. The pattern of awareness is found to be the same across different groups.

Table-5.10: Sources of Awareness of Pre-matric Scholarship among Students

Source	Beneficiary			Non-beneficiary			Total		
	Boys	Girls	Total	Boys	Girls	Total	Boys	Girls	Total
Teachers	22 (47.83)	15 (46.88)	37 (47.44)	12 (46.15)	6 (50.00)	18 (47.37)	34 (47.22)	21 (47.72)	55 (47.42)
Students who got Scholarship	10 (21.74)	8 (25.00)	18 (23.08)	7 (26.92)	3 (25.00)	10 (26.32)	17 (23.61)	11 (25.00)	28 (24.14)
Gram Panchayat Representative	6 (13.04)	4 (12.50)	10 (12.82)	5 (19.23)	1 (8.34)	6 (15.79)	11 (15.28)	5 (11.36)	16 (13.79)
Radio/TV	5 (10.87)	3 (9.37)	8 (10.25)	1 (3.85)	1 (8.33)	2 (5.26)	6 (8.33)	4 (9.10)	10 (8.62)
News Papers	3 (6.52)	2 (6.25)	5 (6.41)	1 (3.85)	1 (8.33)	2 (5.26)	4 (5.56)	3 (6.82)	7 (6.03)
Total	46 (100.00)	32 (100.00)	78 (100.00)	26 (100.00)	12 (100.00)	38 (100.00)	72 (100.00)	44 (100.00)	116 (100.00)

Note: Figures in brackets indicate percentages.
Source: Primary data based.

5.12 Knowledge about Eligibility Conditions:

It has been found above that the teachers are the main source of information of Pre-matric scholarship to students. The teachers generally inform to students that to get the scholarship, a student is to fulfill two conditions. One is that the total annual income of the parents should not exceed more than 1 lakh in the year and other is that the student should have obtained not less than 50 per cent marks in final examination of last class. When sample students were asked to report about their knowledge about these two basic conditions, 53.33 per cent of them reported to be aware of these conditions of Pre-matric scholarship (Table-5.11).

Table-5.11: Students knowing Eligibility Conditions of Pre-matric Scholarship Scheme

Students	Beneficiary	Non- beneficiary	Total
Boys	53 (45.69)	39 (58.21)	92 (50.27)
Girls	53 (63.10)	15 (45.45)	68 (58.12)
Total	106 (53.00)	54 (54.00)	160 (53.33)

Note: Figures in brackets indicate percentages.
Source: Primary data based.

5.13 Knowledge of both Eligibility Conditions:

There are three conditions of getting the Pre-matric scholarship. One is the income limit of Rs. 1 lakh, other is the condition of getting 50 per cent marks in last examination and finally only 2 children are eligible to get the Pre-matric scholarship from a family. When the knowledge of each of the three conditions was enquired from the students, they reported what has been placed in table-5.12. The table shows that the substantial percentage of sample students is not aware of each of the three criterions. There was also no difference between beneficiary and non-beneficiary students.

Table-5.12: Knowledge of Each of the Eligibility Conditions of Pre-matric Scholarship

Conditions	Beneficiary	Non- Beneficiary	Total
Household Income not more than Rs. 1 lakh	35 (33.02)	17 (31.48)	52 (32.50)
Marks not less than 50 per cent in last examination	37 (34.90)	19 (35.19)	56 (35.00)
Only 2 students from one household	34 (32.08)	18 (33.33)	52 (32.50)
Total Respondents	106 (100.00)	54 (100.00)	160 (100.00)

Note: Figures in brackets indicate percentages.
Source: Primary data based.

5.14 Students Receiving Different Amount of Scholarship:

The sample beneficiary students have reported that 79.50 per cent of them received Pre-matric scholarship between Rs. 1000 to 1500 (Table-5.13).

Table-5.13: Classification of Beneficiary Students According to amount of Scholarship

Amount (Rs.)	Number of Beneficiary Students		
	Boys	Girls	Total
1000-1500	100(86.21)	59(70.24)	159(79.50)
1500-2000	6(5.17)	3(3.57)	9(4.50)
More than 2000	10(8.62)	22(26.19)	32(16.00)
Total	116(100.00)	84(100.00)	200(100.00)

5.15 Mode of Payment of Scholarship Amount:

The beneficiary students have reported that 51.50 per cent of them get the scholarship money through the cheque while 48.50 per cent get in cash.

Table-5.14: Mode of Payment of Scholarship Amount

Mode	Number of Beneficairy		
	Boys	Girls	Total
Cash	56 (48.28)	41 (48.80)	97 (48.50)
Cheque	60 (51.72)	43 (51.20)	103 (51.50)
Total	116 (100.00)	84 (100.00)	200 (100.00)

Note: Figures in brackets indicate percentages.

Source: Primary data based.

5.16 Scholarship Given by Different Persons:

The beneficiary students have reported that they get scholarship money from three persons. On the top are their teachers from whom 63 per cent students reported to have got the money. Others are as shown in table-5.15.

Table-5.15: Scholarship Given by Different Persons

Particulars	Number of Beneficiary		
	Boys	Girls	Total
By Teachers	75 (64.66)	51 (60.71)	126 (63.00)
By Sabhasad/Secretary	41 (35.34)	33 (39.29)	74 (37.00)
Total	116 (100.00)	84 (100.00)	200 (100.00)

Note: Figures in brackets indicate percentages.

Source: Primary data based.

5.17 Expenses of Getting Pre-matric Scholarship:

The beneficiary students have reported that they spent around Rs. 361 on different formalities to get Pre-matric scholarship. Getting income certificate and affidavit are the two major items of expenditure (Table-5.16).

Table-5.16: Item wise Expenditure for getting Pre-matric Scholarship

Items	Average Amount (in Rs.) Number of Beneficiary		
	Boys	Girls	Total
Income Certificate	165	161	163
On Making Affidavit	99	103	101
Photos and Travel etc	101	95	98
Total	364	358	361

Note: Figures in brackets indicate percentages.

Source: Primary data based.

5.18 Utilization of Pre-matric Scholarship Amount: Students of Class 1-5:

The beneficiary students of class 1-5 have reported that major part of Pre-matric scholarship is spent on their education (Table-5.17).

Table-5.17: Items wise Average Expenditure of Scholarship Amount : Students of Class 1-5

Items	Average Amount (in Rs.) Number of Students		
	Boys	Girls	Total
Books & Stationary	75	73	74
Learning Material	99	91	95
Travel	51	50	51
Private Tuition Fee	75	69	72
Course Fee	201	201	201
Medical Expenses	167	157	162
Food Expenses	107	97	102
Non Food Expenses	191	183	187
Debt Return	11	3	7
Total	967	923	945

Note: Figures in brackets indicate percentages.

Source: Primary data based.

5.19 Utilization of Pre-matric Scholarship Amount: Students of Class 6-10:

The utilization pattern of scholarship money by the beneficiary students of classes 6-10 as shown in table-5.18 indicates that Pre-matric scholarship has very positive impact on the education of minority students of classes 6-10.The money of scholarship spent on health and food is substantial. Certainly the scholarship is great help to minority students in meeting their educational and health needs.

Table-5.18: Items wise Average Expenditure of Scholarship Amount: Students of Class-6-10

Items	Average Amount (in Rs.)		
	Number of Students		
	Boys	Girls	Total
Books & Stationary	99	94	97
Learning Material	101	102	102
Travel	86	79	83
Private Tuition Fee	99	103	101
Course Fee	213	215	214
Medical Expenses	200	203	202
Food Expenses	141	144	143
Non Food Expenses	208	209	209
Debt Return	3	2	3
Total	1148	1150	1149

Note: Figures in brackets indicate percentages.

Source: Primary data based.

5.20 Effectiveness of Pre-matric Scholarship: Rural Students:

The effectiveness of Pre-matric scholarship is evident in table-5.19.The Pre-matric scholarship

Table-5.19: Effectiveness of Pre-matric Scholarship-Beneficiary Students

Particulars	Boys	Girls	Total
Admission was taken due to Scholarship	6 (5.17)	2 (2.38)	8 (4.00)
Attendance at the School Improved	28 (24.14)	12 (14.28)	40 (20.00)
Scholarship has fulfilled Study Needs	45 (38.79)	35 (41.67)	80 (40.00)
Scholarship has helped in Health Care Needs	67 (57.76)	42 (50.00)	109 (54.50)
Desire to Continue Studies after Getting Scholarship	105 (90.51)	81 (96.43)	186 (93.00)
Educational Skills has Improved	93 (80.17)	75 (89.29)	168 (84.00)
Involvement in the Household Activities has Reduced.	84 (72.41)	69 (82.14)	153 (76.50)
Scholarship has helped in Family Needs	62 (53.45)	34 (40.48)	96 (48.00)
Chances to Continue Study in Higher Class and get a job increased	104 (89.66)	76 (90.48)	180 (90.00)
Total	116 (100.00)	84 (100.00)	200 (100.00)

Note: Figures in brackets indicate percentages.

Source: Primary data based

is very effective in overall educational development, health care and family needs of students and in providing them a silver lining for higher studies and good job prospect.

5.21 Perception of Rural Students about Pre-matric Scholarship:

The table-5.20 shows that near about 85 per cent students both beneficiary and non-beneficiaries feel that there is lack of awareness about the Pre-matric scholarship scheme and language of application form is problem and it is lengthy too. Quite a large number of them feel that documentation is lengthy and income limit is problem to them.

Table-5.20: Views of Students about Pre-matric Scholarship Scheme

Views	No. of Students								
	Beneficiary			Non-Beneficiary			Total		
	Boys	Girls	Total	Boys	Girls	Total	Boys	Girls	Total
Lack of Awareness about the Details of Scheme	98 (84.48)	73 (86.90)	171 (85.50)	57 (85.07)	28 (84.85)	85 (85.00)	155 (84.70)	101 (86.32)	256 (85.33)
Application Form is Lengthy & Language Problems	95 (81.90)	69 (82.14)	164 (82.00)	56 (83.58)	27 (81.81)	83 (83.00)	151 (82.51)	96 (82.05)	247 (82.33)
Too Much Documentation etc.	91 (78.45)	64 (76.19)	155 (77.50)	52 (77.61)	25 (75.76)	77 (77.00)	143 (78.14)	89 (76.07)	232 (77.33)
Income limit of 1 Lakh	84 (72.41)	59 (70.24)	143 (71.50)	49 (73.13)	23 (69.70)	72 (72.00)	133 (72.68)	82 (70.09)	215 (71.67)
50 Percent limit of Marks	70 (60.34)	50 (59.52)	120 (60.00)	38 (56.72)	19 (57.58)	57 (57.00)	108 (59.02)	69 (58.97)	177 (59.00)
Untimely Payment	62 (53.45)	44 (52.38)	106 (53.00)	34 (50.75)	17 (51.51)	51 (51.00)	96 (52.46)	61 (52.14)	157 (52.33)
Total	116 (100.00)	84 (100.00)	200 (100.00)	67 (100.00)	33 (100.00)	100 (100.00)	183 (100.00)	117 (100.00)	300 (100.00)

Note: Figures in brackets indicate percentages.

Source: Primary data based.

5.22 Main Findings:

- Lack of awareness about the details of the Pre-matric Scholarship Scheme was found in majority of beneficiary and non-beneficiary students of Indore district.
- It was found that the school teachers were the most important source of awareness to students followed by the fellow students who got scholarship, representative of gram panchayats/urban bodies and radio.
- Around half of the total sample students were found to be aware of the basic eligibility conditions of Pre-matric Scholarship.

- It was found that around 80 per cent of beneficiary students received Pre-matric Scholarship amount in-between Rs. 1000 to 1500.
- Near about half of the students were paid Pre-matric Scholarship in cash.
- Around 63 per cent of beneficiary students received the scholarship from their teachers.
- The beneficiary students reported that they spent around Rs. 361 on different formalities to get Pre-matric scholarship. Getting income certificate and affidavit were the two major items of expenditure.
- The utilization pattern of scholarship money by the beneficiary students of classes 1-5 and 6-10 indicated that Pre-matric scholarship had very positive impact on the education of minority students. The money of scholarship was largely spent on education, health and food. Hence it can be inferred that the Pre-matric scholarship is a great help to minority students in meeting their educational and health needs.
- It became evident that near about 85 per cent students both beneficiary and non-beneficiaries felt that there was lack of awareness about the Pre-matric scholarship scheme and language of application form was problem and it is lengthy too. Quite a large number of them feel that documentation is lengthy and income limit is problem to them.

Problems in Getting Pre-matric Scholarship and Suggestions of Students

5.23 Students Facing Difficulties while Applying:

The number of students who faced difficulties during the process of application has been shown in table-5.21. The table shows that a high percentage of students faced difficulties. The percentage of students who experienced difficulties were found to be more or less same across boys and girls and beneficiary and non-beneficiary students indicating thereby that most of the applicants of Pre-matric scholarship face difficulties while applying for the scholarship.

Table-5.21: Number of Students Facing Problems while applying for Pre-matric Scholarship

Sex	Beneficiary	Non-beneficiary	Total
Boys	89 (76.72)	51 (76.11)	140 (76.50)
Girls	62 (73.81)	24 (72.72)	86 (73.50)
Total	151 (75.50)	75 (75.00)	226 (75.33)

Note: Figures in brackets indicate percentages.

5.24 Level of Difficulty in Obtaining Application Form for Rural Students:

Around half of the students felt difficulty and more than one-fourth of them found somewhat difficulty in getting application form. 15.67 per cent of them felt high level of difficulty. Thus, obtaining application form for applying the Pre-matric scholarship has been difficult for majority of students (Table-5.22). The pattern did not differ much across different groups.

Table-5.22: Level of Difficulty in Obtaining Application Form: Response of Students

Level of difficulty	Number of Responses								
	Beneficiary			Non-beneficiary			Total		
	Boys	Girls	Total	Boys	Girls	Total	Boys	Girls	Total
Highly difficulty	19 (16.38)	14 (16.67)	33 (16.50)	9 (13.43)	5 (15.15)	14 (14.00)	28 (15.30)	19 (16.24)	47 (15.67)
Difficulty	59 (50.86)	43 (51.19)	102 (51.00)	34 (50.75)	17 (51.51)	51 (51.00)	93 (50.82)	60 (51.28)	153 (51.00)
Somewhat difficulty	31 (26.72)	23 (27.38)	54 (27.00)	19 (28.36)	9 (27.28)	28 (28.00)	50 (27.32)	32 (27.35)	82 (27.33)
No difficulty	7 (6.03)	4 (4.76)	11 (5.50)	5 (7.46)	2 (6.06)	7 (7.00)	12 (6.56)	6 (5.13)	18 (6.00)
Total	116 (100.00)	84 (100.00)	200 (100.00)	67 (100.00)	33 (100.00)	100 (100.00)	183 (100.00)	117 (100.00)	300 (100.00)

Note: Figures in brackets indicate percentages.
Source: Primary data based.

5.25 Level of Difficulty in Filling Application Form:

Around 15.34 percent of all students felt high level of difficulty in filling the application form. The proportion of non-beneficiary students who felt high level of difficulty in filling the form has been higher than the beneficiary students. The proportion of girls versus boys who felt high level of difficulty was lower. However, majority of them (64 per cent) reported that they felt difficulty while 6.33 per cent students felt no problem in filling the form. On the whole, majority of students felt difficulty in filling the application form of Pre-matric scholarship (Table-5.23).

Table-5.23: Level of Difficulty in filling the Application Form: Response of Students

Level of difficulty	Number of Responses								
	Beneficiary			Non-beneficiary			Total		
	Boys	Girls	Total	Boys	Girls	Total	Boys	Girls	Total
High difficulty	21 (18.11)	8 (9.53)	29 (14.50)	12 (17.92)	5 (15.15)	17 (17.00)	33 (18.03)	13 (11.11)	46 (15.34)
Difficulty	67 (57.75)	65 (77.38)	132 (66.00)	43 (64.17)	17 (51.52)	60 (60.00)	110 (60.12)	82 (70.09)	192 (64.00)
Somewhat difficulty	24 (20.69)	7 (8.33)	31 (15.50)	6 (8.95)	6 (18.18)	12 (12.00)	30 (16.39)	13 (11.11)	43 (14.33)
No difficulty	4 (3.45)	4 (4.76)	8 (4.00)	6 (8.96)	5 (15.15)	11 (11.00)	10 (5.46)	9 (7.69)	19 (6.33)
Total	116 (100.00)	84 (100.00)	200 (100.00)	67 (100.00)	33 (100.00)	100 (100.00)	183 (100.00)	117 (100.00)	300 (100.00)

Note: Figures in brackets indicate percentages.
Source: Primary data based.

5.26 Cooperation of Institutions in getting Pre-matric Scholarship:

The table-5.24 shows that around 50 per cent students in Indore district find the role of institution where they study satisfactory in helping them to get Pre-matric scholarship. In this regard, the proportion of boys and girls are roughly the same. There is also no major difference among the beneficiary versus non beneficiary students. It is also to be noted here that those students who find the cooperation of their institutions unsatisfactory and highly unsatisfactory constitute around 37 per cent of all students. These are the good number of students who find the cooperation of their institutions unsatisfactory.

Table-5.24: Level of Cooperation of Institutions in helping Students to get Scholarship : Perception of Students

Items	Number of Students								
	Beneficiary			Non-beneficiary			Total		
	Boys	Girls	Total	Boys	Girls	Total	Boys	Girls	Total
Highly Satisfactory	16 (13.79)	10 (11.90)	26 (13.00)	9 (13.44)	4 (12.12)	13 (13.00)	25 (13.66)	14 (11.97)	39 (13.00)
Satisfactory	63 (54.31)	38 (45.24)	101 (50.50)	29 (43.28)	19 (57.57)	48 (48.00)	92 (50.27)	57 (48.72)	149 (49.67)
Unsatisfactory	29 (25.00)	25 (29.76)	54 (27.00)	18 (26.86)	9 (27.27)	27 (27.00)	47 (25.68)	34 (29.05)	81 (27.00)
Highly Unsatisfactory	8 (6.90)	11 (13.10)	19 (9.50)	11 (16.42)	1 (3.04)	12 (12.00)	19 (10.39)	12 (10.26)	31 (10.33)
Total	116 (100.00)	84 (100.00)	200 (100.00)	67 (100.00)	33 (100.00)	100 (100.00)	183 (100.00)	117 (100.00)	300 (100.00)

Note: Figures in brackets indicate percentages.

Source: Primary data based.

5.27 Role of State Government Officials: Perception of Students:

The table-5.25 indicates that 45.66 per cent of students felt unsatisfied with the role of state

Table-5.25: Role of State Government Officials: Response of Students

Level of Satisfaction	Number of Students								
	Beneficiary			Non-beneficiary			Total		
	Boys	Girls	Total	Boys	Girls	Total	Boys	Girls	Total
Highly Satisfactory	18 (15.52)	12 (14.29)	30 (15.00)	12 (17.91)	4 (12.12)	16 (16.00)	30 (16.39)	16 (13.68)	46 (15.33)
Satisfactory	32 (27.59)	24 (28.57)	56 (28.00)	19 (28.36)	9 (27.27)	28 (28.00)	51 (27.87)	33 (28.21)	84 (28.00)
Unsatisfactory	53 (45.68)	39 (46.43)	92 (46.00)	30 (44.77)	15 (45.45)	45 (45.00)	83 (45.36)	54 (46.15)	137 (45.66)
Highly Unsatisfactory	13 (11.21)	9 (10.71)	22 (11.00)	6 (8.96)	5 (15.16)	11 (11.00)	19 (10.38)	14 (11.96)	33 (11.00)
Total	116 (100.00)	84 (100.00)	200 (100.00)	67 (100.00)	33 (100.00)	100 (100.00)	183 (100.00)	117 (100.00)	300 (100.00)

Note: Figures in brackets indicate percentages.

Source: Primary data based.

government officials in the matter of Pre-matric scholarship. It was 11 per cent of students who felt highly unsatisfied with the role of state government officials. No major difference among beneficiary and non-beneficiary and boys and girls students is evident in this regard.

5.28 Suggestions of Students to Improve the Pre-matric Scholarship Scheme:

The following table shows that six suggestions have been given by the sample students for improvement of Pre-matric Scholarship. These suggestions are that (i) awareness Campaign at community, institutions and panchayat level should be launched, (ii) amount of scholarship should

Table 5.26: Suggestions of Students for Improving the Scheme

Suggestions	No. of Students								
	Beneficiary			Non-beneficiary			Total		
	Boys	Girls	Total	Boys	Girls	Total	Boys	Girls	Total
Awareness Campaign at Community, Institutions and Panchayat Level	106 (91.38)	61 (72.62)	167 (83.50)	58 (86.57)	29 (87.88)	87 (87.00)	164 (89.62)	90 (76.92)	254 (84.67)
Scholarship amount should be Increased.	90 (77.59)	72 (85.71)	162 (81.00)	59 (88.06)	31 (93.94)	90 (90.00)	149 (81.42)	103 (88.03)	252 (84.00)
Income certificate given by Pradhan/Sabhasad should be accepted	91 (78.45)	77 (91.67)	168 (84.00)	52 (77.61)	23 (69.70)	75 (75.00)	143 (78.14)	100 (85.47)	243 (81.00)
More than 2 children should be eligible from onle Family	101 (87.07)	57 (67.86)	158 (79.00)	61 (91.04)	17 (51.52)	78 (78.00)	162 (88.52)	74 (63.25)	236 (78.67)
Application form should be simple and multilingual.	98 (84.48)	68 (80.95)	166 (83.00)	43 (64.18)	13 (39.39)	56 (56.00)	141 (77.05)	81 (69.23)	222 (74.00)
No criteria of percentage of marks	70 (60.34)	67 (79.76)	137 (68.50)	41 (61.19)	20 (60.61)	61 (61.00)	111 (60.66)	87 (74.36)	198 (66.00)
Total Students	116 (100.00)	84 (100.00)	200 (100.00)	67 (100.00)	33 (100.00)	100 (100.00)	183 (100.00)	117 (100.00)	300 (100.00)

Note: Figures in brackets indicate percentages.

Source: Primary data based.

be increased, (iii) income certificate given by Pradhan/Sabhasad should be accepted, (iv) more than 2 children should be eligible for the scholarship from one family and (v) application form should be simplified and be made multilingual.

5.29 Main Findings:

- It became evident that most of the applicants of Pre-matric scholarship faced difficulties while applying for the Pre-matric Scholarship.
- The obtaining of application form for applying the Pre-matric Scholarship has been difficult for majority of students.
- Majority of students felt difficulty in filling the application form of Pre-matric Scholarship.
- Though a high percentage of sample students reported that they were satisfied with the role of their institutions in helping them to get the Pre-matric Scholarship but substantial per cent of them were found to be unsatisfied also.
- It became evident that around 43.33 per cent of the sample students were satisfied and 57 per cent unsatisfied with the role of state government officials in the matter of Pre-matric Scholarship.
- Six suggestions have been given by the sample students for improvement of Pre-matric Scholarship. These suggestions are that (i) awareness Campaign at community, institutions and panchayat level should be launched, (ii) amount of scholarship should be increased, (iii) income certificate given by Pradhan/Sabhasad should be accepted, (iv) more than 2 children should be eligible for the scholarship from one family and (v) application form should be simplified and be made multilingual.

Parents of Beneficiary and Non-Beneficiary Students, Institutions and Officials

5.30 Sample Parents:

The total sample of parents was 150 which included 100 parents of beneficiary students and 50 parents of non-beneficiary students (Table-5.27).

Table-5.27: Sample of the Parents

Particulars	No. of Parents
Beneficiary Parents	100
Non-beneficiary Parents	50
Total	150

Source: Primary data based

5.31 Housing and Family Features:

Housing and family features have been shown in table-5.28. Houses are generally pucca in case of 89.34 per cent families, having 3 and 2 rooms in houses of beneficiary and non-beneficiary parents respectively. The family size is 6 persons in both cases. Around 97.33 per cent houses have electricity and all of them (95 per cent) hold ration card.

Table-5.28: Housing and Family Conditions of Sample Parents

Particulars	Beneficiary Parents	Non-beneficiary Parents	Total
Type of House			
Katchcha	4 (4.00)	2 (4.00)	6 (4.00)
Pucca	91 (91.00)	43 (86.00)	134 (89.34)
Semi Pucca	5 (5.00)	5 (10.00)	10 (6.66)
Total	100 (100.00)	50 (100.00)	150(100.00)
Average Value of House (Rs.)	4,85,000	4,70,000	4,77,500
Average No. of Rooms	3	2	3
Average Family Size	6	6	6
Average Earning Members in the family	2	2	2
House Electrified	98 (98.00)	48 (96.00)	146 (97.33)
Ration Card Holders			
BPL	6 (6.00)	3 (6.00)	9 (6.00)
APL	88 (88.88)	45 (90.00)	132 (88.00)
Total	94 (94.00)	48 (96.00)	142 (94.67)

Note: Figures in brackets indicate percentage.
Source: Primary data based.

5.32 Land Size and Income of Beneficiary Parents:

Beneficiary as well as non-beneficiary parents are mostly the landless (91.33 per cent). It may so because of their urban base.

Table-5.29: Land Size of Parents

Land Holding	Beneficiary Parents	Non-Beneficiary Parents	Total
Land Less	93 (93.00)	44 (88.00)	137 (91.33)
Less than 0.5 acre	5 (5.00)	3 (6.00)	8 (5.33)
0.5 to 1.00 acre	2 (2.00)	3 (6.00)	5 (3.34)
Average	0.60	0.55	0.58
Min	0.28	0.27	0.28
Max	1.00	0.82	0.91

Note: Figures in brackets indicate percentage.
Source: Primary data based.

5.33 Income of Parents:

Most of the beneficiary and non-beneficiary parents (82.67 per cent) have annual income in the range of Rs. 20,001 to 50,000 (Table-5.30).

Table-5.30: Source of Income of Sample Parents

House Hold Income	Beneficiary Parents	Non-beneficiary Parents	Total
Less than 20,000	4 (4.00)	2 (4.00)	6 (4.00)
20001-50000	83 (83.00)	41 (82.00)	124 (82.67)
50001-100000	11 (11.00)	6 (12.00)	17 (11.33)
100001-150000.	2 (2.00)	1 (2.00)	3 (2.00)
Total	100 (100.00)	50 (100.00)	150 (100.00)

Note: Figures in brackets indicate percentage.
Source: Primary data based.

5.34 Awareness about Pre-matric Scholarship:

The awareness about the Pre-matric scholarship is found to be limited among the beneficiary and non-beneficiary parents as evident from the followingtable-5.31.

Table-5.31: Parents Knowledge of the Pre- Scholarship Scheme

Particulars	Number of Parents
Beneficiary	42 (42.00)
Non- Beneficiary	19 (38.00)
Total	61 (40.67)

5.35 Sources of Awareness of Pre-matric Scholarship:

Around half of the sample parents (52.45 per cent) have reported that they could get awareness about the Pre-matric Scholarship from the teachers where their ward studied. The next most important source was the fellow students who were the earlier recipients of the Pre-matric Scholarship (Table-5.32).

Table-5.32: Sources of Awareness of Pre-matric Scholarship Scheme

Source	Number of Parents		
	Beneficiary Parents	Non-beneficiary Parents	Total
Teachers	22 (52.38)	10 (52.63)	32 (52.45)
Students who got Scholarship	12 (28.57)	6 (31.58)	18 (29.51)
Sabhasads	5 (11.90)	2 (10.53)	7 (11.48)
Radio/T.V.	2 (4.76)	1 (5.26)	3 (4.92)
News Papers	1 (2.39)	-	1 (1.64)
Total	42 (100.00)	19 (100.00)	61 (100.00)

Note: Figures in brackets indicate percentage.
Source: Primary data based.

5.36 Reasons of untimely payment of Pre-matric Scholarship:

The beneficiary parents have given three reasons of untimely payment of Pre-matric Scholarship in which delay from the side of district authorities was reported by around half of the respondents as shown in table-5.33.

Table-5.33: Reasons of Untimely Payment of Pre-matric Scholarship: Reasons given by Beneficiaries

Reasons	Number of Parents
Delay by MOMA	15 (27.27)
Delay by District Authorities	27 (49.10)
Delay by the Institutions	13 (23.63)
Total	55 (100.00)

Note: Figures in brackets indicate percentage.
Source: Primary data based.

5.37 Problems Faced by Beneficiary Students: Perception of their Parents:

Majority of parents (67 per cent) of beneficiary students felt that their wards faced problems in getting the Pre-matric scholarship (Table-5.34).

Table-5.34: Problem Faced by Students in Getting the Pre- Matric Scholarship: Parents Response

Particulars	Number of Parents
Yes	67 (67.00)
No	33 (33.00)
Total	100 (100.00)

Note: Figures in brackets indicate percentage.
Source: Primary data based.

5.38 Level of Difficulty Faced in Filling the Application Form: Perception of their Parents:

All the 150 Parents have reported that their wards faced difficulties at different levels in filling the application form as evident in following table-5.35.

Table-5.35: Level of Difficulty in Filling the Application Form

Level of Difficulty	Number of Parents		
	Beneficiary	Non Beneficiary	Total
High Difficulty	28 (28.00)	15 (30.00)	43 (28.67)
Difficulty	48 (48.00)	25 (50.00)	73 (48.67)
Some What Difficulty	17 (17.00)	6 (12.00)	23 (15.33)
Less Difficult	7 (7.00)	4 (8.00)	11 (7.33)
Total	100 (100.00)	50 (100.00)	150 (100.00)

Note: Figures in brackets indicate percentage.
Source: Primary data based.

5.39 Rating of Various Processes of Pre-matric Scholarship: Beneficiary Parents:

The rating to various processes of Pre-matric Scholarship was given by the parents which has been shown in tables-5.36. To all the six aspects of Pre-matric scholarship, average and poor ratings have been given.

Table-5.36: Rating of various Aspects of Pre-matric Scholarship Scheme: Parents

Particulars	Number of Parents					
	Poor	Average	Good	Very good	Excellent	Total
Scholarship Amount	16 (10.67)	67 (44.67)	39 (26.00)	26 (17.33)	2 (1.33)	150 (100.00)
Documentation	43 (28.67)	73 (48.67)	32 (21.33)	2 (1.33)	-	150 (100.00)
Renewal Process	97 (64.67)	53 (35.33)	-	-	-	150 (100.00)
Availability of Application Form	45 (30.00)	67 (44.67)	24 (16.00)	11 (7.33)	3 (2.00)	150 (100.00)
Timeliness of Processing	71 (47.33)	49 (32.67)	21 (14.00)	6 (4.00)	3 (2.00)	150 (100.00)
Support of School Administration	56 (37.34)	69 (46.00)	14 (9.33)	8 (5.33)	3 (2.00)	150 (100.00)

Note: Figures in brackets indicate percentage.
Source: Primary data based.

5.40 Parents Perceptions on Scholarship:

The following views were expressed by the parents about the Pre-matric Scholarship Scheme:

1. Scholarship is helpful for education of Children.
2. Lack of Awareness about the Pre-matric Scholarship Scheme implemented by MOMA Government of India.
3. Lack of Knowledge about important dates of Scheme.
4. Non-Corporative attitude of government educational Institutions.
5. Application form is in English and also lengthy.
6. Applying process is costly due to need of income certificate and Affidavit by Court.
7. Delay processing and late distribution of Scholarship.
8. Conditions of only two children from a family, income and 50 marks of last examination should be relaxed.
9. Scholarship Amount should be increased for girls' students.
10. Regular checking of Scheme at community and institution level should be encouraged.

5.41 Sample Institutions:

The sample institutions are located in urban area of Indore district of Madhya Pradesh as per following table-5.37.

Table-5.37: Location of Sample Institution

Location	Number of Institution
Urban	8 (100.00)
Total	8 (100.00)

Note: Figures in brackets indicate percentage.
Source: Primary data based.

5.42: Type of Sample Institutions

The sample institutions are dispersed in primary, middle, secondary and higher secondary levels (Table-5.38). All the institutions are private as shown in table-16.13.

Table-5.38: Type of Institutions

Particulars	No. of Institutions
Primary	2 (25.00)
Middle	1 (12.50)
Secondary	2 (25.00)
Higher Secondary	3 (37.50)
Total	8 (100.00)

Note: Figures in brackets indicate percentage.
Source: Primary data based.

Table-5.39: Type of Institutions

Particulars	No. of Institutions
Private	8 (100.00)
Total	8 (100.00)

Note: Figures in brackets indicate percentage.
Source: Primary data based.

5.43: Enrolment, Applied and Award of Pre-matric Scholarship:

Among the total enrolled students, very low proportion of them (12.42 per cent) applied for Pre-matric Scholarship in the year 2010-11. In the year 2009-10, only 7.88 per cent of enrolled students applied for the Pre-matric Scholarship. The percentage of girl applicants was higher in

Table-5.40: Year-wise Enrolment, Applied and Pre-matric Scholarship Awarded to Students in Sample Institutions

Year	Enrolled			Applied			Awarded		
	Boys	Girls	Total	Boys	Girls	Total	Boys	Girls	Total
2009-10	1426 (100.00)	1189 (100.00)	2615 (100.00)	102 (7.15)	104 (8.75)	206 (7.88)	14 (13.73)	27 (25.96)	41 (19.90)
2010-11	2485 (100.00)	2014 (100.00)	4499 (100.00)	241 (9.70)	318 (15.79)	559 (12.42)	73 (30.29)	123 (38.68)	196 (35.06)
Total	3911 (100.00)	3203 (100.00)	7114 (100.00)	343 (8.77)	422 (13.18)	765 (10.75)	87 (25.36)	150 (35.55)	237 (30.98)

Note: Figures in brackets indicate percentage.
Source: Records of Sample Institutions.

comparison with the boy applicants. Out of those who applied, only 35.06 succeeded in getting the Pre-matric Scholarship in 2010-11 while only 19.90 per cent succeeded in getting the Pre-matric Scholarship in the year 2009-10. Thus, the percentages of applicants in total enrolment and those awarded have been quite low in Indore district of Madhya Pradesh.

5.44 Reasons of not getting Scholarship: Perspective of Institutions:

The sample institutions have given the following reasons due to which the Pre-matric scholarship could not be given to all its applicants.

Table-5.41: Reasons of not getting Scholarship

Reasons	Total
Lack of awareness in the community	8 (100.00)
Lengthy and expensive paper work	8 (100.00)
Language problem in filling the application form	8 (100.00)
Follow up of application is not easily accessible	6 (75.00)
Lack of monitoring about the scholarship	6 (75.00)

Note: Figures in brackets indicate percentage.
Source: Records of Sample Institutions.

5.45 Mode of Payment of Scholarship Amount:

The mode of payment of scholarship money was found to be in cash in 25 per cent institutions (Table-5.42).

Table-5.42: Mode of Payment of Scholarship Amount

Mode	Number of Institutions
Cash	2 (25.00)
Cheque	6 (75.00)
Total	8 (100.00)

Note: Figures in brackets indicate percentage.
Source: Records of Sample Institutions.

5.46 Time taken in Processing:

All the institutions have reported that entire processing of application takes more than 15 days.

Table-5.43: Average Time Taken in Processing of Application

Time Taken	Number of Institutions
10-15 Days	-
More than 15 Days	8 (100.00)
Total	8 (100.00)

Note: Figures in brackets indicate percentage.
Source: Records of Sample Institutions.

5.47 Level of Difficulty in Processing:

Only 25 per cent of sample institutions have reported no difficulty in processing of applications while rest finds different levels of difficulties as shown in table-5.44

Table-5.44: Level of Difficulty in Processing the Application

Level of Difficulty	Number of Institutions
Difficult	3 (37.50)
Somewhat Difficult	3 (37.50)
Not Difficult	2 (25.00)
Total	8 (100.00)

Note: Figures in brackets indicate percentage.
Source: Records of Sample Institutions.

5.48 Time taken from Proposal to Disbursement of Pre-matric Scholarship:

The sample institutions have reported that considerable time (6-7months) is taken in the sanction of the scholarship. The entire time duration is as shown in table-5.45.

Table-5.45: Duration of Pre-matric Scholarship Distribution

Proposal sent to MOMA	September 2009-10
Sectioned	November-December 2009-10
Scholarship Reached the District	January-February 2010-11
Distributed	February-March 2010- 11

5.49 Improvement in Enrolment and Drop out:

The records of sample institutions showed that there was negligible growth in the Enrolment of minority students in 2010-11 over 2009-10.

5.50 Level of Satisfaction of Institutions with State and Central Government Agencies:

On the three items of satisfaction as shown in table-5.20, majority of institutions reported their dissatisfaction.(Table-5.46).

Table-5.46: Level of Satisfaction with State and Central Government Agencies

Heads	Satisfied	Dissatisfied	Total No. of Institutions
Satisfaction with State Government			
Timely Processing and Approval	2 (25.00)	6 (75.00)	8 (100.00)
Timely Release of Funds	1 (12.50)	7 (87.50)	8 (100.00)
Staff Behavior	3 (37.50)	5 (62.50)	8 (100.00)
Satisfaction with Central Government			
Timely Processing and Approval	3 (37.50)	5 (62.50)	8 (100.00)
Timely Release of Funds	2 (25.00)	6 (75.00)	8 (100.00)
Staff Behavior	3 (37.50)	5 (62.50)	8 (100.00)

Note: Figures in brackets indicate percentage.
Source: Records of Sample Institutions.

5.51 Data Management:

In half of the institutes data management of Pre-matric Scholarship was manual and in half institutes it was semi-computerized (Table-5.47).

Table-5.47: System of Data Management of Pre-matric Scholarship

Procedure	No. of Institutions
Manual	4 (50.00)
Semi- Computerized	4(50.00)
Number of Institution	8(100.00)

Note: Figures in brackets indicate percentage.
Source: Records of Sample Institutions.

5.52 Impact of Pre-matric Scholarship Scheme:

The staff of the sample institutions reported that the beneficiary students have become more regular in attending their classes and the interest of the beneficiary students in their studies has increased. The Pre-matric scholarship is great help to students in meeting their educational needs as felt by the management of instructions.

5.53 Assessment of Pre-matric Scholarship: Views of Institutions

It appears that institutions have no clear cut idea about the Pre-matric Scholarship in Indore district. As a result their assessment about the Pre-matric Scholarship is way warded and leads to no definite conclusion (Table-5.48).

Table-5.48: Overall Assessment of Pre-matric Scholarship Scheme

Level of Satisfaction	No. of Institutions
Highly Satisfied	-
Satisfied	3 (37.50)
Somewhat Satisfied	3 (37.50)
Dissatisfied	2 (25.00)
Number of Institution	8 (100.00)

Note: Figures in brackets indicate percentage.
Source: Records of Sample Institutions.

5.54 Main Suggestions of Institutions for Improvement of Scheme:

- Mass awareness campaign should be launched in the community about the scheme.
- Application forms should be made available in Hindi and Urdu.
- Timely distribution of scholarship.
- Less Documentation should be required with application of Pre-matric Scholarship.

District Level Official:

5.55 On the Guidelines:

The clerks in the office of Coordinator, Department of Scheduled Tribes Welfare, Government of Madhya Pradesh at Indore reported that guidelines of the Pre-matric Scholarship are available in their office.

5.56 Selection Criteria:

The two clerks in the office of Coordinator, Department of Scheduled Tribes Welfare, Government of Madhya Pradesh at Indore provided official version of implementation of Pre-matric Scholarship and reported that selection criteria is followed.

5.57 Awardees of Pre-matric Scholarship:

The office of Coordinator, Department of Scheduled Tribes Welfare, Government of Madhya

Table-5.49: Number of Awardee Students of Pre Matric Scholarship in IndoreDistrict

Year	Total No. of Students
2009-10	192
2010-11	723
Total	915

Source: Department of Schedule Tribe Welfare, Indore.
Note: Religion and Sex wise Data not available with office of the Schedule Tribe Welfare.

Pradesh at Indorewho looks after the Pre-matric Scholarship Scheme in the district has provided the number of awardee students for the year 2009-10 and 2010-11 as shown in table-5.49.

5.58 Grants of Pre-matric Scholarship:

All the grants allocated was approved and then used in 2009-10 and 2010-11 as shown in table-5.50.

Table-5.50: Grant Allocation, Approval and Utilization (Rs. In Lakhs)

Year	Amount allocated	Grants Approved/ Sanctioned	Grants Utilized
2009-10	3.73	3.73	3.73
2010-11	10.52	10.52	10.52

Source: Department of Schedule Tribe Welfare, Indore.

5.59 Time Spent in Disbursement of Pre-matric Scholarship:

The official version is that six months are spent in the whole process of disbursement of Pre-matric Scholarship.

Table-5.51: Time Spent in Disbursement of Pre-matric Scholarship:

Proposal sent to MOMA	October
Sanctioned	January
Scholarship reached the District	February
Scholarship Disbursed	March

Source: Department of Schedule Tribe Welfare, Indore.

5.60 Impact of Pre-matric Scholarship Scheme: Officer's Views

- Scholarship scheme enhanced Enrolment of student belonging to minority communities.
- Scholarship amount provided adequate cover to students in their study needs.
- Improved the educational achievement level of students.

5.61 Problems in Implementation of Scheme: Officer's Views

- No fund for advertisement
- Lack of awareness
- Delay in processing of Central Government Scholarship Schemes as compared with the State Government schemes.
- Lengthy process and language problem.

5.62 Suggestions for Improvement:

- Less documentation work.
- Separate staff should be provided.
- Application form should be easy and in Hindi.

5.63 Main Findings: Parents

- Housing conditions of Muslims are better in Indore district. Around 90 per cent of their houses are pucca and 97 per cent houses are electrified and most of them have ration cards.
- Because of their urban base, parents are mostly the landless.
- Most of the beneficiary and non-beneficiary parents have annual income in the range of Rs. 20,001 to 50,000.
- The awareness about the Pre-matric scholarship is poor among the beneficiary, and non-beneficiary parents.
- There were two main important sources of awareness of Pre-matric Scholarship to the parents. One is the teachers and other is the students who got the Pre-matric scholarship earlier.
- The substantial percentage of parents has held responsible the district officials for the delay in Pre-matric Scholarship.
- Majority of parents of beneficiary students felt that their wards faced problems in getting the Pre-matric scholarship.
- All the sample parents have reported that their wards faced difficulties at different levels in filling the application form.
- The parents have given average and poor rating to all the aspects of Pre-matric Scholarship.
- The parents have found the role of Pre-matric positive in the education of their wards.

5.64 Main Findings: Institutions

- The sample institutions are located in urban areas of Indore district and all are private.
- The percentage of applied students in total enrolled students was very low. At the same time that got the Pre-matric scholarship, their percentage in total applicants was also found to be quite low in Indore district.
- Lack of awareness in the community, lengthy and expensive paper work, language problem in filling the application form, difficult follow up of application and lack of monitoring of scholarship are reasons given by the institutions for the poor award of Pre-matric Scholarships in Indore district.
- The mode of payment of scholarship money was found to be in cash in 25 per cent institutions.
- The sample institutions have reported that 6-7 months are taken in the entire process of sanction of Pre-matric scholarship.
- The records of sample institutions showed that there was negligible growth in the enrolment of minority students in 2010-11 over 2009-10.
- The majority of institutions reported their dissatisfaction with the state and central government departments dealing with the Pre-matric Scholarship.

- There is no computerization of data of Pre-matric Scholarship in Indore district.
- It appears that institutions have no clear cut idea about the functioning of Pre-matric Scholarship in Indore district. As a result their assessment of the Pre-matric Scholarship is way warded and leads to no definite conclusion.

5.65 Main Findings: District Officials

- The official record showed that only 192 and 723 number of Pre-matric Scholarships was given during 2009-10 and 2010-11 in Indore district which is quite a few numbers.
- All the allocated and approved grant of Pre-matric Scholarship was used in 2009-10 and 2010-11 in Indore district.
- The official version is that six months are spent in the whole process of disbursement of Pre-matric Scholarship in the district.
- The officials felt that the Pre-matric Scholarship scheme enhanced enrolment of students belonging to minority community, provided adequate cover to students in their study needs and improved the educational achievement of students.
- The officials viewed the lack of fund for advertisement, lack of awareness, delay in processing of Central Government Scholarship Schemes as compared with the State Government schemes and lengthy process and language problem as major problems of Pre-matric Scholarship in the district.
- The officials have suggested less documentation work, need of separate staff for Central Government Scholarships Schemes and the application form should be made easy and in Hindi.

Field Observations, Key Issues and Suggestions: Pre-matric Scholarship

5.66 Field Observations:

It was observed during the field investigation of the present study in Indore district of Madhya Pradesh that the implementation of Scholarship Schemes of the Ministry of Minority Welfare, Government of India has been poor in the district. The Department of Tribal Welfare which is responsible for the implementation of these schemes in the State of Madhya Pradesh seems to have no interest in their proper implementation. This can be assessed from the fact that out of five development blocks of Indore district, these scholarships schemes have been implemented only in Indore Sadar block. When we asked to the officials that why these schemes could not by be extended to other blocks of the district, they replied that staff is not there to look after the work of these schemes. There is three member staff of Tribal Welfare Department at Indore. One is the coordinator who rarely comes to the office and two others are the clerks who look after the official work. They have no interest that the benefit of these schemes reaches to the students of minorities. When the matter was discussed with other stakeholders like parents and institutions, they all blamed the district officials for their inaction and unwillingness to help them to get these scholarships. The parents of students eligible for the Pre-matric Scholarship face much difficulty as their wards cannot go to officials time and again. The parents told that they get application form of Pre-matric Scholarship with difficulty. They devote much of their time in completing the formalities of the application.

Thereafter, parents go to concerned institution for submissions. The institutions reported that they visit the office for submission which takes many visits as concerned officials remain non-available many times. The parents told us that they never remain sure that when the scholarship will reach to them. The institutions also blamed district officials for their inaction.

5.67 Key Issues of Pre-matric Scholarship:

- The concerned officials at the district level have no interest to implement the Scholarship Schemes of the Ministry of Minority Affairs, Government of India.
- The outreach of the Pre-matric Scholarship to minorities is very low in Indore district.
- There is absolute lack of awareness about the Pre-matric Scholarship among the students and their parents.
- Substantial percentages of awardee students are being paid their scholarship money in cash.
- Substantial number of students felt difficulty in obtaining application form, filling it and submitting it.
- Considerable time is also spent during application to award of scholarship.
- Income certificate and affidavit are also problems.

5.68 Suggestions:

- There is need that the management of Scholarship Schemes of the Ministry of Minority Affairs, Government of India should be taken away from the Department of Tribal Welfare in Madhya Pradesh and may be entrusted to the other departments like Waqf, education etc. or a separate department on the lines of Department of Minority Welfare, Government of Uttar Pradesh should be established in Madhya Pradesh.
- There is need of rigorous orientation training of state and district level officials who oversee the scheme.
- Simultaneously need is to generate awareness among the minority community about the scholarship scheme.
- The teachers of schools should be made aware of the scheme and they should be made to encourage their students to apply for the Pre-matric scholarship. The state officials may also be asked to involve village panchayats/urban bodies in this matter.
- The income limit of parents should be raised to Rs. 1,50,000/. The amount of Pre-matric Scholarship should reasonably be increased.
- The application form should be in Hindi and be simplified.
- The data management should be computerized.
- The issue of renewal is not clearly to the students, parents and district officials. This needs to be made clear to district officials in particular.
- The payment of scholarship in cash must be stopped and bulk payment to schools should be prohibited. All students should be asked to open an account in the bank and scholarship money should be electronically transferred in their account directly from the state level.
- In some way accountability clause should be added in the scheme and District Collectors should be held responsible if poor and inefficient implementation is found.

Chapter-VI

Introduction : Post-matric Scholarship—Indore District

6.1 Sample of the Study:

It has been mentioned in the sampling methodology of Post-matric Scholarship that institution based sampling technique was adopted in the selection of beneficiary and non-beneficiary students and sampling was confined to urban areas of Indore district as no scholarship was given in the rural areas of the district. Following the same methodology, beneficiary and non-beneficiary students of Post-matric Scholarship were also selected from the same urban areas of Indore district from where the sample was taken for the Post-matric Scholarship. It was decided that 10 per cent of all beneficiary and non-beneficiary students of pre-matric scholarship will be taken as sample if the number of such students exceeds 50 but in our sample wards, the number was found to be less than 50. Therefore, all the beneficiary and non-beneficiary students of Post-matric Scholarship were selected on census basis as sample which is as follows:

Table-6.1: Sample Size of the Post-Matric Scholarship: Students

Sex	Beneficiary	Non Beneficiary	Total
Boys	11	14	25
Girls	7	2	9
Total	18	16	34

Characteristics of Sample Students-Post-Matric Scholarship

6.2 Age of Students:

There are two age-groups of beneficiary and non-beneficiary students as shown in table-6.2. The beneficiary students are 72.22 per cent in age group of 16-18 years and 27.78 per cent in age group of 19-21 years while majority (81.25 per cent) of non-beneficiaries is in the age group of 16-18 years. The boys and girls of both groups are mostly in the age group of 16-18 years. On the whole, more than 76 per cent of the sample students are in the age group of 16-18 years.

Table-6.2: Age wise Number of Sample Students

Sex	Students	16-18 Year	19-21 Year	Total
Boys	Beneficiaries	7 (63.64)	4 (36.36)	11 (100.00)
	Non-Beneficiaries	11 (78.57)	3 (21.43)	14 (100.00)
	Total	18 (72.00)	7 (28.00)	25 (100.00)
Girls	Beneficiaries	6 (85.71)	1 (14.29)	7 (100.00)
	Non-Beneficiaries	2 (100.00)	0 (0.00)	2 (100.00)
	Total	8 (88.89)	1 (11.11)	9 (100.00)
Total	Beneficiaries	13 (72.22)	5 (27.78)	18 (100.00)
	Non-Beneficiaries	13 (81.25)	3 (18.75)	16 (100.00)
	All Total	26 (76.47)	8 (23.53)	34 (100.00)

Note: Figures in brackets indicate percentages.

Source: Primary data based.

6.3 Level of Schools:

Out of total sample students, 47.06 per cent are in graduate followed by 35.29 per cent in intermediate and 17.65 per cent in post-graduate. Non-beneficiaries are not studying at post graduate level so 56 per cent of them are studying in graduation and rest 44 per cent in intermediate.

Table-6.3: Institution Where Sample Students are Studying

Sex	Students	Intermediate	Graduation	Post-Graduation	Total
Boys	Beneficiaries	1 (9.10)	5 (45.45)	5 (45.45)	11 (100.00)
	Non-Beneficiaries	6 (42.86)	8 (57.14)	0 (0.00)	14 (100.00)
	Total	7 (28.00)	13 (52.00)	5 (20.00)	25 (100.00)
Girls	Beneficiaries	4 (57.14)	2 (28.57)	1 (14.29)	7 (100.00)
	Non-Beneficiaries	1 (50.00)	1 (50.00)	0 (0.00)	2 (100.00)
	Total	5 (55.56)	3 (33.33)	1 (11.11)	9 (100.00)
Total	Beneficiaries	5 (27.78)	7 (38.89)	6 (33.33)	18 (100.00)
	Non-Beneficiaries	7 (43.75)	9 (56.25)	0 (0.00)	16 (100.00)
	All Total	12 (35.29)	16 (47.06)	6 (17.65)	34 (100.00)

Note: Figures in brackets indicate percentages.

Source: Primary data based.

6.4 Type of Institutions:

Out of totals sample students, 73.53 per cent are studying in government institutions, 14.71 per cent in private and 11.76 per cent in government aided institutions (Table-6.4).

Table-6.4: Institution Where Sample Students are Studying

Type of Institution	Type of Institution			
	Government	Private	Aided	Total
Intermediate	10 (83.33)	0 (0.00)	2 (16.67)	12 (100.00)
Graduation	9 (56.25)	5 (31.25)	2 (12.50)	16 (100.00)
Post- Graduation	6 (100.00)	0 (0.00)	0 (0.00)	6 (100.00)
Total	25 (73.53)	5 (14.71)	4 (11.76)	34 (100.00)

Note: Figures in brackets indicate percentages.

Source: Primary data based.

6.5 Sources of Income:

Small business/trade is the main occupation of 50 per cent beneficiary students while for 43.75 per cent of non-beneficiary student's artisan based activities are the main occupation (Table-6.5).

Table-6.5: Sources of Income of Sample Students

	Source	Beneficiary	Non-Beneficiary	Total
1	Casual Labour	1 (100.00)	0 (0.00)	1 (100.00)
2	Small Farmer	0 (0.00)	1 (100.00)	1 (100.00)
3	Artisan	4 (36.36)	7 (63.64)	11 (100.00)
4	Salaried (Government /Private)	4 (44.44)	5 (55.56)	9 (100.00)
5	Small Business/Trade	9 (75.00)	3 (25.00)	12 (100.00)
	Total	18 (52.94)	16 (47.06)	34 (100.00)

Note: Figures in brackets indicate percentages.
Source: Primary data based.

6.6 Income of Students:

All the students of Post-matric Scholarship which included beneficiary and non-beneficiary both are classified according their income in table-6.6 which indicated that 55.56 per cent of beneficiary students and 68.75 per cent of non-beneficiary students have average annual income in the range of Rs. 20,001 to Rs. 50,000.

Table-6.6: Classification of Students According to their Income

	Source	Beneficiary	Non-Beneficiary	Total
1	Casual Labour	1 (100.00)	0 (0.00)	1 (100.00)
2	Small Farmer	0 (0.00)	1 (100.00)	1 (100.00)
3	Artisan	4 (36.36)	7 (63.64)	11 (100.00)
4	Salaried (Government /Private)	4 (44.44)	5 (55.56)	9 (100.00)
5	Small Business/Trade	9 (75.00)	3 (25.00)	12 (100.00)
	Total	18 (52.94)	16 (47.06)	34 (100.00)

Note: Figures in brackets indicate percentages.
Source: Primary data based.

6.7 Expenditure on Education:

The average expenditure per student on Post-matric education has been calculated in table-6.7 which shows that more than 10 thousands are spent per students and there is no major difference between the beneficiary and non-beneficiary students.

Table-6.7: Average Expenditure of Education per Student on Different Items

Item	Amounts (in Rs.)		
	Beneficiary	Non- Beneficiary	Total
Course Fee	2085	1955	2022
Teaching Learning Materials	1610	1485	1548
Travel	1990	1778	1883
Tuition	2900	2380	2641
Others	1980	1920	1949
Total	10565	9518	10042

Note: Figures in brackets indicate percentages.

Source: Primary data based.

6.8 Attending Schools, Getting Scholarship and Family Features:

In the families of students getting Post-matric scholarship, around 54 per cent of eligible adults are found to be going to schools. The percentage of girls is lower than the boys and only 37.50 per cent of them could get Post-matric Scholarship. In the age structure, around half is in the age group of less than 5 years and 47 per cent family member have highest qualification of graduation. In this way, percentage of schooling going adults in schools age adults is quite low among Muslims of Indore district and those getting Post-matric Scholarship are also few (Table-6.8).

Table-6.8: Children Going to Schools, Getting Scholarships and Family Structure

Number of Students	
Children Going to School	
Boys	31 (54.60)
Girls	17 (52.51)
Total	48 (53.54)
Students Getting Scholarships	
Boys	11 (34.48)
Girls	7 (41.18)
Total	18 (37.50)
Age Structure of Family Members	
Less than 5 Years	104 (51.49)
5-14 Years	28 (13.86)
15-23 Years	20 (9.91)
24-35 Years	15 (7.42)
36-59 years	10 (4.95)
60 + years	25 (12.37)
All Members	202 (100.00)
No. of Earning Members in the Family	38 (18.81)
Highest Educational Status of a Member in Family	
Intermediate	12 (35.29)
Graduate	16 (47.06)
Post Graduate	6 (17.65)
Total	34 (100.00)

Note: Figures in brackets indicate percentages.
Source: Primary data based.

6.9 Housing:

Housing conditions in terms of pucca houses and electricity is good (Table-6.9).

Table-6.9: Housing and other Conditions of Sample Students

Housing Type	No. of Response
Kachcha	2 (5.88)
Pucca	29 (85.30)
Mix	3 (8.82)
Total	34(100.00)
Ownership of the House	
1. Owned	29 (85.29)
2. Rented	2 (5.88)
Given by Employer	3(8.23)
Value of the House, if owned (Average)	481193
Average Number of Rooms	3
Houses with Electricity	33 (97.06)
No. of Households with Ration Cards	32 (94.12)
Percentage of Marginal and Small Land owning Households	3 (8.82)

Note: Figures in brackets indicate percentages.

Source: Primary data based.

6.10 Main Findings:

- In the entire sample, more than 76 per cent of the sample students are in the age group of 16-18 years.
- Out of total sample students, 47.06 per cent are in graduation followed by 35.29 per cent in intermediate and 17.65 per cent in post-graduation. Non-beneficiaries are not studying at post graduate level so 56 per cent of them are studying in graduation and rest 44 per cent in intermediate.
- Out of totals sample students majority of them are studying in government institutions.
- Small business/trade is the main occupation of 50 per cent beneficiary students while for 43.75 per cent of non-beneficiary student's artisan based activities are the main occupation.
- 55.56 per cent of beneficiary students and 68.75 per cent of non-beneficiary students have average annual income in the range of Rs. 20,001 to Rs. 50,000.
- The average expenditure per student on Post-matric education is more than 10 thousands per students and there is no major difference between the beneficiary and non-beneficiary students.
- The percentage of schooling going adults in schools age adults is quite low among Muslims of Indore district and those getting Post-matric Scholarship are also few.
- Housing conditions of Muslims in Indore district may be termed as good.

Awareness, Utilization and Impact of Post-matric Scholarship

6.11 Complete Awareness about Post-matric Scholarship

The complete awareness about the details of Post-matric Scholarship is limited to only 38.24 per cent of the sample students (Table-6.10).

Table-6.10: Students who are Completely Aware of the Post -matric Scholarship Scheme

Sex	Benefiacjob	Non- beneficiary	Total
Boys	4 (36.36)	5 (35.71)	9 (36.00)
Girls	3 (42.86)	1 (50.00)	4 (44.44)
Total	7 (38.89)	6 (37.50)	13 (38.24)

Note: Figures in brackets indicate percentages.
Source: Primary data based.

6.12 Sources of Awareness of Post-matric Scholarship to Rural Students:

The main source of awareness of Post-matric scholarship to students is the teachers of the institutions where the students study followed by the students who earlier got the scholarship (Table-6.11).

Table -6.11: Sources of Awareness of Post- matric Scholarship

Source	Students								
	Beneficiary			Non-Beneficiary			Total		
	Boys	Girls	Total	Boys	Girls	Total	Boys	Girls	Total
Teachers	2 (50.00)	2 (66.67)	4 (57.14)	2 (40.00)	-	2 (33.33)	4 (44.44)	2 (50.00)	6 (46.16)
Students who Scholarship	1 (25.00)	1 (33.33)	2 (28.57)	2 (40.00)	1 (100.00)	3 (50.00)	3 (33.34)	2 (50.00)	5 (38.46)
Radio /TV	-	-	-	1 (20.00)	-	1 (16.67)	1 (11.11)	-	1 (7.69)
News Papers	1 (25.00)	-	1 (14.29)	-	-	-	1 (11.11)	-	1 (7.69)
Total	4 (100.00)	3 (100.00)	7 (100.00)	5 (100.00)	1 (100.00)	6 (100.00)	9 (100.00)	4 (100.00)	13 (100.00)

Note: Figures in brackets indicate percentages.
Source: Primary data based.

6.13 Student's Knowledge of Eligibility Conditions:

It is reported by 44.12 per cent of sample students that they are aware of the eligibility conditions of Post-matric Scholarship (Table-6.12).

Table-6.12: Students Knowing Eligibility Conditions of Post-matric Scholarship Scheme

Students	Number of Students		
	Beneficiary	Non- Beneficiary	Total
Boys	5 (45.45)	6 (42.86)	11 (44.00)
Girls	3 (42.86)	1 (50.00)	4 (44.44)
Total	8 (44.45)	7 (43.75)	15 (44.12)

Note: Figures in brackets indicate percentages.

Source: Primary data based.

6.14 Knowledge about Each Eligibility Condition:

It reflects from table-6.13 that majority of students both beneficiary and non-beneficiary as well is not aware of each the three conditions of Post-matric Scholarship.

Table-6.13: Knowledge of Sample Students about Each of the Eligibility Conditions of Post-matric Scholarship

Conditions	Number of Students		
	Beneficiary	Non Beneficiary	Total
Household Income not more than Rs. 2 Lakh	3 (37.50)	3 (42.86)	6 (40.00)
Marks not less than 50 per cent in last exam	3 (37.50)	2 (28.57)	5 (33.33)
Only 2 Student from one household	2 (25.00)	2 (28.57)	4 (26.67)
Total	8 (100.00)	7 (100.00)	15 (100.00)

Note: Figures in brackets indicate percentages.

Source: Primary data based.

6.15 Students Receiving Different Amount of Post-matric Scholarship:

The sample students have reported that 88.89 per cent of them received the Post-matric Scholarship of Rs.3000 to 4000 (Table-6.14).

Table-6.14: Classification of Beneficiary students According to amount of Scholarship

Amount(Rs.)	Number of Beneficiary Students
2000-3000	1 (5.56)
3000-4000	16 (88.89)
4000-5000	1 (5.55)
Total	18 (100.00)

Note : Figures in brackets indicate percentage .

Source : Primary data based

6.16 Mode of Payment:

The mode of payment of Post-matric Scholarship is through cheque only as all the sample students have reported it.

Table–6.15: Mode of Payment of Scholarship Amount

Mode	No. of Beneficiary		
	Boys	Girls	Total
Cash	-	-	-
Cheque	11 (100.00)	7 (100.00)	18 (100.00)
Total	11 (100.00)	7 (100.00)	18 (100.00)

Note : Figures in brackets indicate percentage .

Source : Primary data based

6.17 Scholarship Given by Different Persons:

The beneficiary students have reported that they are given their Post-matric Scholarships by their teachers (Table-6.16).

Table-6.16: Scholarship Given by Different Persons

Particulars	Number of Benificairy		
	Boys	Girls	Total
By Teachers	11 (100.00)	7 (100.00)	18 (100.00)
Total	11 (100.00)	7 (100.00)	18 (100.00)

Note: Figures in brackets indicate percentages.

Source: Primary data based.

6.18 Expenses for Applying the Post-matric Scholarship:

The total expenditure of Rs. 185 is required to apply for the Post-matric Scholarship. There are two main items of expenditure. One is on getting income certificate and other on getting affidavit (Table 6.17).

Table-6.17: Item wise Expenditure for getting Post-matric Scholarship

Items	Average Amount (in Rs.)		
	Boys	Girls	Total
Income Certificate	85	96	91
On Making Affidavit	70	60	65
Photos and Travel etc	30	27	29
Total	185	184	185

Source: Primary data based.

6.19 Utilization of Post-matric Scholarship Money : Students of Class 11-12 :

The students have reported that most part of the money they get as Post-matric Scholarship is spent on the items related to their education (Table-6.18). In this way, the role of Post-matric Scholarship in the educational development of minority students of classes 11-12 is paramount.

Table-6.18: Items wise Average Expenditure of Scholarship Amount: Students of Class-11-12

Item	Average Amount (In Rs)
Books & Stationary	850
Learning Material	565
Travel	270
Private Tuition Fee	700
Course Fee	1000
Medical Expenses	200
Food Expenses	294
Non Food Expenses	203
Debt Return	12
Total	4094

Source: Primary data based.

6.20 Utilization of Post-matric Scholarship Money: Graduation and above:

The role of Post-matric Scholarship in the educational development of minority students in graduation and above is paramount as major part of the Post-matric Scholarship money is reported to be spent on their education related needs (Table 6.19).

Table-6.19: Items wise Average Expenditure of Scholarship Amount: Students of Graduation and above

Item	Average Amount (In Rs)
Books & Stationary	920
Learning Material	645
Travel	280
Private Tuition Fee	600
Course Fee	1500
6- Medical Expenses	250
7- Food Expenses	395
8- Non Food Expenses	250
9- Debt Return	20
Total	4860

Source: Primary data based.

6.21 Effectiveness of Post-matric Scholarship:

The students have been very straight forth in replying about the effectiveness of Post-matric Scholarship. All of them said that they did not take the admission due to Post-matric Scholarship. There has been no improvement in their school attendance but all of them reported that the Post-matric Scholarship has been very useful to them in meeting their educational, family and health care needs (Table-6.20).

Table-6.20 Responses of Students on Effectiveness of Post-matric Scholarship

Particulars	Yes	No	Total
Admission Taken due to Scholarship	-	18 (100.00)	18 (100.00)
Attendance at the School Improved	-	18 (100.00)	18 (100.00)
Scholarship has Fulfilled Study Needs	18 (100.00)		18 (100.00)
Scholarship has Helped in Health Care Needs	15 (83.33)	3 (16.67)	18 (100.00)
Desire to Continue Studies after Getting Scholarship	18 (100.00)	-	18 (100.00)
Educational Skills has Improved	18 (100.00)	-	18 (100.00)
Involvement in the Household Activities has Reduced.	16 (88.89)	2 (11.11)	18 (100.00)
Scholarship has Helped in Family Needs	12 (66.67)	6 (33.33)	18 (100.00)
Chances to Continue Study in Higher Class and get a job increased	16 (88.89)	2 (11.11)	18 (100.00)

Note: Figures in brackets indicate percentages.

Source: Primary data based.

6.22 Perception of Students about Post-matric Scholarship:

The students feel that lack of awareness about Post-matric Scholarship, lengthy application form and it's language, too much documentation, untimely payment and limit of 50 per cent marks are the major problems associated with the Post-matric Scholarship (Table-6.21).

Table-6.21: Views of Students about Post-matric Scholarship Scheme

Views	Number of Students		
	Beneficiary	Non-beneficiary	Total
Lack of Awareness about the Detail of Scheme	16 (88.89)	14 (87.50)	30 (88.23)
Application Form is Lengthy & Language Problems	15 (83.33)	13 (81.25)	28 (82.35)
Too Much Documentation etc.	14 (77.77)	12 (75.00)	26 (76.47)
Untimely Payment	13 (72.22)	11 (68.75)	24 (70.59)
50 Percent limit of Marks	12 (66.67)	11 (68.75)	23 (67.65)
Income limit of 2 Lakh	9 (50.00)	8 (50.00)	17 (50.00)
Total Students	18 (100.00)	16 (100.00)	34 (100.00)

Note: Figures in brackets indicate percentages.
Source: Primary data based.

6.23 Main Findings:

- The complete awareness about the details of Post-matric Scholarship is limited to only 38.24 per cent of the sample students.
- The main source of awareness of Post-matric scholarship to students is the teachers of the institutions where the students study followed by the students who earlier got the scholarship.
- It is reported by 44.12 per cent of sample students that they are aware of the eligibility conditions of Post-matric Scholarship.
- It is evident that majority of students both beneficiary and non-beneficiary as well are not aware of each the three conditions of Post-matric Scholarship.
- The sample students have reported that 88.89 per cent of them received the Post-matric Scholarship of Rs.3000 to 4000.
- The mode of payment of Post-matric Scholarship is through cheque only as all the sample students have reported it.
- The beneficiary students have reported that they are given their Post-matric Scholarships by their teachers.
- There are two main items of expenditure. One is on getting income certificate and other on getting affidavit.
- The students have reported that most part of the money they get as Post-matric Scholarship is spent on the items related to their education. In this way, the role of Post-matric Scholarship in the educational development of minority students of classes 11-12 is paramount.

- The role of Post-matric Scholarship in the educational development of minority students in graduation and above is paramount as major part of the Post-matric Scholarship money is reported to be spent on their education related needs.
- The students have reported that the Post-matric Scholarship has been very useful to them in meeting their educational, family and health care needs.
- The students feel that lack of awareness about Post-matric Scholarship, lengthy application form and it's language, too much documentation, untimely payment and limit of 50 per cent marks, are the major problems associated with the Post-matric Scholarship

Problems in Getting Post-matric Scholarship and Suggestions of Students

6.24 Students Facing Difficulties while Applying:

Around 73 per cent of the sample students face problems while applying for the Post-matric Scholarship (Table-6.22).

Table-6.22: Number of Students Facing problems while applying for Post-matric cholarship

Students	Number
Beneficiary	13 (72.22)
Non-beneficiary	12 (75.00)
Total	25 (73.53)

Note: Figures in brackets indicate percentages.

Source: Primary data based.

6.25 Level of Difficulty in Obtaining Application Form:

The students have reported that around 65 per cent of them face difficulty while obtaining the

Table-6.23: Level of Difficulty in Obtaining Application Form: Response of Students

Level of difficulty	Number of Students		
	Beneficiary	Non-beneficiary	Total
Highly difficulty	2 (11.11)	2 (12.50)	4 (11.76)
Difficulty	13 (72.22)	9 (56.25)	22 (64.71)
Somewhat difficulty	2 (11.11)	4 (25.00)	6 (17.65)
No difficulty	1 (5.56)	1 (6.25)	2 (5.88)
Total	18 (100.00)	16 (100.00)	34 (100.00)

Note: Figures in brackets indicate percentages.

Source: Primary data base

application form of Post—matric Scholarship. Around 12 per cent of them also reported high level of difficulty in obtaining the application form of Post—matric Scholarship (Table-6.23).

6.26 Level of Difficulty in Filling Application Form:

In filling the application form, more than 60 per cent felt difficulty. Around 12 per cent of sample students reported high level of difficulty in filling the application form (Table-6.24).

Table-6.24: Level of Difficulty in Filling the Application Form: Response of Students

Level of difficulty	Number of Students		
	Beneficiary	Non-beneficiary	Total
Highly difficulty	2 (11.11)	2 (12.50)	4 (11.77)
Difficulty	11 (61.11)	10 (62.50)	21 (61.76)
Somewhat difficulty	3 (16.67)	3 (18.75)	6 (17.65)
No difficulty	2 (11.11)	1 (6.25)	3 (8.82)
Total	18 (100.00)	16 (100.00)	34 (100.00)

Note: Figures in brackets indicate percentages.
Source: Primary data based.

6.27 Level of Cooperation of Institutions:

The majority of beneficiary as well as non-beneficiary students reported to be satisfied with the cooperation of their institutions in helping them to get the Post-matric Scholarship to them.

Table-6.25: Level of Cooperation of Institutions in helping Students to get Post-matric Scholarship: Perception of Students

Level of Satisfaction	Number of Students		
	Beneficiary	Non-beneficiary	Total
Highly Satisfactory	3 (16.67)	2 (12.50)	5 (14.71)
Satisfactory	10 (55.55)	10 (62.50)	20 (58.82)
Unsatisfactory	3 (16.67)	3 (18.75)	6 (17.65)
Highly Unsatisfactory	2 (11.11)	1 (6.25)	3 (8.82)
Total	18 (100.00)	16 (100.00)	34 (100.00)

Note: Figures in brackets indicate percentages.
Source: Primary data based.

6.28 Role of State Government Officials:

Around 64 per cent of sample students are reported to be satisfied with the role of state government officials in getting the Post-matric Scholarship.

Table-6.26: Role of State Government Officials

Level of Satisfaction	Number of Students		
	Beneficiary	Non-beneficiary	Total
Highly Satisfactory	1 (5.56)	2 (12.50)	3 (8.82)
Satisfactory	12 (66.67)	10 (62.50)	22 (64.71)
Unsatisfactory	3 (16.66)	3 (18.75)	6 (17.65)
Highly Unsatisfactory	2 (11.11)	1 (6.25)	3 (8.82)
Total	18 (100.00)	16 (100.00)	34 (100.00)

Note: Figures in brackets indicate percentages.
Source: Primary data based.

6.29 Suggestions of Students for Improving the Post-matric Scholarship Scheme:

Six suggestions to improve the Post-matric Scholarship have been given by the students. These have been shown in table-6.27. The most important is that the income certificate given by the Sabhasad should be acceptable.

Table 6.27: Suggestions of Students in Improving the Scheme

Suggestions	Number of Students		
	Beneficiary	Non-beneficiary	Total
Awareness Campaign at Community, Institutions and Panchayat Level	16 (88.89)	16 (100.00)	32 (94.11)
Scholarship amount should be Increased.	18 (100.00)	14 (87.50)	32 (94.11)
Income certificate given by Sabhasad should be accepted	18 (100.00)	16 (100.00)	34 (100.00)
More than 2 children should be eligible from onle Family	17 (94.44)	9 (56.25)	26 (76.47)
Application form should be simple and multilingual.	17 (94.44)	12 (75.00)	29 (82.29)
No criteria of percentage of marks	16 (88.89)	12 (75.00)	28 (82.35)
Total Students	18 (100.00)	16 (100.00)	34 (100.00)

Note: Figures in brackets indicate percentages.
Source: Primary data based.

6.30 Main Findings:

- Around 73 per cent of the sample students face problems while applying for the Post-matric Scholarship.
- The students have reported that around 65 per cent of them face difficulty while obtaining the application form of Post—matric Scholarship. Around 12 per cent of them also reported high level of difficulty in obtaining the application form of Post—matric Scholarship.
- In filling the application form, more than 60 per cent felt difficulty. Around 12 per cent of sample students reported high level of difficulty in filling the application form.
- The majority of beneficiary as well as non-beneficiary students reported to be satisfied with the cooperation of their institutions in helping them to get the Post-matric Scholarship.
- Around 64 per cent of sample students are reported to be satisfied with the role of state government officials in helping them to get the Post-matric Scholarship.
- Six suggestions have been given by the students to improve the Post-matric Scholarship Scheme. The most important is that the income certificate given by the Sabhasad should be acceptable.

Parents of Beneficiary and Non-Beneficiary Students, Institutions and Officials

6.31 Sample Parents:

The total sample of parents was 19. The beneficiary parents were 10 and non-beneficiary parents were 9 as shown in the following table-6.28.

Table-6.28 Sample of the Parents

Particular	No. of Parents
Beneficiary Parents	10
Non-beneficiary Parents	9
Total	19

Note: Figures in brackets indicate percentages.
Source: Primary data based

6.32 Housing and Family Features:

Housing and family features have been shown in table-6.29. 84.21 per cent houses are pucca and 10.53 per cent are semi-pucca, having 3 rooms. The family size is of 6 persons. 89.47 per cent houses have electricity and all of them hold ration card.

Table-6.29: Housing and Family Conditions of Sample Parents

Particular	Beneficiary	Non-beneficiary Parents	Total
Type of House			
Kachcha	-	1 (11.11)	1 (5.26)
Pucca	9 (90.00)	7 (77.78)	16 (84.21)
Semi Pucca	1 (10.00)	1 (11.11)	2 (10.53)
Average Value of House (Rs.)	440615	455467	448038
Average No. of Rooms	3	3	3
Average Family Size	6	6	6
Average Earning Members in the family	2	2	2
House Electrified	9 (90.00)	8 (88.88)	17 (89.47)
Ration Card Holders			
BPL	1 (10.00)	1 (11.11)	2 (10.53)
APL	9 (90.00)	8 (88.89)	17 (89.47)
Total	10 (100.00)	9 (100.00)	19 (100.00)

Note: Figures in brackets indicate percentages.
Source: Primary data based

6.33 Land Size of Parents:

Being the urban based, land holdings are nominal (Table-6.30).

Table-6.30: Land Size of Parents

Land Holding	Beneficiary	Non-beneficiary Parents	Total
Less than 0.5 acre	1	-	1 (5.26)
0.5 to 1.00 acre	-	(11.11)	1 (5.26)
Average	0.27	1.00	0.64
Min	0.27	1.00	0.64
Max	0.27	1.00	0.64

Note: Figures in brackets indicate percentages.
Source: Primary data based.

6.34 Annual Income of Parents:

The table-6.31 shows that more than half of the sample parents have average annual income in the range of Rs. 20,001 to Rs, 50,000. Around one-fourth of them are also in the income range of Rs. 50,001 to Rs. 1,00,000. The percentage of beneficiaries in the income range of Rs. 50,001 to Rs. 1,00,000 are higher in comparison with non-beneficiaries.

Table-6.31: Annual Income of Parents

Income (Rs.)	Beneficiary	Non-beneficiary Parents	Total
Less than Rs. 20,000	1 (10.00)	-	1 (5.26)
20,001-50,000	5 (50.00)	6 (66.67)	11 (57.89)
50,001-1,00,000	3 (30.00)	2 (22.22)	5 (26.32)
1,00,001-1,50,000	1 (10.00)	1 (11.11)	2 (10.53)
Total	10 (100.00)	9 (100.00)	19 (100.00)

Note: Figures in brackets indicate percentages.
Source: Primary data based

6.35 Awareness about Post-matric Scholarship:

The awareness about the Post-matric scholarship is found to limited among parents. While 50 per cent parents of beneficiaries reported their awareness about the Post-matric Scholarship, 44.44 per cent parents of non-beneficiary reported their awareness about the Post-matric Scholarship.

Table-6.32: Parents Knowing the Post-Matric Scholarship Scheme

Particulars	Number of Parents
Beneficiary	5 (50.00)
Non- Beneficiary	4 (44.44)
Total	9 (47.37)

Note: Figures in brackets indicate percentages.
Source: Primary data based

6.36 Sources of Awareness of Post-matric Scholarship:

For majority of parents of beneficiary and non-beneficiary students, major sources of awareness of Post-matric scholarship are teachers, radio/TV and other students who did receive Post-matric Scholarship earlier (Table-6.33).

Table-6.33: Source of Awareness of Post-Matric Scholarship Scheme

Source	Number of Parents		
	Beneficiary	Non-beneficiary Parents	Total
Teachers	2 (40.00)	2 (50.00)	4 (44.45)
Radio/T.V	1 (20.00)	1 (25.00)	2 (22.22)
News Paper	1 (20.00)	-	1 (11.11)
Other students who have previously received the scholarship	1 (20.00)	1 (25.00)	2 (22.22)
Total Responses	5 (100.00)	4 (100.00)	9 (100.00)

Note: Figures in brackets indicate percentages.

Source: Primary data based.

6.37 Reasons of untimely payment of Post-matric Scholarship:

The beneficiary parents have given three reasons of untimely payment of post-matric scholarship which are as shown in table-6.34. On the top is the district officials followed by the Ministry of Minority Affairs for the delay in timely payment of Post-matric Scholarship.

Table-6.34: Reasons of Post-matric Scholarship not getting Timely

Reasons	Number of Parents
Delay by MOMA	2 (20.00)
Delay by District Authorities	4 (40.00)
Delay by the Institutions	1 (10.00)
Total	7 (70.00)

Note: Figures in brackets indicate percentages.

Source: Primary data based.

6.38 Problems Faced by Beneficiary Students: Perception of Parents:

53 per cent parents of beneficiary students felt that their ward faced problems in getting the post-matric scholarship (Table-6.35).

Table-6.35: Problems Faced by Students in getting the post-matric Scholarship: Parents Responses

Particulars	Number of Parents
	Total
Yes	10 (52.63)
No	9 (47.37)
Total	19 (100.00)

Note: Figures in brackets indicate percentages.
Source: Primary data based

6.39 Level of Difficulty Faced in Filling the Application Form: Perception of Parents:

All sample Parents are facing difficulties of various levels in filling the application form as evident in following table-6.36.

Table-6.36: Level of Difficulty in Filling the Application Form

Level of Difficulty	Number of Parents		
	Beneficiary	Non beneficiary	Total
High Difficulty	1 (10.00)	1 (11.11)	2 (10.52)
Difficulty	6 (60.00)	6 (66.67)	12 (63.16)
Some What Difficulty	2 (20.00)	1 (11.11)	3 (15.79)
Less Difficult	1 (10.00)	1 (11.11)	2 (10.53)
Total	10 (100.00)	9 (100.00)	19 (100.00)

Note: Figures in brackets indicate percentages.
Source: Primary data based.

6.40 Rating of Various Aspects of Post-matric Scholarship by Beneficiary Parents:

The rating of various aspects of Post-matric Scholarship by the beneficiary parents has been given in table-26.10. All the parents have given poor rating to the renewal process while amount of scholarship and support of school administration have been given average rating by 60 per cent parents. The availability of application form has received poor rating by 50 per cent parents. (Table-6.37)

Table-6.37 Rating of various Aspects of Post-matric Scholarship Scheme by Beneficiary Parents

Particulars	Number of Parents			
	Poor	Average	Good	Total
Scholarship Amount	3 (30.00)	6 (60.00)	1 (10.00)	10 (100.00)
Documentation	6 (60.00)	2 (20.00)	2 (20.00)	10 (100.00)
Renewal Process	10 (100.00)	-	-	10 (100.00)
Availability of Application Form	5 (50.00)	4 (40.00)	1 (10.00)	10 (100.00)
Timeliness of Processing	3 (30.00)	5 (50.00)	2 (20.00)	10 (100.00)
Support of School Administration	3 (30.00)	6 (60.00)	1 (10.00)	10 (100.00)

Note: Figures in brackets indicate percentages.

Source: Primary data based.

6.41 Rating of Various Aspects of Post-matric Scholarship by Non-beneficiary Parents:

The non-beneficiary parents have given the following rating to various aspects of Post-matric Scholarship which has been shown in table-6.38. The timeliness of processing has got poor rating by all non-beneficiary parents while 56 per cent has given poor rating to documentation. The

Table-6.38: Rating of various Aspects of Post-matric Scholarship Scheme by Non-beneficiary Parents

Particulars	Number of Parents				
	Poor	Average	Good	Very good	Total
Scholarship Amount	2 (22.22)	5 (55.56)	1 (11.11)	1 (11.11)	9 (100.00)
Documentation	5 (55.56)	2 (22.22)	1 (11.11)	1 (11.11)	9 (100.00)
Renewal Process	3 (33.33)	-	-	-	9 (100.00)
Availability of Application Form	3 (33.33)	3 (33.33)	2 (22.22)	1 (11.12)	9 (100.00)
Timeliness of Processing	9 (100.00)	3 (33.33)	3 (33.34)	-	9 (100.00)
Support of School Administration	2 (22.22)	6 (66.67)	1 (11.11)	-	9 (100.00)

Note: Figures in brackets indicate percentages.

Source: Primary data based

scholarship amount and support of school administration have received average rating by 67 per cent and 56 per cent parents respectively.

6.42 Parents Perceptions on Scholarship:

The following views were expressed by the parents about the Post-matric Scholarship Scheme:

Table-6.39: Observations of Sample Parents about Post-matric Scholarship Scheme

1.	Scholarship is helpful for students in their education.
2.	Lack of Awareness about Post-Matric Scholarship Scheme implemented by MOMA Government of India.
3.	Lack of Knowledge about important dates of Scheme.
4.	Non-Corporative attitude of Government educational Institutions.
5.	Application Form is lengthy.
6.	Applying process is costly due to arrangement of various types of certificates like Income Certificate, Affidavit etc.
7.	Delayed processing and late distribution of Scholarship.

6.43 Main Findings:

- **Housing and family features indicate that 84.21 per cent houses are pucca and 10.53 per cent are semi-pucca, having 3 rooms. The family size is of 6 persons. 89.47 per cent houses are electricity and all of them hold ration card.**
- **Being the urban based, land holdings are nominal.**
- More than half of the sample parents have average annual income in the range of Rs. 20,001 to Rs, 50,000. Around one-fourth of them are also in the income range of Rs. 50,001 to Rs. 1, 00,000.
- While 50 per cent parents of beneficiaries reported their awareness about the Post-matric Scholarship, 44.44 per cent parents of non-beneficiary reported their awareness about the Post-matric Scholarship.
- For majority of parents of beneficiary and non-beneficiary students, major sources of awareness of Post-matric scholarship are teachers, radio/TV and other students who did receive Post-matric Scholarship earlier.
- The beneficiary parents have given three reasons of untimely payment of Post-matric scholarship. On the top is the district officials followed by the Ministry of Minority Affairs for the delay in timely payment of Post-matric Scholarship.
- 53 per cent parents of beneficiary students felt that their ward faced problems in getting the Post-matric scholarship.

- All sample Parents are facing difficulties of various levels in filling the application form.
- All the parents have given poor rating to the renewal process while amount of scholarship and support of school administration have been given average rating by 60 per cent parents. The availability of application form has received poor rating by 50 per cent parents.
- The timeliness of processing has got poor rating by all non-beneficiary parents while 56 per cent has given poor rating to documentation. The scholarship amount and support of school administration have received average rating by 67 per cent and 56 per cent parents respectively.
- The parents made the observations that Post-matric Scholarship is helpful for students in their educational needs, there is lack of awareness among the minority community about the scheme, there is non-cooperative attitude of the institutions where their wards study, application form is lengthy, application process is costly and there are delays in processing and distribution of Post-matric Scholarship.

6.44 Sample Institutions:

The two sample institutions are government owned and two are private located in urban part of the Indore district as per following table-6.40.

Table-6.40: Basic Information on Surveyed Institutions

Name of School	Category of the Institutions	Type
Government Holkar Science College, Indore	Degree College	Government
Government Kasturba Girls Higher Secondary School, Indore	Inter College	Government
Mata JijaBai Girls P.G. College	P.G. College	Private
Naurilal Senior Secondary School, Indore	Inter College	Private

6.45 Award of Post-matric Scholarship to Muslim Students:

In Government Holkar Science College, Indore 11.46 per cent and 11.18 per cent of all enrolled Muslim students applied for the Post-matric Scholarship during 2009-10 and 2010-11. Out of those who applied, 10.20 per cent in 2009-10 and 11.32 in 2010-11 received the Post-matric Scholarship.

Table-6.41: Students Enrolled, Applied and Awarded Scholarship: Government Holkar Science

Year	Muslim Students								
	Enrolled			Applied			Awarded		
	Male	Female	Total	Male	Female	Total	Male	Female	Total
2009-2010	282 (100.00)	145 (100.00)	427 (100.00)	30 (10.64)	19 (13.10)	49 (11.46)	3 (10.00)	2 (10.53)	5 (10.20)
2010-2011	302 (100.00)	172 (100.00)	474 (100.00)	32 (10.60)	21 (12.21)	53 (11.18)	4 (12.50)	2 (9.52)	6 (11.32)

Source: Records of the Institutions.

6.46 Award of Post-matric Scholarship to Muslim Students:

In Government Kasturba Girls Higher Secondary School, Indore, 22.94 per cent of all enrolled Muslim girl students applied for the Post-matric Scholarship during 2010-11. Out of those who applied, 16.98 per cent received the Post-matric Scholarship.

Table-6.42: Students Enrolled, Applied and Awarded Scholarship: Government Kasturba Girls

Years	Muslim Students								
	Enrolled			Applied			Awarded		
	Male	Female	Total	Male	Female	Total	Male	Female	Total
2010-11	-	462 (100.00)	462 (100.00)	-	106 (22.94)	106 (22.94)		18 (16.98)	18 (16.98)

Source: Records of the Institutions

6.47 Award of Post-matric Scholarship to Muslim Students:

In Mata JijaBai Girls P.G. College, Indore 22.84 per cent of all enrolled Muslim girl students applied for the Post-matric Scholarship during 2010-11. Out of those who applied, only 3.57 per cent received the Post-matric Scholarship.

Table-6.43: Students Enrolled, Applied and Awarded Scholarship : Mata JijaBai Girls P.G. College

Years	Muslim Students								
	Enrolled			Applied			Awarded		
	Male	Female	Total	Male	Female	Total	Male	Female	Total
2010-11	-	612 (100.00)	612 (100.00)	-	140 (22.88)	140 (22.88)	-	5 (3.57)	5 (3.57)

Source: Records of the Institutions

6.48 Award of Post-matric Scholarship to Muslim Students:

In Naurilal Senior Secondary School, Indore, Indore, 14.82 per cent and 22.86 per cent of all enrolled Muslim students applied for the Post-matric Scholarship during 2009-10 and 2010-11. Out of those who applied, 12.05 per cent in 2009-10 and 14.71 per cent in 2010-11 received the Post-matric Scholarship.

Table-6.44 Students Enrolled, Applied and Awarded Scholarship : Naurilal Senior Secondary

Years	Muslim Students								
	Enrolled			Applied			Awarded		
	Male	Female	Total	Male	Female	Total	Male	Female	Total
2009-10	390 (100.00)	170 (100.00)	560 (100.00)	60 (15.38)	23 (13.53)	83 (14.82)	6 (10.00)	4 (17.39)	10 (12.05)
2010-11	398 (100.00)	197 (100.00)	595 (100.00)	100 (25.13)	36 (18.27)	136 (22.86)	11 (11.00)	9 (25.00)	20 (14.71)

Source: Records of the Institutions.

6.49 Reasons for Non- Award of Scholarship:

Lack of awareness about the scheme, lengthy application form and language problem and too much formality are the three most important reasons given by the institutions for non-award of Post-matric Scholarship to Muslim students.

Table-6.45: Important Reasons for Students Not being Awarded Scholarship

Reasons	No. of Institutions
Lack of Awarness About the Scheme	4 (100.00)
Lenthy Application Form And Language Problem	4 (100.00)
To Much Formality	4 (100.00)
Delay Payment of Schlorship	3 (75.00)

Source: Staff of the Institutions

6.50 Level of satisfaction of Institutions with State Government:

No sample institution has reported dissatisfaction with the state government as far the timely processing of applications, timely release of fund, and staff behavior is concerned. The institutions are very satisfied or satisfied with the involvement of state government in different processes of Post-matric scholarship.

Table-6.46: Satisfaction Level of Institutions with State Government

Heads	Level of Satisfaction	
	Very Satisfied	Satisfied
Timely Processing of Applications	1 (25.00)	3 (75.00)
Timely Release of Funds	3 (75.00)	1 (25.00)
Staff Behaviour	2 (50.00)	2 (50.00)
No. of Institutions	4	

6.51 Level of satisfaction of Institutions with Central Government:

No sample institution has reported dissatisfaction with the central government as far the timely processing of applications, timely release of fund, and staff behavior is concerned. The institutions are very satisfied or satisfied with the involvement of central government in different processes of Post-matric scholarship.

Table-6.47: Institutions' Level of Satisfaction with Central Government Agencies

Heads	Level of Satisfaction	
	Very Satisfied	Satisfied
Timely Processing of Approval	3 (75.00)	1 (25.00)
Timely Release of Funds	2 (50.00)	2 (50.00)
Staff Behaviour	1 (25.00)	3 (75.00)

6.52 Bottlenecks in the Education System:

Majority of institutions have reported that they face the bottleneck of lack of qualified teachers.

Table-6.48: Bottlenecks Faced in the Education System

Bottlenecks	No. of Institutions
Inefficient Teaching Methods	1 (25.00)
Lack of Qualified Teachers	3 (75.00)
Number of Institutions	4 (100.00)

6.53. Data Management:

In 3 out 4 sample institutions, method of data management is manual.

Table-6.49: Methods of Data Management

Procedure	No. of Institutions
Manual	3 (75.00)
Semi- Computerized	1 (25.00)
Fully Computer	-
Number of Institutions	4 (100.00)

6.54 Availability of Guidelines of Post-matric Scholarship:

All the sample institutions have reported that they have the guidelines of the Post-matric Scholarship.

Table-6.50: Availability of Guidelines of Post-matric Scholarship

Particulars	Responses	
	Yes	No
Guidelines Available about the Scheme with District Minority Welfare Officer	√	
Scheme Implemented as per Guidelines	√	
Guidelines Followed Easily	√	

Source: District Schedule Tribe Welfare Coordinator, Indore

6.55 Problems of Post-matric Scholarship: Institutions Views:

Table-6.51 Problems Regarding Implementation of the Scheme

Application form is lengthy and complicated.
Language problem
No fund allotted by MOMA for advertisement of the scheme
Separate staff not available for managing the Scheme
Required computers not provided by MOMA

6.56 Main Findings:

- In the total Enrolment of Muslim students in all the four sample institutions, 13.14 per cent of them applied for the Post-matric Scholarship and 11.13 of those applied were awarded the Post- Matric Scholarship in 2009-10. In 2010-11, 14.24 per cent of enrolled students applied but 11.65 per cent of applied got the Post-matric scholarship. Thus, the outreach of minority students for the Post-matric Scholarship has been very limited in Indore district.
- Lack of awareness about the scheme, lengthy application form, language problem and too much formality are the four most important reasons given by the institutions for few award of Post-matric Scholarships to Muslim students in Indore district.
- All sample institution has reported satisfaction with the state government as far the timely processing of applications, timely release of fund, and staff behavior is concerned.
- The institutions are very satisfied or satisfied with the MOMA in different processes of Post-matric scholarship.
- The data management of Post-matric Scholarship at the institutions level is mostly manual.

District Officials

6.57 On the Guidelines:

The Officers of District Scheduled Tribes Welfare Department at Indore reported that guidelines of the Post- matric Scholarship are available and the scheme is implemented as per guidelines.

Table-6.52: Availability of Guidelines of Post-matric Scholarship

Particular	Responses	
	Yes	No
Guidelines Available about the Scheme with District Minority Welfare Officer	√	
Scheme Implemented as per Guidelines	√	
Guidelines Followed Easily	√	

Source: Response of District Minority Welfare Officer, Indore

6.58 Selection Criteria:

The officials reported that in selection process, apart from the marks obtained in the previous examination, poverty and girls students are given the preference.

6.59 Problems Regarding Implementations the Scheme:

The shortage of staff and non-availability of computers are the two man problems faced in course of implementation of scheme in the district

6.60 Awardees of Post-matric Scholarship:

The number of awardees of the Post-matric Scholarship was just 27 in 2009-10 which increased to 40 during 2010-11 in entire Indore district which indicates poor implementation of scheme in the district.

Table-6.53.: Year and Religion wise Number of Awardee Students of Post-matric Scholarship

Year	Religion	Number of Awardee Students		
		Boys	Girls	Total
2009-2010	Muslim	9	5	14
	Sikh	7	6	13
	Total	16	11	27
2010-11	Muslim	4	25	29
	Sikh	6	5	11
	Total	10	30	40

Source: District Schedule Tribe Welfare, Indore

6.61 Utilization of Grant of Post-matric Scholarship:

In both the years, meager grant was sanctioned and it was utilized entirely.

Table-6.54: Grant Approval and utilization (In Rs. Lakh)

Year	Grants Approved/Sanctioned	Grants Utilized
2009-10	3.36	3.36
2010-11	13.14	13.14

Source: District Schedule Tribe Welfare, Indore

6.62 Satisfaction with MOMA

The district officials reported to be satisfied with the MOMA as shown in following table-26.28.

Table 6.55: Satisfaction Level with MOMA

Major Head	Satisfaction Level
Timely Processing of approval	Satisfied
Timely Release of Funds	Satisfied
Staff Behavior	Very Satisfied

Source: Response of District Schedule Tribe Welfare Coordinator, Indore

6.63 Time Spent in Disbursement of Post- matric Scholarship:

The officials have reported that six months' time is required in entire processing of Post-matric Scholarship.

Table-6.56: Time Spent in Disbursement of Post- matric Scholarship

Proposal sent to MOMA:	October
Sanctioned:	January
Scholarship Reached the District:	February
Scholarship Disbursed:	March

6.64 Impact of Post- Matric Scholarship:

A .Scholarship scheme has enhanced Enrolment of student belonging to minority communities.
B. Scholarship amount provided adequate cover to the student to meet their study needs.
C. Improving the educational achievement level of students.
6.65 Suggestions for Improvement of Post-matric Scholarship:
4. Funds for awareness of the Scheme should be allotted by MOMA
5. Staff should be recruited under the scholarship scheme
6. Availability of application form to ensued in easy way and Hindi version.

6.65 Main Findings:

- The Officers of District Scheduled Tribes Welfare Department at Indore reported that guidelines of the Post- matric Scholarship are available and the scheme is implemented as per guidelines.
- The officials reported that in selection process, apart from the marks obtained in the previous examination, poverty and girls students are given the preference.

- The shortage of staff and non-availability of computers are the two man problems faced in course of implementation of scheme in the district
- The number of awardees of the Post-matric Scholarship was just 27 in 2009-10 which increased to 40 during 2010-11 in entire Indore district which indicates poor implementation of scheme in the district.
- In 2009-10 and 2010-11, meager grant was sanctioned and it was utilized entirely.
- The district officials reported to be satisfied with the MOMA as shown in following table-5.30.
- The officials have reported that six months' time is required in entire processing of Post-matric Scholarship.
- The officials felt that the impact of Post-Matric Scholarship was positive in enhancing the Enrolment of students belonging to minority communities, the scholarship provided adequate cover to the student to meet their study needs and it helped in improving the educational achievement level of students.
- The officials also Suggested that funds for awareness of the Scheme should be allotted by MOMA, Staff should be recruited under the scholarship scheme and availability of application form should be ensured and it should be Hindi language.

Chapter-VII

Introduction : Merit cum Means based Scholarship—Indore District

7.1 Sample of the Study:

The institution based methodology was adopted for the study of Merit cum Means based Scholarship as was done in case of earlier two schemes of scholorships. The sample for the evaluation of Scheme of Merit cum Means based Scholarship was drawn from the same urban wards of Indore district from where the sample of previous two scholarship scheme was taken. Thus, sample size to study the Scheme of Merit cum Means Scholarship is as shown in following table-7.1. All recipients of the Merit cum Means based Scholarship were taken in the sample on census basis.

Table-7.1: Sample Size of the Study of Merit cum Means based Scholarship: Students

Particular	Beneficiary	Non-beneficiary	Total
Boys	2 (50.00)	3 (100.00)	5 (71.43)
Girls	2 (50.00)	-	2 (28.57)
Total	4 (100.00)	3 (100.00)	7 (100.00)

Note: Figures in brackets indicate percentages.
Source: Primary data based.

Characteristics of Sample Students of Merit cum Means based Scholarship

7.2 Age of Students:

The classification of sample students as per their age indicated that majority of them (beneficiaries as well non-beneficiaries) is in the age group of 18-21 years (Table-7.2).

Table-7.2: Classification of Sample Students according to their Age

Age-Group	Beneficiary	Non-beneficiary	Total
18-21 Years	2 (50.00)	2 (66.67)	4 (57.14)
22-23 Years	2 (50.00)	1 (33.33)	3 (42.86)
Total	4 (100.00)	3 (100.00)	7 (100.00)

Note: Figures in brackets indicate percentages.

Source: Primary data based.

7.3 Occupations:

Trade and salaried jobs are the two main occupations of the families of sample students.

Table-7.3: Classification of Sample Students according to their Family Occupations

Occupation	Beneficiary	Non-beneficiary	Total
Agriculture	-	1 (33.33)	1 (14.28)
Trade	2 (50.00)	1 (33.33)	3 (42.86)
Salaried (Private/ Government)	2 (50.00)	1 (33.34)	3 (42.86)
Total	4 (100.00)	3 (100.00)	7 (100.00)

Note: Figures in brackets indicate percentages.

Source: Primary data based.

7.4 Type of Institutions:

More than half of the students are from the private institutions.

Table-7.4: Type of Institutions of Students

Type of Institution	No. of Students
Government	3 (42.86)
Private	4 (57.14)
Total	7 (100.00)

Note: Figures in brackets indicate percentages.

Source: Primary data based.

7.5 Family Income of Students:

The average annual income of all students' families was between Rs. 1, 50,000 to Rs. 2,00,000.

Table-7.5: Annual Income of Students Households

Category of Income (Rs.)	Beneficiary	Non-Beneficiary	Total
150000-200000	4 (100.00)	3 (100.00)	7 (100.00)
Above 200000	-	-	-
Total	4 (100.00)	3 (100.00)	7 (100.00)

Note: Figures in brackets indicate percentages.

Source: Primary data based.

7.6 Courses of Study of Students:

It reflects from table-7.6 that students are studying in various types of technical/professional courses. But 71.42 per cent of them are studying management course of MBA.

Table-7.6: Students Studying in Different Courses

Particulars		MBA	MCA	BCA	Total
Boys	Beneficiary	1 (50.00)	1 (50.00)	-	2 (100.00)
	Non-beneficiary	2 (66.67)	-	1 (33.33)	3 (100.00)
	Total	3 (60.00)	1 (20.00)	1 (20.00)	5 (100.00)
Girls	Beneficiary	2 (100.00)	-	-	2 (100.00)
	Non Beneficiary	-	-	-	-
	Total	2 (100.00)	-	-	2 (100.00)
All Students		5 (71.42)	1 (14.29)	1 (14.29)	7 (100.00)

Note: Figures in brackets indicate percentages.

Source: Primary data based.

7.7 Main Findings:

- It was evident that indicated that majority of beneficiaries and non-beneficiaries students of Merit cum Means based Scholarship was in the age group of 18-21 years
- Trade and salaried jobs were the two main occupations of the families of sample students.
- More than half of the students were studying in the private institutions.

- The average annual income of all students' families was between **Rs. 1,50,000 to Rs.** 2,00,000.
- The sample students were studying in various types of technical/professional courses and 71.42 per cent of them were studying management course of MBA.

Students Views about Merit cum Means based Scholarship

7.8 Amount of Scholarship:

The students have reported that they received average amount of Rs, 23,300 **under this** scholarship.

Table-7.7 : Amount of Scholarship Received

Sex	Amount (in Rs.)		
	Course Fee	Maintenance Fee	Total
Boys	13500	10800	24300
Girls	12600	9600	22200
Total	13060	10240	23300

Source: Primary data based.

7.9 Items of expenditure:

Most of the amount of scholarship was spent on education related items.

Table-7.8: Item wise Average Expenditure of Scholarship Amount : Beneficiary Students

Item	Average Amount (Rs.)
Book & Stationary etc.	3250
School Dress	1150
Learning Materials	2250
Travelling Expenditure	2000
Course Fees	3850
Medical Expenditure	1200
Total	13700

Source: Primary data based.

7.10 Sources of Information of Merit cum Means Scholarship:

For more than half of the students, institutions are the source of information about the scheme.

Table-7.9: Sources of Information about the Scheme to Students

Sources	Number of Student		
	Beneficiary	Non-beneficiary	Total
Institutions	2 (50.00)	2 (66.67)	4 (57.14)
News Papers	2 (50.00)	1 (33.33)	3 (42.86)
Total	4 (100.00)	3 (100.00)	7 (100.00)

Note: Figures in brackets indicate percentages.

Source: Primary data based.

7.11 Level of Difficulty Faced by the Students in getting the Scholarship:

50 per cent students reported that they faced no difficulty while 50 per cent faced somewhat difficulty in receiving the scholarship.

Table-7.10: Level of Difficulty Faced by Students in receiving the Scholarship

Level of Difficulty	Number of Students
High Difficulty	-
Difficulty	-
Somewhat Difficulty	2 (50.00)
No Difficulty	2 (50.00)
Total	4 (100.00)

Note: Figures in brackets indicate percentages.

Source: Primary data based.

7.12 Satisfaction with Scholarship Amount:

50 per cent students are reported to be satisfied and 50 per cent unsatisfied with the scholarship amount.

Table-7.11: Response of Beneficiary Students on the Satisfaction with Scholarship Amount

Particular	Number of Response		
	Yes	No	Total
Boys	1 (50.00)	1 (50.00)	2 (100.00)
Girls	1 (50.00)	1 (50.00)	2 (100.00)
Total	2 (50.00)	2 (50.00)	4 (100.00)

Note: Figures in brackets indicate percentages.

Source: Primary data based.

7.13 Level of Satisfaction:

All the students have reported average level of satisfaction with the reimbursement of course fee.

Table-7.12: Level of Satisfaction with Method of Reimbursement of Course Fee : Beneficiary Students

Items	Boys	Girls	Total
Satisfaction	-	-	-
Average	2 (100.00)	2 (100.00)	4 (100.00)
Poor	-	-	-
Total	2 (100.00)	2 (100.00)	4 (100.00)

Note: Figures in brackets indicate percentages.
Source: Primary data based.

7.14 Perception about Merit cum Means based Scholarship:

Around 57 per cent students have given poor rating to various aspects of merit cum Means based Scholarship.

Table-7.13: Perception about various Aspects of Merit Cum Means Scholarship

Particular	Good	Average	Poor	Total
Documentation	-	3 (50.00)	3 (50.00)	6 (100.00)
Eligibility	2 (28.57)	3 (42.86)	2 (28.57)	7 (100.00)
Scholarship Amount	2 (28.57)	2 (28.57)	3 (42.86)	7 (100.00)
Mode of Payment	1 (14.29)	2 (28.57)	4 (57.14)	7 (100.00)
Time of Reimbursement of Scholarship	1 (14.29)	2 (28.57)	4 (57.14)	7 (100.00)

Note: Figures in brackets indicate percentages.
Source: Primary data based.

7.15 Future Plan of Students:

More than 71 per cent students want to search job in future.

Table-7.14: Future Plans of Students

Plans	Beneficiary Students			Non-beneficiary Students			Total Students		
	Boys	Girls	Total	Boys	Girls	Total	Boys	Girls	Total
Search of Employment	2 (100.00)	1 (50.00)	3 (75.00)	2 (66.67)	-	2 (66.67)	4 (80.00)	1 (50.00)	5 (71.43)
Start Self Employment	-	1 (50.00)	1 (25.00)	1 (33.33)	-	1 (33.33)	1 (20.00)	1 (50.00)	2 (28.57)
Total	2 (100.00)	2 (100.00)	4 (100.00)	3 (100.00)	-	3 (100.00)	5 (100.00)	2 (100.00)	7 (100.00)

Note: Figures in brackets indicate percentages.

Source: Primary data based.

7.16 Level of satisfaction with Institutions:

Around 43 per cent students are found to be dissatisfied with their institutions.

Table-7.15: Level of Satisfaction with Institutions

Level of Satisfaction	Beneficiary Students	Non-beneficiary Students	Total Students
Very Satisfied	2 (50.00)	-	2 (28.57)
Satisfied	1 (25.00)	1 (33.33)	2 (28.57)
Dissatisfied	1 (25.00)	2 (66.67)	3 (42.86)
Total	4 (100.00)	3 (100.00)	7 (100.00)

Note: Figures in brackets indicate percentages.

Source: Primary data based.

7.17 Level of Satisfaction with the State Government:

More than half of the students have reported to be dissatisfied with the state government officials who oversee the Merit cum Means Scholarship.

Table-7.16: Level of Satisfaction with State Government

Level of Satisfaction	Beneficiary Students	Non-beneficiary Students	Total Students
Very Satisfaction	2 (50.00)		2 (28.57)
Satisfaction	1 (25.00)	-	1 (14.29)
Dissatisfaction	1 (25.00)	3 (100.00)	4 (57.14)
Total	4 (100.00)	3 (100.00)	7 (100.00)

Note: Figures in brackets indicate percentages.

Source: Primary data based.

7.18 Impact of the Scheme:

The students find the impact of Merit cum means Scholarship very helpful and positive in their education.

Table-7.17: Impact of Merit cum Means based Scholarship: Students Views

Particular	No. of Beneficiary		
	Boys	Girls	Total
Great help in continuation of education	1 (50.00)	1 (50.00)	2 (50.00)
Scholarship helped them to get higher education	1 (50.00)	1 (50.00)	2 (50.00)
Improvement in quality of education	-	-	-
Total Sample Beneficiaries	2 (100.00)	2 (100.00)	4 (100.00)

Note: Figures in brackets indicate percentages.
Source: Primary data based.

7.19 Suggestions:

Following Suggestions have been given by the students for improvement of Merit cum Means based Scholarship:

1. Distribution of Scholarship should be timely.
2. 50 percent mark should not be compulsory for getting scholarship.
3. Processes of application should be made easy.
4. The scholarship should be distributed at the time of admission.
5. Scholarship Scheme should be for all students of Minorities.

7.20 Main Findings:

- The students have reported that they received average amount of Rs, 23,300 under Merit cum Means based Scholarship.
- Most of the amount of scholarship was spent on education related items.
- For more than half of the students, institutions were the source of information about the scheme.
- 50 per cent students reported that they faced no default while 50 per cent faced somewhat difficulty in receiving the scholarship.
- 50 per cent students reported to be satisfied and 50 per cent unsatisfied with the scholarship amount.
- All the students reported average level of satisfaction with the reimbursement of course fee.
- Around 57 per cent students have given poor rating to various aspects of merit cum Means based Scholarship.
- Around 43 per cent students were found to be dissatisfied with their institutions.

- **More than half of the students have reported to be dissatisfied with the state government officials who oversee the Merit cum Means Scholarship.**
- **The students find the impact of Merit cum means Scholarship very helpful and positive in their education.**
- **The students have suggested that distribution of scholarship should be timely, 50 percent mark should not be compulsory for getting scholarship, process of application should be made easy, the scholarship should be distributed at the time of admission and scholarship scheme should be for all students of Minorities.**

Merit cum Means based Scholarship: Role and Views of Institutions and District Officials

7.21 Award of MCM:

Around 3 per cent of enrolled minority students applied for MCM and all of them got the scholarship.

Table-7.18: Enrolment of Minority Students and their Application for MCM

Name of Institute	Knowledge of MCM		Total Students Enrolled	% of Minority Students	No. of Students applied for Scholarship		Application Forwarded to State Department	
	Yes	No			2009-10	2010-11	2009-10	2010-11
School of Computer Science, Indore	1	-	430 (100.00)	8.35	12 (2.79)	14 (3.26)	12 (2.79)	14 (3.26)
Devi Ahilya Vishwavidhyal, Indore	1	-	740 (100.00)	9.35	22 (2.97)	26 (3.51)	22 (2.967)	26 (3.51)
M.B. Khalsa, Indore	1	-	540 (100.00)	16.52	15 (2.78)	18 (3.33)	15 (2.78)	18 (3.33)

Source: Sample Institutions.

7.22 Processing of Applications:

Processing time was 30 days and institutions were satisfied with the reimbursement after getting the money from the state government department. The processing was manual in 1 out of 3 institutes.

Table-7.19: Processing of Applications

Name of Institute	Method of Processing of Application	If through Computer, By whom	No. of computer used	Ave. no. of days involved in processing of Application	Time taken in reimbursement of course fee after getting from state department	satisfaction with the co-operation of state department
School of Computer Science, Indore	Computer	Institution Employee	2	30	Satisfied	Satisfied
Devi Ahilya Vishwavidhyal, Indore	Manually	-	-	30	Satisfied	Satisfied
M.B. Khalsa, Indore	Computer	Institution Employee	2	30	Satisfied	Satisfied

Source: Sample Institutions.

7.23 Impact of Merit cum Means scholarship:

The institutions have reported that improvement in education level of recipient students was good and there was no drop out of students who got the scholarship.

Table-7.20: Impact of Merit cum Means based Scholarship

Name of Institute	Time taken for reimbursement of course fee to students	Any student dropout from course		Improvement in level of education	Impact of MCM scheme
		Yes	No		
School of Computer Science, Indore	30 days	-	✓	Good	Improvement in admission of Minority Students
Devi Ahilya Vishwavidhyal, Indore	30 days	-	✓	Good	Improvement in admission of Minority Students
M.B. Khalsa, Indore	30 days	-	✓	Very Good	Improvement in admission of Minority Students

Source: Sample Institutions.

7.24 Assessment of Scholarship:

The assessment of institutions about the MCM Scholarship was satisfactory as evident in following table.

Table-7.21: Assessment of MCM Scheme

Very Satisfied	Satisfied	Little Satisfied	Unsatisfied
-	✓	-	-
-	✓	-	-

Source: Sample Institutions.

District Level Official :

7.25 Selection of Candidates :

The district officials have reported that appointment of a nodal officer was done by the State government and number of candidates to be given MCM Scholarship was decided as per population of minorities in the state.

Table-7.22: Selection of Candidates

Particulars	Responses	
	Yes	No
Appointment of Nodal Officer by State Govt. for implementation of the scheme	✓	
Sufficient time has been given for applying the scheme	✓	
Number of student applied for the scholarship	NA	
Number of awardees students of scholarship	NA	
Scholarship provided to Girls student	NA	
Selection of candidate on the basis of minority population of the State.	✓	

Source: District Schedule Tribes Welfare Department, Indore.

7.26 Process of Selection:

The list is loaded on website and linked with the website of the MOMA. Online applications are invited. There is full computerization of data.

Table-7.23: Process of Selection

Particulars	Responses	
	Yes	No
The list of selected candidate has been floated on website	✓	
Website hyperlinked with the Ministry of Minority Affairs' Website	✓	
Applications have been invited online for scholarship	✓	
Process of sorting of application form is manually		✓
Status of computerization of data	Fully computerized	

Source: District Schedule Tribes Welfare Department, Indore.

7.27 Distribution of Scholarship:

The distribution is through the cheques.

Table-7.24: Distribution Method of Scholarship Amount

Particulars	Responses	
	Yes	No
Mode of Scholarship Amount	Through Cheque	
Progress Report sent to Central Govt.	✓	
Satisfaction level of cooperation of Central Govt.	Satisfied	
Status of computerization of data management in College/Institutions	Fully Computer	
Any separate bank account and record available	✓	

Source: District Schedule Tribes Welfare Department, Indore.

7.28 Main Findings:

- The classification of sample students as per their age indicated that majority of them (beneficiaries as well non-beneficiaries) was in the age group of 18-21 years.
- Trade and salaried jobs were the two main occupations of the families of sample students.
- More than half of the students were from private institutions.
- The average annual income of around all students families was between Rs. 1,50,000 to Rs. 2,00,000.
- It reflects that students were studying in various types of technical/professional courses. But around 71.42 per cent of them were studying management course of MBA.
- The average amount of Rs, 23,300 was received in this scholarship.
- Most of the amount of scholarship was spent on education related items.
- For more than half of the students, institutions are the source of information about the scheme.
- 50 per cent students reported that they faced no default while 50 per cent faced somewhat difficulty in receiving the scholarship.
- 50 per cent students reported to be satisfied and 50 per cent unsatisfied with the scholarship amount.
- The students have reported average level of satisfaction with the reimbursement of course fee.
- Around 57 per cent students have given poor rating to various aspects of merit cum Means based Scholarship.
- More than 71 per cent wants to search job in future.
- Around 43 per cent students were dissatisfied with their institutions.
- More than half of the students have reported to be dissatisfied with the state government officials who oversee the merit cum Means Scholarship.
- The students find the impact of merit cum means Scholarship very helpful and positive in their education.
- Distribution of Scholarship should be timely, 50 percent mark should not be compulsory for getting scholarship, Easy Processes for scholarship Scheme, scholarship should be

distributed at the time of admission and Scholarship Scheme should be for all students of Minorities are the suggestions of the students.

- Around 3 per cent of enrolled minority students applied for MCM and all of them got the scholarship.
- The improvement in education was good and there was no drop out of students who got the scholarship.

Field Observations, Key Issues and Suggestions: Merit cum Means based Scholarship

7.29 Field Observations:

The discussion with the recipient students of Merit cum Means based Scholarship in the field indicated that untimely payment of scholarship amount is great problem to them. Generally the students take admission in the month of April/May. But the payment of scholarship to them takes many months. The second problem is that the amount of scholarship is quite meager in view of high course fee paid by them. The renewal is also problem to them. One more observation in case of Indore district is that the reach of MCM Scholarship has been very poor in the district and the role of concerned officials has also been inactive. The concerned officials as has been observed in case of other scholarships of MOMA take very little interest in MCM Scholarship also. As result, students and institutions face harassment. In this way entire process of scholarship distribution is slowed down and ultimately the students suffer.

7.30 Key Issues of MCM Scholarship:

- Untimely payment to students as a result of delayed processing of applications.
- The amount of Scholarship is meager in comparison with the course fee.
- Renewal of scholarship is problematic.
- There is official apathy in managing the scholarship schemes of the MOMA in the Indore district.

7.31 Suggestions:

- There is utmost need of revamping of district and state level management system of scholarships of MOMA.
- The amount of scholarship needs revision in view of course fee and other expenses being incurred by the students.
- There is need of orientation training of district officials on certain key aspects of scholarship like the renewal because concerned officials themselves are not aware of the process involved.

Chapter-VIII

Free Coaching and Allied Scheme

8.1 Religion-wise Students:

In sample students of Free Coaching and Allied Scheme, 90 per cent are Muslims and 10 per cent are Sikhs.

Table-8.1: Sample Students of Free Coaching and Allied Scheme

Gender	Religions		
	Muslims	Sikhs	Total
Boys	2 (66.67)	1 (33.33)	3 (100.00)
Girls	7 (100.00)	-	7 (100.00)
Total	9 (90.00)	1 (10.00)	10 (100.00)

Note: Figures in brackets are the percentages.
Source: Primary data based.

8.2 Type of Courses Attended in Coaching:

All students are attending the coaching for getting admission in engineering course.

Table-8.2: Type of Coaching attended by Sample Students

Gender	Type of Coaching				
	Engineer	Medical	Management	Competitive	Total
Boys	3 (100.00)	-	-	-	3 (100.00)
Girls	7 (100.00)	-	-	-	7 (100.00)
Total	10 (100.00)	-	-	-	10 (100.00)

Note: Figures in brackets are the percentages.
Source: Primary data based

8.3 Annual Income:

50 per cent households of sample students have average annual income in the range of Rs. 50,000 to Rs. Rs. 100,000 and to all of them service is the only occupation.

Table-8.3: Annual Income of Households of Sample Students

Occupation	Average Annual Income (Rs.)/ Number of Students				
	Less Than 25000	25000-50,000	50000-100000	100000-150000	Total
Service	1 (10.00)	3 (30.00)	5 (50.00)	1 (10.00)	10 (100.00)
Total	1 (10.00)	3 (30.00)	5 (50.00)	1 (10.00)	10 (100.00)

Note: Figures in brackets are the percentages.
Source: Primary data based.

8.4 Type of Coaching Institution:

The coaching institution is private.

Table-8.4: Type of Coaching Institution

Type of Institute	Number		
	Boys	Girls	Total
Private	3 (100.00)	7 (100.00)	10 (100.00)
Total	3 (100.00)	7 (100.00)	10 (100.00)

Note: Figures in brackets are the percentages.
Source: Primary data based

8.5 Sources of Awareness:

For 100 per cent boys, 57 per cent girls and 70 per cent all students, the main source of awareness about the Free coaching Scheme is the friends.

Table-8.5: Sources of Awareness about Free Coaching Scheme among Students

Source	Number of Students		
	Boys	Girls	Total
News Papers	2 (66.67)	5 (71.43)	7 (70.00)
Schools/ Institution	2 (66.67)	3 (42.86)	5 (50.00)
Friends	3 (100.00)	4 (57.14)	7 (70.00)
Parents	1 (33.33)	2 (28.57)	3 (30.00)
Home Tutors / Coaching Center	2 (66.67)	4 (57.14)	6 (60.00)
website of Ministry	-	2 (28.57)	2 (20.00)
Total	3 (100.00)	7 (100.00)	10 (100.00)

Note: Figures in brackets are the percentages.
Source: Primary data based.

8.6 Purpose of Joining Free Coaching:

All the students have reported that they joined the Free Coaching for ensuring their employability.

Table-8.6: Purpose of Joining the Free Coaching

Views	Number of Students		
	Boys	Girls	Total
To ensure our employability	3 (100.00)	7 (100.00)	10 (100.00)
To ensure well-being of our families in future	1 (33.33)	2 (28.57)	3 (30.00)
To enable us to enter into institution of higher Studies	1 (33.33)	1 (14.29)	2 (2.00)
Total	3 (100.00)	7 (100.00)	10 (100.00)

Note: Figures in brackets are the percentages.
Source: Primary data based.

8.7 Increase in confidence in Competitive Exams:

60 per cent students reported that their confidence level increased significantly in competitive examination after taking free coaching.

Table-8.7: Increase in Confidence of Students in Competitive Examinations

Responses	Number of Students		
	Boys	Girls	Total
To an extent	1 (33.33)	3 (42.86)	4 (40.00)
Significantly	2 (66.67)	4 (57.14)	6 (60.00)
Total	3 (100.00)	7 (100.00)	10 (100.00)

Note: Figures in brackets are the percentages.

Source: Primary data based.

8.8 Utility Level of Free Coaching Scheme:

50 per cent students find utility of Free Coaching Scheme useful and very useful.

Table-8.8: Utility of Free Coaching Scheme

Utility	Boys	Girls	Total
Utterly Useless	-	-	-
Useless	1 (33.33)	-	1 (10.00)
Average	1 (33.34)	3 (42.85)	4 (40.00)
Useful	1 (33.33)	3 (42.86)	4 (40.00)
Very Useful	-	1 (14.29)	1 (10.00)
Total	3 (100.00)	7 (100.00)	10 (100.00)

Note: Figures in brackets are the percentages.

Source: Primary data based.

8.9 Level of Satisfaction of Students with Facilities/ Infrastructure of Coaching Centre:

The students have reported satisfaction with facilities/infrastructure of the coaching Centre as shown in table-8.9.

Table-8.9: Level of Satisfaction with Facilities/Infrastructure in Coaching Center : Students Responses

Facilities	Responses / Number of Students				
	Highly Dissatisfaction	Dissatisfaction	Satisfaction	Highly satisfaction	Total
Physical Infrastructure	-	-	7 (70.00)	3 (30.00)	10 (100.00)
Course Module	-	-	9 (90.00)	1 (10.00)	10 (100.00)
Course Timing & Duration	-	-	5 (150.00)	5 (50.00)	10 (100.00)
Faculty	-	-	8 (8.00)	2 (20.00)	10 (100.00)
Library & Reading	-	-	7 (70.00)	3 (30.00)	10 (100.00)
Access to Computer / Internet	-	-	8 (8.00)	2 (20.00)	10 (100.00)
Success Rates of Yours Predecessors	-	-	9 (90.00)	1 (10.00)	10 (100.00)

Note: Figures in brackets are the percentages.

Source: Primary data based.

8.10 Average Expenditure of Scholarship Amount:

The average expenditure of scholarship amount is Rs. 6750. The major items of expenditure is related to their education but part of other important needs of students is also met from scholarship amount (Table-8.10).

Table-8.10: Items wise Average Expenditure of Stipend: Students Responses

Items	Annual Average Expenditure (Rs.)
Food	800
Accommodation	1600
Books and Stationary	2250
Clothing	900
Medicines	500
Application for jobs	300
Phone	400
Total	6750

Source: Primary data based.

8.11 Mode of Payment of Scholarship:

The students have reported that entire amount of scholarship is paid to them by cheque.

Table-8.11: Mode of Payment of Scholarship

Mode	Number of Students
Cheque	10 (100.00)
Cash	-
Total	10 (100.00)

Note: Figures in brackets are the percentages.
Source: Primary data based.

8.12 Processing of Application:

66.67 per cent of boys, 42.85 per cent of girls and 50 per cent of all students have reported that the process of application and documentation is tedious (Table-8.12).

Table-8.12: Responses of Students about Processing of Application and Documentation

Process	Number of Students		
	Boys	Girls	Total
Very Tedious	1 (33.33)	2 (28.57)	3 (30.00)
Tedious	2 (66.67)	3 (42.85)	5 (50.00)
Average	-	1 (14.29)	1 (10.00)
Smooth	-	1 (14.29)	1 (10.00)
Total	3 (100.00)	7 (100.00)	10 (100.00)

Note: Figures in brackets are the percentages.
Source: Primary data based.

Coaching Institution

8.13 Coaching Institute:

One Coaching Institute namely the Brain Smiths Education Pvt. Ltd is the only coaching institute in the entire Indore district which was supported by the MOMA for imparting free coaching to minority students for different professional courses during the year 2009-10.

Table-8.13: About the Coaching Institution

Name of Institutions	Brain Smith Education Pvt. Ltd, Indore, M.P.
Training Provided	Pre-engineering Test
Year	2009-10

Source: Sample Coaching Institute.

8.14 Enrolment of Minority Students in Coaching Centre:

The sample Coaching Centre runs the Pre-engineering coaching of 8 months duration with a capacity of 1000 intake. During 2009-10, 25 minority students were enrolled in which boys were 12 and gild were 13.

Table-8.14: Total Enrolment and Enrolment of Minority Students

Type of Training	Duration of Coaching	Total Enrolment	Enrolment of Minority Students	Enrolment of Minority Boys	Enrolment of Minority Girls
Pre Engineering Entrance Test	8 Months	1000	25	12	13

Source: Sample Coaching Institute.

8.15 Infrastructure of Coaching Centre:

The Coaching Centre has entire required infrastructure as shown in table-8.15. It was physical verified by the spot visit that the Centre was well equipped to impart pre-engineering coaching.

Table-8.15: Availability of infrastructures in the institute

Infrastructure	Total
Class Rooms- Number and Area	8/3000sq feet
Teachers (Number)	12
Computer Laboratory with Internet (Computer in Numbers)	10
Number of Books, Journal and News Papers	3000
Audio-Visual aids	Yes
Photo Copiers	Yes

Source: Primary data based.

8.16 Qualification of Faculty:

The Coaching Centre has qualified panel of faculty as shown in table-8.16.

Table-8.16: Qualification of the Faculty of Coaching Centre

Qualification		No of Faculty
M. Tech		1 (10.00)
M.B.B.S		1 (10.00)
MCA		1 (10.00)
MSC		3 (30.00)
MBA		1 (10.00)
BE		3 (30.00)
Total		10 (100.00)

Note: Figures in brackets are the percentages.
Source: Primary data based.

8.17 Experience of Faculty:

The faculty of the Coaching Centre has sufficient teaching experience as shown in table-8.17.

Table-8.17: Teaching Experience of Faculty

Experience (in Years)	Number of Faculty
Up to 3 Years	2 (20.00)
3-5 Years	3 (30.00)
5-7 Years	4 (40.00)
7 Years and more	1(10.00)
Total	10 (100.00)

Note: Figures in brackets are the percentages.
Source: Primary data based.

8.18 Selection Criteria of Students:

1- Annual Household Income
2- Maximum Marks Criteria
3- Qualification

8.19 Suggestions of Students for better implementation of Free Coaching Scheme

1. Increase the number of centers for free coaching scheme in the district.
2. Free coaching scheme should also be provided for different streams like NDA, Geology etc.
3. Amount of Stipend should be increased.
4. Books & Stationary should be provided by the institution.
5. Session should bĕ started timely i.e. April/ May by the institutions.

8.20 Main Findings:

- 90 per cent Muslims and 10 per cent Sikhs students were enrolled in sample coaching.
- All students were attending the coaching for getting admission in engineering course.
- 50 per cent households of sample students had average annual income in the range of Rs.
- 50,000 to Rs. Rs. 100,000 and to all of them service was thé only occupation.
- For majority of students, the main source of awareness about the Free coaching Scheme was the friends.
- All the students reported that they joined the Free Coaching for ensuring their employability and majority of them found that their confidence level increased significantly in competitive examination after taking free coaching.
- 50 per cent students found utility of Free Coaching Scheme useful and very useful.
- The students reported their satisfaction with facilities/infrastructure at the coaching Centre.
- Around half of all students reported that the process of application and documentation was tedious.
- It was physical verified by the spot visit that the Centre was well equipped to impart pre-engineering coaching.
- Increase the number of centers for free coaching scheme in the district, free coaching scheme should also be provided for different streams like NDA, Geology etc., amount of stipend should be increased, books and stationary should be provided by the institution and session should be started timely i.e. April/ May by the institutions, were the some suggestions given by the manager of the sample coaching.

Field Observations, Key Issues and Suggestions: Free Coaching and Allied Scheme

8.21 Field Observations:

During the field investigation, officials of the Department of Tribal Welfare at Indore were asked to provide the list of coaching centers which were assisted by the MOMA to provide free coaching to the minority students for getting admission in various professional/technical courses. But the officials said that in the entire Indore district, only three Scholarships Schemes of the MOMA, Government of India has been implemented so far and the Free Coaching Scheme has not been implemented in the district as yet. However, when our research team discussed the matter with some of the prominent coaching centres of the Indore city, we came to know that one centre has received financial support from the MOMA to impart free coaching to minority students. Thereafter, we contacted this centre and obtained all details for the evaluation of the Free Coaching Scheme. This goes to prove that how ignorant and careless the concerned district officials of Indore district are about the implementation of the scholarship schemes of the MOMA.

Our field observation on the basis of spot visit and discussion with the manager of coaching centre indicated that coaching centre was doing well. It came out during the discussion that 25 students of minorities were admitted under Free Coaching Scheme of MOMA to prepare them to seek admission in engineering course during 2009-10. Out of these 25 candidates, 22 candidates succeeded in getting admission in engineering course after their coaching. On the basis, it can be said that success rate has been well. It was also observed that the teaching faculty was competent and centre was equipped with all required infrastructure.

8.22 Key Issues of Free Coaching and Allied Scheme:

- The key issue is that the district officials who have been assigned the task of implementation of Free Coaching Scheme of the MOMA are totally ignorant about the Free Coaching Scheme itself. This calls for immediate action on the part of state and MOMA.
- The outreach of the Free Coaching Scheme is very limited in the district.
- Despite being a good scheme for the minorities to obtain technical/professional education, the poor implementation has debarred the minority student's to get its full benefit.

8.33 Suggestions:

- The scholarship Schemes of the MOMA should be taken away from the Department of Tribal Welfare and be given to any other related department.
- The immediate need is that the State Government of Madhya Pradesh should be asked to issue directives to the Department of Tribal Welfare for identification of some coaching centers not only in Indore district and in other districts of the state so as to increase the reach of minority students to free coaching.
- The funding support to coaching centres should also be increased so that genuine institutions are involved and quality coaching is ensured.

Index

A

Age of Students, 3, 53, 86, 101, 166
Amount of Scholarship, 169
Annual Income, 180
Annual Income of Parents, 151
Assessment of Merit-cum-Means Scheme, 96
Assessment of Scholarship, 175
Attending Schools, 137
Availability and Accessibility of the Scheme, 83
Availability of Guidelines of post-matric Scholarship, 161
Average Expenditure of Scholarship Amount, 183
Award of Merit cum Means Scholorship, 174
Award of post-matric Scholarship to Muslim Students, 157
Awardees of pre-matric Scholarship, 46
Awardees of post-matric Scholarship, 82, 163
Awareness about pre-metric Scholarship, 36
Awareness, Utilization and Impact of Pre-matric Scholarship, 10

B

Bottlenecks in the Education System, 161
Bottleness Faced in the Teaching Process and Education System, 80

C

Central Government, 92
Characteristics of Sample Students: Post-matric Scholarship, 53, 133
Children Attending Schools, Getting Scholarship and Family Features, 7, 104
Coaching Centre, 185
Coaching Institution, 180, 184
Complete Awareness about Pre-matric Scholarship, 10, 107, 139
Co-operation of Institutions in Gatting Pre-matric Scholarship, 116
Co-operation of Institution in Gatting Pre-matric Scholarship: Rural Students, 26
Co-operation of Institution in Gatting Pre-matric Scholarship: Urban Students, 27
Courses of Study of Students, 87, 168
Criteria, 81, 163
Criteria for Selecting Institutions, 82

D

Data Management, 45
Department of Tribal Welfare, 187
Distribution Method of Scholarship Amount, 97
Distribution of Scholarship, 177
District Minority Welfare Officer, 50

E

Education Institutions, 76, 94
Effectiveness of pre-matric Scholarship: All Students, 19
Effectiveness of pre-matric Scholarship, 64
Effectiveness of pre-matric Scholarship: Rural Students, 18, 112
Effectiveness of pre-matric Scholarship: Urban Students, 18
Enrolment, 41, 124
Expenditure on pre-matric Education, 6, 104
Expenses for Applying the post-matric Scholarship, 142
Expenses of Getting pre-matric Scholarship, 16, 110
Expenditure on Education, 55
Expenditure of Scholarship Amount, 89
Expenditure on Education, 136
Experience of Faculty, 186

F

Family Income of Students, 87, 168
Field Observations, 49, 84, 99, 131, 178, 187
Filling Application Form, 115
Free Coaching Scheme, 188
Future Plan of Students, 91, 171

G
Gatting Scholarship and Family Features, 56, 137
Government Holkar Science College Indore, 157
Government of India, 2
Grants of Pre-matric Scholarship, 47, 129
Grants of post-matric Scholarship, 82
Guidelines, 81

H
Housing, 8, 57, 138, 105
Housing and Family Features, 34, 69, 118, 150

I
Impact of pre-matric Scholarship Scheme, 45
Improvement in Enrolment and Drop Out, 44, 126
Impact of Merit-cum-Means Scholarship, 95
Impact of Merit-cum-Means Scholarship, 92
Income of Families, 5, 103
Income of Parents, 120
Income of Students, 55, 136
Institutions, 40

K
Key Issues of Free Coaching and Allied Scheme, 188
Key Issues of pre-matric Scholarship, 50, 132
Key Issues of post-matric Scholarship, 84
Knowledge about Eligibility Conditions, 13, 61, 108
Knowledge of both Eligibility Conditions, 14

L
Land Size and Income of Beneficiary Parents, 35, 119
Land Size and Income of Non-Beneficiary Parents, 35
Land Size of Parents, 70, 151
Level of Co-operation of Institutions, 67, 148
Level of Difficulty in Obtaining Application Form for All Students, 24
Level of Difficulty in Filling Application Form for Rural Students, 24
Level of Difficulty in Filling Application Form for Urban Students, 25
Level of Difficulty in Obtaining Form for Rural Students, 22, 114
Level of Difficulty in Obtaining Application Form for Urban Students, 23
Level of Satisfaction of Institutions with Central Government, 160
Level of Satisfaction with Reimbursement of Course Free, 90
Level of Satisfaction of Institutions with State and Central Government Agencies, 45
Level of Scholars, 4, 102. 134
Location of Previous Institutions, 87

M
Main Findings, 130
Mechanisms of Community Awareness, 82
Merit-cum-Means Bases Scholarship, 99
Method of Scholarship Payment and Processing of Application, 79
Ministry of Minority Affairs, 1
Mode of Payment, 62
Mode of Payment of Scholarship Amount, 15, 53, 109, 125, 184
Most Important Problem and Overall Assessment of pre-matric Scholarship Scheme, 46
Murari, Krishna, 96
Muslim Children, 106

N
Number of Male and Female Candidates Received Scholarship, 98

O
Objectives of Evaluation, 1
Observations of Parents, 75
Occupations, 86, 167

P
Parents of Beneficiary and Non-Beneficiary Students, 118, 150
Parents of Beneficiary and Non-Beneficiary Students, Institutions and Officials, 34
Parents perceptions on Scholarship, 40, 123, 156
Perception of All Students about pre-matric Scholarship, 20
Perception of All parents about Various Aspects of Post-metric Scholarship, 74
Perception of Students about Post-matric Scholarship, 145
Perception of Students about Various Aspects of Scholarship, 90
Perspective of Institution, 125
Perception of Rural Students about pre-matric Scholarship, 19] 64, 113

Perception of Urban Students about pre-matric Scholarship, 20
Problems Faced by Beneficiary Students, 121
Problems Faced by Beneficiary Students: Perception of their parents, 37
Problems in getting pre-matric Scholarship and Suggestions of Students, 22
Problems of Getting post-matric Scholarship and Suggestion of Students, 66
Problems of Implementation of Scheme, 129
Problems Regarding Implementations of the Scheme, 81
Processing of Applications, 174, 184
Process of Selection, 176
Purpose of Joining Free Coaching, 181

Q

Qualification of Faculty, 186

R

Radio, 12-13
Rating of various Aspects of post-matric Scholarship by Beneficiary parents, 154
Rating of Various process of pre-matric Scholarship, 38, 122
Reasons for Non-Award of Scholarship, 78, 159
Reasons of Untimely payment of pre-matric Scholarship, 37, 121
Reasons of Untimely payment of post-matric Scholarship, 71, 153
Religion-wise Students, 179
Response of District Minority Welfare Officer, 83
Role of State Government Officials, 67, 116, 149
Role of State Government Officials: Perception of All Students, 29
Role of State Government Officials: Perception of Rural Students, 28
Role of State Government Officials: Perception of Urban Students, 29

S

Sample Institutions, 123
Sample parents, 34
Satisfaction Level with Ministry of Minority Welfare, 83
Satisfaction of Students with their Institutions, 91
Satisfaction with Scholarship Amount, 170
Satisfaction with Ministry of Minority Welfare, 163
Scholarship Amount Received, 88
Scholarship Application and Grant, 97
Scholarship Given by Different persons, 15, 142
Selection of Beneficiary students, 80
Selection of Candidates, 176
Selection process of Candidates, 91
Sources of Income, 54
Sources of Income and Schooling, 5, 103
Sources of Information of the Scheme, 89
Sources of Awareness, 180
Sources of Awareness of pre-matric Scholarship, 36
Sources of Awareness of pre-matric Scholarship to all Students, 2, 60
Sources of Awareness of post-matric Scholarship to Rural Students, 11, 59, 107, 140
Sources of Awareness of pre-matric Scholarship to Urban Students, 10, 12
State Government, 92
Students Facing Difficulties while Applying, 114, 141, 147
Students Knowledge of Eligibility Conditions, 140
Students of Class, 111
Students Perception, 89
Students Receiving Different Amount of Scholarship, 14
Students Receiving Different Amount of post-matric Scholarship, 62
Students Satisfied with the Amount of Scholarship, 90
Suggestions of Students to Improve the pre-matric Scholarship, 30

T

Television, 12-13
Time taken in Processing, 125
Time take from proposal to Disbursement of pre-matric Scholarship, 44, 126
Trend in Enrolment and Processing of Applications for Scholarship, 94
Type of Course Attended in Coaching, 180
Type of Institutions, 135
Type of Schools, 4, 102

U

Urdu language, 81
Utility of Free Coaching Scheme, 182
Utilization of pre-matric Scholarship Amount, 11, 16-17
Utilization of pre-matric Scholarship Money, 63, 143

